THE WORLD'S FAIR

A Picaresque Novel

JOAN FERRY

Copyright © 2017 by Joan Ferry

All rights reserved. No part of this publication may be reproduced, stored in a retrieval system, or transmitted, in any form or by any means, electronic, mechanical, photocopying, recording, or otherwise, without the written prior permission of the publisher.

For more information please visit Joan's page at
www.joanferryauthor.com

ISBN: 978-0-9958983-0-1

Cover Design: Iryna Spica
Typeset in *Arno* at SpicaBookDesign

to my mother and father

TABLE OF CONTENTS

1	Prologue	1
2	Prospect Street	19
3	Michael	37
4	Maura	56
5	Alma	77
6	Two Visits	98
7	Moving On	116
8	Bella	128
9	Silvy	152
10	Next Door	174
11	Emerald	193
12	The Theatre	217
13	The Businesswoman	236
14	Other Dimensions	250
15	The Pointe	260
16	Downriver	276
17	Two Greats	293
18	The Arrivals	301
19	Epilogue	321

CHAPTER ONE

Prologue

EMER WATCHES THEM through the car window as they run up the church steps. The baby sleeps beside her on the back seat. Her mother returns to the car as if she's forgotten something.

Emer rolls down the window and looks at her questioningly. Her mother whispers, "We're getting married. We won't be long. Just look after Zack." Emer rolls the window up quickly. The air is a little cool in Ottawa for May. She studies the date over the portals of the United Church. "1937." It's a brand new church, she thinks. Wow! I'm six years older than this church.

Later that night she remembers standing at the foot of her father's bed. Her feet were cold. Her father was shouting and coughing. She saw his chest heaving. His feverish body contorted as he struggled to control the wracking cough. His black curly hair glistened with sweat. His body was drenched. He shouts as his fists thud against the mattress. "No! No! No!"

Her mother sits up in the bed. "Michael, what is it? Wake up!" She looks worried. "Is it because we got married?"

He slowly sits up and spits into a handkerchief. "Nothing to do with that."

"Not the same dream, Michael? Not the same dream?"

Zack starts to cry from the next room.

Michael slumps back, too exhausted to tell her. "That tasted like blood, Bella. Where's the sputum cup?"

Bella hands it to him.

"Can I get you a glass of water, Dad?" Emer asks.

Together they go to the kitchen.

Emer wraps her toes around the spindle legs of the chair and watches him as he pours each of them a glass of water. He is tall and thin with dark brown hair, brown eyes, and a straight nose. They look alike. What she loves best about him is his kindhearted eyes. To her they are regal. They radiate the warmth of a king. That and the variety of ways he finds to express himself.

"What happened, Dad?"

"I just had a bad dream, that's all."

His cough subsides.

Emer sees him trying to shrug it off.

He changes the subject, "You know that tomorrow I'm going into the hospital. The sanatorium. I have tuberculosis." He enunciates every word clearly.

Emer feels the urgency in his voice and whispers, "What's that?"

How can he explain to his six-year-old? "It's a disease of the lungs." He repeats, "a disease of the lungs," to reassure himself that he had actually said it.

"Will you get better?"

He pulls himself together. "Yes, of course I will."

The doctor said that even with plenty of rest, cod liver oil, and sunshine, "getting better" would still be in the lap of the gods. But he is determined that he will beat this thing, if for no other reason than to confront his mother and grandmother. One of them has to tell him the truth. He has to get to the bottom of these damnable recurring dreams. He knows that the TB diagnosis has something to do with unresolved issues. He feels sure of it. It isn't only his lifestyle that had brought it on.

PROLOGUE

As he looks at her querying eyes, he knows that he also must secure a future for his family.

"There's nothing to worry about, really. Your life will continue here with your mother and Zack, much the same as always."

"But without you?"

"Yes, for the present."

"Is that what made you shout in your sleep?" she asks.

"Not exactly." He looks away. "I don't know. I just know that I had a nightmare. It keeps coming back." He lowers his voice as if he were talking to himself. "Has for years now."

"What is it?"

"It's a dream I have of me as a baby, sitting on the floor. Two women are fighting over me."

"Who, Dad?"

"Your grandmother Silvy and your great-grandmother Alma."

"Why are they fighting?"

"They're saying bad things, Emer. I don't quite hear what they say but I hear that they are bad things."

"What, Dad?"

Michael bites his lips, knowing he can't tell his young daughter the dream. It is too shocking even for him to absorb.

He shudders. Their voices still ring in his ears.

Alma repeatedly screamed to his mother, "You don't even know who the father is." She pointed to the baby sitting on the floor. Him. Michael.

And then Silvy's recurring chant of "I couldn't help it! I couldn't help it! I couldn't help it!"

"The hell you couldn't! He's a bastard!" Alma shouted.

And then in the midst of his wails his Aunt Maura scooped him up off the floor and ran away with him to her house.

To Emer, he says, "I don't really know who my father is."

Her young voice cracks. "Is that important, Dad?"

"Yes, Emer. Very."

The reason why he'd married Bella the day before, he thought.

His children at least would know who their father was. Even if he did die.

Emer sips her water. "But it's Grandfather Maguire, Aunt Maura's brother."

"That is no longer clear to me."

Emer folds both legs up on the chair and hunches her shoulders over them in deep thought. She loves her father. He always speaks his deepest truth, no matter what. It hurts to see him in such pain. In her heart she resolves to watch her family closely. She is determined to get to the bottom of it.

Life was not the same after her father left. In her view, her eighth birthday came and went almost unnoticed. Almost two years had passed and the excitement of his presence had vanished. Her mother was totally wrapped up in three-year-old Zack.

Emer felt as though she no longer existed.

She dipped her fingers into Bella's emollients, unguents, and face creams in the hope that if she rubbed them on her skin her mother would smell them on her and grow to love her too. She even painted her toenails in imitation of her mother, though she herself didn't favour the look of it. Still, nothing happened.

One night she woke up screaming. Bella came rushing in.

"What is it?"

"There's a rat crawling up my arm."

Her mother felt her forehead. She was feverish and sweating.

PROLOGUE

The next day they went to see Doctor Carmichael at the Sanatorium. All three of them had X-rays, including Zack.

Emer was admitted to the San a week later with a shadow on her lung. She was delighted. She didn't feel sick. She felt perfectly fine. She could see her father once a week!

In the beginning he was in the Perley Building, but after she arrived he moved to the Grey Building to be closer to her. This gave everyone reason to hope that he would make it. Admission to the Grey indicated that the disease was beginning to go into remission.

On Saturdays they walked together hand in hand in the deep snow along the boulevard lined with ghostly maple trees shorn of leaves, their branches draped in snow and icicles. The maple was a sacred tree in his view, "because in spring it gives us its sap, which when boiled turns into a beautiful syrup. It's relatively more nutritious than straight sugar, you know." They walked all the way to the frozen creek and back through the middle of a pine forest covered in pancake-sized clumps of snow.

"We're having a good run at life in the country, aren't we?" They may be in there to die, but they are going to have a good time doing it.

"The snow stays so much whiter, longer," she whispered, enchanted with the silence of this new sparkling world, away from the city and apartment living.

The San had given her a winter snowsuit of tomato-red woollen leggings with a matching sweater, toque, and mittens. The snowsuit was a size five but it was still a bit big for her. At eight she was small for her age.

He held her hand tightly as he spoke. It was important to him that she should know the details of family folklore, however inglorious they might be.

"You see, Emer, it goes this way," he began. "Silvy, my mother, ran away to the circus when I was three months old."

"Wow! What a wonderful thing to do!"

"Yes, but I was very young, and I needed her." His knowledge of basic psychology told him that a nurturing mother was a necessity to the infant child. Where else would he learn love except at his mother's side?

She could tell from his serious tone that it wasn't the right thing for Granny to have done. "Did you love her, Dad?"

He smiled sadly. "At three months old? I suppose so. I don't know. I needed her, let's put it that way. I suppose she was too young to have known any better," he said in a forgiving tone.

"So then what happened?"

"Aunt Maura raised me."

Michael suddenly whirled his daughter around, threw her up in the air with gales of laughter, and caught her, shouting, "I lived with Aunt Maura and we all lived happily ever after, so there!" He was forever grateful to the woman who had taken on the responsibility of mothering him when she herself at sixteen barely had enough to live on. Maura was the only woman he knew who could translate spiritual values into pragmatic action with detachment.

Emer loved her father's spontaneity. She wasn't sure what motivated his excitement, but if it was like hers, it came from a passionate love of life.

He continued to talk about himself.

She watched his words forming vapour puffs that disappeared into the blue-white air. The new snow scrunched underfoot. Emer watched thick scatterings of snowflake words forming intricate lacework connections in mid-air.

PROLOGUE

"You see, I entered Ottawa University when I was eighteen, and majored in mathematics. I was pretty successful, so much so that when I began graduate studies, my advisors told me that if I went on and completed a doctorate I'd be granted tenure as a professor. First, of course, I'd have to complete my Master of Science degree…"

"And have you?"

"No, darling, I haven't."

She thought about this for a moment. "What's tenure, Dad?"

"Tenure is a position that is bestowed upon you for life."

"Bestowed?"

He straightened her toque. "Well, yes. It's given to you for as long as you live."

She clapped her mittens together. "A gift forever? Can you make it happen?"

He cleared his throat and looked away. There were some complications here, of course, if and when he got better: the solving of Fermat's last theorem for the master's degree, the church's sanctions on marrying Bella in the United Church, and his precarious health. He would clear up the mess with Father Bruneau, the Dean of Science Studies. The pink-cheeked priest had no room in his heart for non-conformists. To Emer he said, "We will only know that when I get out." He hoped it was going to be the case. He intended to realize this goal, if he lived.

He talked about his student days at Ottawa University, and how he'd met her mother when he was playing violin in the orchestra at the Standish Hall in Hull.

"Where is that?"

"On the other side of the provincial bridge."

"That's in Quebec, huh?"

"Yes, that's where your mother is from, Gatineau Pointe, Quebec."

Emer felt as if she was a grown woman. She didn't understand a lot of what he said, but she absorbed all of his words much as a flower absorbs the sun and the rain.

Sometimes the walks were spent catching up on her schoolwork. He made a game out of every subject he taught her. She knew from his laughter that he loved to teach.

Under cold, crisp, blue sunlit skies he drew triangles in the glittering snow, to explain the Pythagorean theorem. On other days it would be *Hamlet*, or Plato's *Republic*, or a one-sided discussion on the theory of relativity. One Saturday she watched as his leather-gloved hand meticulously wrote Fermat's last theorem into the crusty snow.

"One day," he said, standing back to study the equation, "I will resolve this problem, make some money, and then we will move to Peru, where the sun shines the year round. Where there's pounding surf, palm trees, and warmth in the very air we breathe. And that's a promise!" He squeezed her hand tight. She never forgot this. On still other days, it was meditative walks and quiet talks about their future lives in Peru. "Oh Daddy, imagine that. Just imagine it!" She could barely breathe with the thought of it.

"Imagination is reality, so yes, let's just work on that." She followed the word-puffs as they travelled, merging into the ice-blue sky.

Her mother came to visit her every Sunday. She came with Grandmaman, or Mémère, as Emer calls her. They drape themselves around the white wrought-iron knobs at the foot of her bed.

Mémère's gold ciborium-shaped pendants dangled into the prickly wire fur of her brown muskrat. Her mother wore a brown tweed coat, her golden brown curls piled high in the manner of a

PROLOGUE

movie actress. Was it Barbara Stanwyck or Irene Dunne? Hard to tell. The upswept hairdo looks stunning with her sea-green eyes.

Emer lay flat on her back in a tent the nurses made for her because she had bronchitis. They placed a little steamer inside the tent so that she could breathe more easily. As she lay there in the euphoric haze of friar's balsam, she could see their anxious faces through the mist.

"*Penses-tu qu'a va mourir?*" Memère said. Do you think she'll die?

Emer's attention riveted on her mother's response.

Bella merely shrugged, appearing indifferent.

Emer's heart stopped for a second. She felt nothing coming from her mother. Absolutely nothing. Silence.

Bella died for Emer, then and there, standing right at the foot of her bed.

Both of them dissolved into puddles under their coats like the bad witch in *The Wizard of Oz*. She raged inside, screaming soundlessly. "You fools! Insensitive fools! I'm going to live! I will live!"

They were too lost in their own "mellow-drama" to hear her. That much she knew.

Emer's shutdown toward her mother and Memère was complete by age eight. From that moment on she became her own best support. No bitterness. No rancour.

The day her father walked through the grey-stone Sanatorium gates, both thumbs up, would live in her memory forever. He knew how to turn darkness into light. He let her see that he was unafraid to experience his own darkness from within himself and move forward from that point.

"We have the ability to transform ourselves, Emer. Life is a gift. We are here to experience it fully. Good, bad, or indifferent. We have the power within ourselves to change our so-called negative emotions by experiencing them fully. The trick is to catch myself ignoring them. From that point, I can then move forward into a healthy body. All is energy, including thoughts and feelings. They are neither 'good' nor 'bad.' All of life's experience is power at our disposal to use consciously."

At the time, all Emer understood was that, although he might have been going into the hospital to die, he chose to go down like the *Titanic*, "with all his lights on."

"No defeats," he'd said. "Only powerful lessons to learn."

Emer chose to make the family incident at the foot of her bed serve her. Death's door was death's door.

―

Aunt Maura sits in a chair by his bed. He watches her snow-white head bent attentively over the makeshift bookcase on the window ledge.

She smiles. "Still reading all your books, Michael?"

He whispers, "Got it from you, I guess."

"I see your interests are more varied than ever," she says, reading the titles. "Books on magic tricks, chess, theatre; where are the ones on music?"

"Over here. And I brought the violin with me to keep in practice."

"That was a good added income, wasn't it? Best to keep it up."

"Yup. Never know what's around the old corner." Friends that helped him through the day.

"You've got several books on mathematics."

"Was thinking I'd work on Fermat's theorem while I'm here. This episode kind of cut me off at the starting post."

"It will happen. It will and you know that!"

PROLOGUE

"I want to crack that one day."

"Is that a vow?"

"Actually, yes."

"Then it will happen," she says matter-of-factly.

He is thankful for her light touch.

She looks at him quizzically. "What's this one?"

"It's a book on yoga. The exercises. How to breathe."

"Yes, well, breathing is of the essence, isn't it?"

Michael laughs. He feels her gentle comfort as if they were back home in Clarkstown. "A chap in this wing happens to be a yoga instructor. He's teaching me about breathing. Pranayama, he calls it."

"What does the doctor say to this?"

"The more oxygen I get into this the better, he says."

"Good, you're on the right track then, aren't you?" There is a moment of silence between them.

"Conscious breathing is it then?"

"Yes." Her knowledge always surprises him. "How do you know?"

"Toussaint," she says. And then, as if to remind herself to be quiet, she puts a finger to her lips.

His name startles Michael. He scans Maura's face, trying to detect her intention behind mentioning him. "Could I have the glass of milk on the cabinet there?"

"Certainly," she says.

He drinks the cool liquid down and sinks back into the pillow. Some mistakes you never forget, he thinks.

He remembers his mother's brother, Uncle Toussaint, making a slingshot for him. From the moment he got it, he was a natural shot. Could knock any milk bottle clear off its pedestal by the age of six. Ping! The bottles resounded and echoed into the back woods.

THE WORLD'S FAIR

The kids had thought he was a marvel. He'd thought so too! Such satisfaction in being able to make a thing vanish. Magical feeling. He loved his old slingshot.

Uncle Toussaint, though, was another matter. Michael had not liked the brusque way he treated his mother. He was mean to her.

He was called Toussaint because he'd been born November first, All Saints' Day. "A holy day of obligation," he would say leeringly. A masher with the women, he brought a few home every Saturday night to Alma's house from the Byward Market. His taxi service was especially busy on weekends. Whether the girls paid him or not, they got free lodgings and food. Toussaint's excuse to his mother was always the same. "They have no place to sleep on the weekend, Ma." The less fortunate in Alma's and Choe's house had always been given a big welcome on Murray Street. The recollection of the girls sitting around his grandmother's kitchen table on a Sunday afternoon eating thick, homemade soup and bread made Michael smile in spite of himself. It had been an exciting place for a boy of nine, despite the admonitions from Aunt Maura and her sister Meg. "The Longprés!" they exclaimed almost in unison, with Meg always adding, "Toussaint, indeed!"

One summer day when Michael was eight, Maura's radio antenna fell over after a bad thunderstorm. It needed repairs.

The Maguire house, a duplex in Clarkstown, was minutes away from Eastview, where Toussaint lived and ran his business. He was known locally to be the only man in the neighbourhood that did that kind of work.

Toussaint arrived on the Maguire doorstep, all French charm and grace. Michael saw that Aunt Maura was hypnotized by his uncle's reverence for her.

PROLOGUE

The house had a peaked roof. Toussaint reached it through an attic trap door and walked up its steep, wet slope. Michael was in the backyard watching him work. Maura was in the back summer kitchen baking some pies for Toussaint, as payment. Every now and again her face appeared at the screen door. To Michael she looked overly concerned. She even came out on the back porch, shading her eyes against the sun to make sure of his uncle's safety, for God's sake! The practical joker, the prankster in him, ran into the wet bushes, took out his slingshot, the one Toussaint had made for him, and delicately "pinged" the antenna. Toussaint turned his head abruptly to see where the sound had come from, and in so doing, rolled down the roof to the ground, where his body fell in a crumpled heap. Maura ran screaming for help. Terrified, Michael hid in the bushes, crying, "I didn't mean it! I didn't mean it! Please, God, let him be okay. It was just a joke," over and over again as he writhed in anguish.

The ambulance came, but it was too late. Toussaint's neck was broken. He was already dead.

Michael had cried in the bushes for hours while Maura ran for help. He never knew whether she had seen him do it. She never mentioned it. Life in her home continued as if nothing had ever happened. If anything, her love and support for him increased, until he graduated from Ottawa University with a four-year Bachelor of Arts degree, majoring in mathematics. She had helped initially with his violin fees by working at St. Brigid's Orphanage. Later on she even paid for his tuition at university when his father refused to do so.

He looked at Maura long and hard, feeling the pain once again of what he had done as a child. Tears roll down his face.

"There now," she says, taking his hand and squeezing it hard, "everything has a reason. We don't always see the larger canvas."

Michael didn't know if she was talking about Toussaint. Had she in fact seen him do it, or was she talking about the tuberculosis that had taken a turn for the worse? He was too tired to ask.

She sat beside his bed, well past visiting hours, her legs crossed at thin ankles, hands clasped together in her lap.

She had always been present for him in all of his growing crises and she was present now. He wondered where she got the strength.

Michael fell asleep in a state of exhaustion.

The leaves of the poplar outside his window started their rustling sound, throwing dappled shadows interspersed with glimmers of light across the white counterpane on his bed.

Maura gazed on his beloved face. She rose and gently wiped his forehead with a cool face cloth. He resembled him so much that she thought her heart would break with the pain.

Remembering her promise to the only man she had ever loved, she gathered herself up staunchly and tiptoed out of the room.

As she walked back through the tree-lined boulevard to the stone gate, the coolness of the October breeze forced her to gather her cardigan tightly around her hunched shoulders.

Maura thought of Emerald, and silently prayed that she would make it. Her one and only godchild, whom she herself had named. The brilliant little chess player with the big brown all-seeing eyes. She was sure Emerald had a tremendous future ahead of her. She glanced up at the second storey of the Children's Building. The ghostly dimness of the night lights in the main corridor cast long shadows. Shadows of nurses on the walls as they moved in and out of rooms, tucking the children in. It reminded her of the nights when she was on duty at St. Brigid's Orphanage caring for the youngsters in the Babies' Wing. Unwanted babies. The babies of young unwed mothers and fathers who didn't have the means of supporting their child.

PROLOGUE

He'd come to visit his daughter, three-month-old Jesse. The smiling baby that welcomed you at any time of the day or night. She handed him her favourite baby.

The picture of this strong, dark, curly-headed man gazing into his infant's face touched her deeply.

He had allowed Maura to see his vulnerability. In that moment she fell in love with him. They were both twenty-one years old.

The month previously, Sister Walter Marie had scanned her application form. "Your experience with children fully qualifies you for a job caring for the babies at our orphanage." As she stood up, her headdress made her look three feet taller. She extended her hand warmly. "Welcome to the staff!"

By then Michael was six and had been living with her since she was fifteen. Her brother John had brought him to her at three months old.

That had been her "qualification," as the nun put it.

Then came laughing Jesse. Then Jesse's father. Her face was wet with tears. She wondered if she would ever forget him. A tinkling melody of some old jazz tune wafted to her from somewhere. Everywhere. Nowhere. A melody they had danced to. God knows.

Leaving Michael behind her after a visit always left her limp.

Michael was packing his books when Dr. Carmichael entered the room. He hitched up his long white smock and sat down at the end of Michael's bed. "Well, it's been a long time coming, hasn't it?" he said drily.

Michael threw some books into the box. "Feels like three years," he said sardonically, not entirely able to hide the bitterness in his words.

He could hardly forget the date. 1937, the year he'd married Bella and also the date he'd admitted himself into the care of the Sanatorium.

The old man knew Michael's story. He puffed on his glasses and polished them on his handkerchief. "Congratulations, anyway," he said to his glasses with an air of restraint.

Michael caught his acerbic tone but knew that it wasn't directed at him. His doctor hid behind an expressionless tone the way some people hide behind an expressionless mask. It was his protection against the experience of so many lives lost, thought Michael. "Lots of water under the bridge," he said, thinking of the thirty-one others in his ward who hadn't made it.

The doctor shrugged. "Yup! One in thirty-one. Not great odds. You win some. You lose a lot."

Michael saw his shoulders slump under the oversized smock and knew that he took the losses personally.

Carmichael looked up, peering at him intently over his glasses. "But maybe you'll do all the living you can for them."

Michael paused to breathe into the pain of the lost ones, many of them friends. "Sure, will give it a good try."

"You can drop in for X-rays every once in a while. Just to make sure there's no recurrence." He cleared his throat. "Emer too, of course. And here are the sputum cups for testing." He dropped them into the suitcase.

Michael mimicked a military salute. "Yes, Sir!"

"You can tell Bella," he added, "that there's to be no sharing of towels, utensils, or linens. Just in case." He got up to go and turned at the doorway. "And as usual, as I mentioned when you and Emer came in here, no hugs, no kisses. No physical contact. Remember, she had a shadow, you had definite scarring."

Michael laughed. "I know. "Germs, germs, germs!"

PROLOGUE

"This is serious, Michael. I'm talking about lives now. I don't want to see either one of you in here again. Take care of yourself and your family. That is my pleasure."

"I will, Doctor."

As he turned to leave he said, "I cleared Emer a month ago, as you know."

Michael nods.

There is a silence, then, "No heavy work of any kind and definitely no cigarettes." He fondles the stethoscope at his neck. "Also, I want you to examine the possibilities of another job. One that takes you away from the classroom. Preferably a job that is done in the fresh air."

Michael looks up from his suitcase in shock. "But teaching math is what I'm trained for. How am I supposed to find a job in the fresh air?"

"Well, look at it, Michael. The world has changed since you arrived here."

"Not that much. Only a few years ago."

"When you arrived in May of '37, Hitler's strategists were testing new weapons in the Spanish Civil War, and Franco in consequence won." Dr. Carmichael looks out the window. "Unlike the Spaniards, we got through that war here in Canada unscathed, but I'd say that at this very moment the war machine is in full production, with Krupp at the helm, producing guns for the Germans to aim at the rest of Europe. We might just have to get involved. The depression here has gotten worse. I have a feeling that we'll either go to hell in a wheelbarrow or it will explode."

Doctor Carmichael looked around the room, avoiding Michael's gaze. Normally a very conservative man, he cleared his throat, embarrassed that he'd said so much.

Michael was astonished at this sudden display of verbiage. He snapped his suitcase shut. "I think you're being too pessimistic. After all, the World's Fair just opened in New York a few weeks ago; the exhibits in those pavilions are from all over the globe—Czechoslovakia, USSR, Britain, to name a few. In my world the Fair sees the future in a very positive light. The combination of those images of the Trylon, the Perisphere, and the Helicline—the sphere and the tower, with the bridge connecting them—spells futuristic to me. Reason for hope about the developing ingenuity we on the American continent display through our creative inventions. War spells gloom and doom."

"Well, anyway, congratulations." The interview was over. "And ... good luck to you!" the doctor called as he sped out of the room. His starched smock flapped loudly at his legs.

"Maybe we'll go to hell in a wheelbarrow and explode!" Michael said to the four walls as he threw the last of his books into the box.

His attention shifted to Bella and the children as he placed their photograph on top of the books.

With the suitcase in one hand and a box in the other, Michael walked out the front door to the waiting cab. "We stumble toward success," he thundered into the curtain of rain.

His strength restored, he relaxed into the back seat. Staring into the May downpour, he readied himself to face the challenge of his new world.

CHAPTER TWO

Prospect Street

THE FAINT IRONY of its name hung over all the flattened, tumbledown, clapboard houses of Prospect Street. It served as a great leveller for the families who moved there all on the same day in the summer of 1939, the Maguires among them.

The Depression had ceased to be merely a low ebb in the tide of economic history. For these people, it had become a state of mind endured to the point of desperation, then accepted past enduring, and finally resigned to. It was the body-blow of poverty without prospect. It had crushed even the strongest optimism. It was here now and to stay. It was true that they had come separately and at different times of the day, having decided independently of one another to move from their self-contained and heated flats in Ottawa's Uppertown to this dead end of a street at a dead end in time. But as one truck after another pulled up before the empty drab-faced houses, and blank-faced people stood on the sidewalks surrounded by their knocked-about furniture, they seemed by their very presence to confront the world and one another with a statement of fact.

A generation had become adults in the shadow of the Depression. They had survived without money, married without money, and now would raise their children without money. They would live and die broke but not broken, secure against nothing, but grimly holding out for holding's sake. They would let a smile be their umbrella and laugh the devil away.

THE WORLD'S FAIR

The demanding urgency of life, yes, had to be satisfied somehow, and if it meant only a few beers at the end of the week, a pack of cigarettes and a Carol Lombard movie, or a gamble with chance at the penny arcades, then that was it, and you couldn't have everything. Who could? The state of mind remained unaltered, and while politicians argued the vicious problem of the slump, the unemployed fingered their monthly relief cheques, and thought, yes, of life, not of politics.

Prospect Street, in the city of Ottawa, parliamentless for the summer of 1939.

All this was before the holocaust that no one suspected was imminent, that no one suspected would bring an end to what was felt to be a permanent state of mind and introduce another, even less funny. All this was before that, and in comparison with that, it could have been much worse.

A moving truck comes to a lurching stop before 268 Prospect Street. Emer Maguire jumps off the back and nibbles her lips with the tense excitement of a young rabbit.

There are five other trucks along the street erupting furniture. Back from the street are houses of a snugness she had not expected. The trees along the street came as a vast surprise, but most of all the people scuddering up and down the broken wooden walkways. She had not expected people. Families pass boxes of pots and pans through windows and back doors. Children race along the sunburned, trodden grass with bundles of clothes; overalled men trot up with overstuffed furniture; harassed men give directions from their porches on where to set it down; women hang curtains and, with children following, run around searching for brooms and mops and all the other aids to quick and ordered domestic entrenchment.

Emer stood transfixed to the spot where the lurch had thrown her. She remembered the rooming house they had just left, a crumbling red brick building squeezed between a penitentiary on one side and a convent on the other, on Waller Street, a street without people.

Her mother nudged her, and her brother's pudgy little hand slipped into hers. Both were propelled up the wooden path to the porch of 268, where they assembled while Michael Maguire fitted a key into the rusted Yale lock and threw open the front door. He stood aside and the children scuttled past him into the empty, dusty, dank-with-darkness hallway. Bella set foot on the step and peered in. The head of the family retraced his steps down the path, jingling the keys, and directed the moving men to bring the cardboard boxes first and stack them on the porch.

The movers grinned, then got on with it.

Michael tried to impose some kind of order from the beginning, but after a while the furniture is dropped with dull unconcerned thuds all over the available floor space.

The men had been through this before, and nod sympathetically while they drop the things wherever they can. Bella watched dejectedly from her collapsed position in an armchair in the hall and bit her nails.

Finally Michael moved her into the kitchen, where he had set up the table, and they sat together over a bottle of beer waiting until the job was over. "I wonder where the kids have gone," he said.

"There's a yard in the back—that's nice. I guess they went to have a look around." She relaxed a little. "I'm glad they've got a yard, anyway."

"We'll be all right," he said. "It's no palace, but it's better than the place you had on Waller Street."

"I couldn't find a place by myself," she said. "I would have had to look alone." She smiled palely.

"I know, dear. All that's over with now. That part of it anyhow. So long as I look after myself and we can all stay together. That's the important thing." He heard the stern voice of Dr. Carmichael warning him: no strenuous work of any kind for at least a year. He looked at the chaos of heavy furniture and wondered how he was going to organize it. If he couldn't get help, he'd have to get the stuff upstairs by himself ... but that was life, and how could it be avoided? With a family.

"It's been hard on you," he said. "Don't think I don't understand that. But it's been tough for me too, wasting three years. Not knowing whether I'd come out of it or not. And knowing Emer was in the same shape. I kept blaming myself for that, but it was nobody's fault. I know that now. We've got to be thankful I'm better, and that with Emer it wasn't anything more than a shadow. We've got a lot to be thankful for, haven't we? Really."

She thought a moment. "Yes, I think we have."

"Sure we have. And if we can live down what's past we can make a good future, too. A good future for the kids." He made rings on the table with the wet beer glass, waiting for her to say something, then remembering that she was a woman who had little to say when the subject was not basic, or concrete, or founded on everyday realities. Theorizing was foreign to her. He recalled that every visiting day she had filled the time talking about the real and useful things, had avoided any speculation about the future. Their communication skills at that point had been basically good, but after the years away from her he was back with a woman, a new wife, he did not fully know. The illness and the lifestyle that had precipitated the illness became a gulf between them. The experience was something he wasn't able to verbally share with her. Or so he felt. But with Emer he had shared part of it and that would always be something between them.

"We must be very careful with Emer," he said. "She hasn't as much resistance as I have. A child never has."

She nodded and seemed to think deeply about it.

He gets up quickly. "I'll help you get organized, Bella. Tell me where you want things and I'll get started."

She rose to this suggestion and he felt on safer ground. It was up to him to make his own assumptions and examine them and make them work in terms of their lives, and he must not merely talk about what he planned to do. His voice rose.

"We have to put the house in order. It's better to start with the kitchen, too." He moved a small table and two chairs to the window. "You know, there are no mistakes in the universe. I see this as an opportunity for you and I to start over again. Fresh. From the beginning. We'll entrench solidly this time. Once we get our bearings."

"Will you help me unpack the boxes?"

"Better than that! I'll do it myself!"

He would help to get things settled around the house over the weekend, maybe rest a little on Sunday, and then look up Bert Buckingham at the university to sound out his prospects for getting his job back.

"Maybe Monday I'll arrange to see the Dean about working into the summer program somewhere."

Bella proudly imitated Bruneau's voice. "Something can always be arranged for a man with an academic background."

Michael laughed, remembering the Jesuit's propensity for dictum.

"There's no need for us to accept relief money any more," he said. "I'll go into mental and physical training during the summer, so that when the academic year begins in September I'll be ready to make up for lost time." Michael felt a surge of energy at his second chance to make "a successful go of family life."

"We stumble toward success," he whispered, as a reminder that there was nothing wrong in stumbling.

Emer sat with her brother on the step of the red corrugated garage and let a trickle of sunflower seeds pour into his cupped hands. They chewed contentedly awhile, spitting the shucks onto the hot earth, and explored with their eyes the infinite possibilities of the yard. They had already investigated both sides of Prospect Street, counting the trees and observing the neighbours. A neighbour on the other side of the duplex had given them a crumpled paper bag with a handful of speckled seeds in it. They returned to the yard to munch them, having seen as much as they could of what was going on in the other houses, what kind of furniture was coming out of the trucks, and who the children were. While they sat, something flashed through a broken slat in the fence. Emer sprang to her feet, took Zack by the wrist, and pulled him into the garage.

He crammed his mouth with the rest of the seeds and whispered in the dark. "Whatsa matter, Emer?"

She pinched his arm and waited. They strained to see through a knot in the wood.

He caught sight of the white mass of feathers and the brilliant red comb. Suddenly he was out the door and off after the chicken.

"Woof, woof!" He zigzagged after the distraught bird and made a violent grab for its tail.

"Leave him alone! Leave him!" Emer cried, running ahead and jumping around to avoid the spiteful-looking beak.

A girl shouted from over the fence, "Hermione, *viens ici!*"

But the chicken strutted and squawked around, half trying to fly.

Emer shouted, "Come and get him before he pecks us to death!"

The girl squeezed through the broken slat, crept up on the bird, and grabbed it by a leg, very expertly Emer thought. She swung the chicken over her shoulder and disappeared through the opening.

The children stood in the middle of the yard guarding their squinted eyes against the shimmering sun, hoping the French girl would come back. The bells in the Parliament Tower tolled the hour of six as they stared at one another.

Inside the house, Michael and Bella watched from the window. Eventually the Baillargeon Brothers truck pulled out. They were left alone in the tiny kitchen to rest over their glass of beer. It was suddenly quiet; they could look at one another again. The house had the heavy smell of soot, mothballs, and stuffiness, yet they sat there well past six o'clock, toasting their new home, happy to be together again. Because the house was strange to them and they felt the awesomeness of being together again, they spoke in whispers, about the children, the six-room duplex, and Michael's chances of teaching. Their voices hummed on, one into the other in contentment, punctuated by the distant chiming of bells.

In the yard, Emer asked, "What's all that ringing for?"

"The Gubmint bells," Zack said.

She smiled. Sometimes he talked as if he had a mouthful of marbles. The consonants seemed to obstruct the vowel sounds. "Who told you it was Government?"

"Mommy told me when you were far, far away," he indicated grandly with his hand, then ran to the loose slat in the fence and shouted after the girl, "Hey, I'm not afraid of a ol' chicken!"

"Shut up!" Emer climbed up and sat on the fence. "Hey, why don't you come back?" she hollered.

The thin girl disappeared into her back shed. Her black dress melded into the darkness. Her pasty face suddenly reappeared through the crack in the doorway. Sweat trickled down her temple and found a resting place in her clavicle. The chicken heat of the shed must be suffocating her. She opened the door a crack. "What … you … want?"

It sounded as if she was chewing with her front teeth. She probably felt very stupid. She puckered and forced her lips to stretch over her teeth in ways foreign to her, angling her jaw unusually forward. Emer hesitated on the fence top, not knowing what to say. Close by, a phone started to ring. The urgency of the ringing made Emer wish she could say something to the girl to drown it out. But instead she stared down at the blue-green print of her dress until it subsided. Looking up, she found the girl in the doorway fanning herself with a yellowed front page of *Allô Police*.

She cleared her throat behind the newspaper and shrugged, "Bye. I go."

"I'll bet you can't climb up this fence," Emer shouted.

"*Quoi?*" She looked back.

"Oh, never mind." She looked down at her brother to discover that he was crossing his eyes and sticking his tongue out at the girl. She swung her foot down and gave his behind a swift kick that almost set her off balance. "How ignorant can you be?"

His head went flying between the slats. He struggled to free himself and wailed, "Fix you! Fix you, Emer!"

Emer had already transferred her interest to a red truck sitting up on blocks in the middle of scattered white chicken feathers. She pointed. "Is that yours?"

Hesitantly the French girl came toward them and inspected Zack's predicament.

Perched up high, Emer gets a good look at her—a thin angular frame and long flaxen hair, curlicued and limply hugging the nape of her damp neck. The black cotton dress is too big for her.

"My name's Emer, and we've just moved in," she barely whispered, nodding her head toward the house.

"*Tu es anglaise?*" Her black eyes flashed.

Emer hesitated. "Well, my mother is French but my father speaks English."

"Oh." The pale face nodded. "*Ma mère pis mon père sont français.*"

"My mother speaks French." Emer frowned as if in deep thought. "I think she must be French."

"*Pis ton Père?*"

"My father's Irish, I think." With all the "Begorras" and "Top o' the morning to yez" that came out of her Great-Aunt Maura, Emer surmises he must be Irish. Plus of course her name, Emerald. She'd been named for the old Emerald Isle. Not that she'd ever been to Ireland, nor had she ever seen a real green emerald. Only a fake one that Gran Silvy showed her when she accompanied her father on one of his visiting jaunts. Finally, she said, "But he speaks French too, so I'm not really sure." She bit her lower lip, pensively.

"Oh." The flaxen head nodded.

"Understand? Capiche?"

THE WORLD'S FAIR

The girl threw her palms skyward in a question mark and walked toward the remains of an old barn on her side of the fence. Her bare feet came down hard on the sharp stones. At the foot of the ladder that led to the loft, she lifted her chin and gazed directly at Emer. "You want see more chickens?"

Emer shifted uncomfortably on the sharp wooden edge of the fence; her face tilted upward as she listened to the irritated squawks from above. "Why don't we drive your truck instead?"

The bare feet tense their toes in the hot sand, clutching the gravel, releasing and waiting. She isn't sure she understands the request, but she understands the gesture. "Non," she says. "My father no like."

Zack started to wail that his head was stuck. Emer, glad of an excuse to avoid the pecking chickens, shinnied down the fence and pretended annoyance. "Tiresome. That's what you are. Serves you right for making faces."

Zack tried to wriggle around to punch her, but his arms flailed the fence instead.

The girl climbed up to the middle of the ladder to get a better look. The dead dress fluttered limply about her knees. She snickered.

"Stay still a minute, will ya? How can I get you out if you keep acting like a wet hen?"

"Yur hurting me, yur hurting me!"

She stifled his screams and looked toward the house.

The French girl laughed as she came down the ladder.

"Why do you not stop to pull?" She ambled gracefully toward the fence.

Puffing and straining, Emer gritted her teeth. She hated the girl for laughing.

The girl's pale face leaned close to Zack's by-now-purple one. She turned her head to one side. "*Tourne-la de côté.*"

Emer released her brother's shoulders and without any more fuss he pulled his head through. He rubbed his scratched face, forgetting he was mad at Emer.

She climbed back to her perch.

Taking his anger out on the loose boards, he kicked as hard as he could with his high-laced boots. "Mean ol' fence!"

The girl giggled on the other side, joining in and banging the rotted wood with her back in response to his banging.

The fence shook so hard with the two of them pounding that Emer jumped off and peered at the girl through the opening. The girl caught Emer staring and stopped.

The sun was beginning to go down and already birds were chattering for limbs for the night. Emer grumbled into the silence. "I hate it when the sun goes down. Birds are going to bed. It means I have to go in. The old seven o'clock curfew."

From the kitchen window Bella watched the orange sunset. "Better call the children in. It's getting late." She drank the last of her beer. "Shall we unpack tonight?"

"No, let's just unpack the dishes and put up the beds for now. The rest can wait 'til tomorrow."

"Call them in. I'll heat something up."

Outside at the fence, the silence lengthens.

Emer murmured, "What's your name?"

The girl fingered the ends of her straight hair.

"Roberta." And she added, *"Mais tout le monde m'appelle Poupoune."*

"Poopoon, Poopoon," the boy purred delightedly, plunking down on the ground closer, to see her face.

"'Poupée' means doll, right?" Emer said thoughtfully. "But you are Poupoune. Pretty close, isn't it?"

THE WORLD'S FAIR

The girl seemed satisfied. She smiled and sat on the ground as close to the opening as she could, smoothing the faded material delicately over her bony knees, her legs extended in front of her. Zack's pumpkin face reflected the orange of the setting sun. He picked at the slivers in the wood. Emer sat crouched with her knees under her chin and hummed a tune she heard on the nickelodeon in the Queen's Hotel. A hotel that her mother's cousin owned in Gatineau Pointe.

"*C'est 'Mexicali Rose.' Je l'ai déjà entendu à la radio.*" Poupoune had heard it on radio.

Somewhere nearby a fire truck reeled by. Emer stopped humming. Their hearts beat faster but no one moved. Poupoune crossed herself. The shrill sound died in the distance.

"Gee, I thought they were coming here for a minute an' we've just moved in," Emer said to no one in particular.

The girl grabbed a handful of gravel and nervously shifted it from one hand to the other. "You have radio?" She held her breath for an answer.

Emer shrugged and brushed the sand from her cotton dress. She countered with another question: "Do you want to play chess?" She'd learned the game from her father while she was in the San and played with everybody who'd play with her.

Poupoune scrutinized her thumb. "*Non*, Maman say to me, stay in yard."

Emer cast a glance at Poupoune's thumb to see what is so interesting. "What are those white specks on your nail?"

Poupoune clenched her fists, hiding her nails. "Maman, she say they are white lie marks because I tell lie. But that is not true."

Emer examined her own nails for lie specks but was disappointed. "That's funny, I tell a lotta lies and I don't have any specks." The three heads came closer together to check each other out.

"Maybe you have on your toes."

Emer frowned, thinking of the red polish on her toes and that she would have to take it off to have a good look. "Hmmm, maybe." Three heads nodded reflectively.

Back inside the house, Bella said, "The children must be getting hungry for their supper."

Michael nodded distractedly. He stared into the amber liquid, trying to piece the fragments of his life into a formal pattern.

Order it. I must order it. There had been a pattern before the San. As vague as it was, studying for his Master's degree had held him in a pattern. He hadn't been able to finish it because of the illness. But now that he was cured, he would get back to work on it, first chance he got. Order. I must order my existence.

Bella found a can opener in one of the cardboard boxes. "A tin of soup will have to do. I don't have any bread."

Outside, in the vanishing light, three pairs of eyes strained to see one another. The crows made their peculiar double-sounding cawing as they swooped down for their prey. No one made a move. The kitchen light in Poupoune's house flickered on, throwing a buttery yellow reflection on the garbage cans underneath the window. Suddenly a vicious yank was given to the shade, rolling it to the bottom. Poupoune giggled nervously. Just as swiftly, the blind rolled to the top again with a resounding bang, as if the spring had broken. There were loud screams and shouts as pandemonium broke loose in the kitchen. The children freeze. Unconsciously they huddle closer together.

Poupoune spits on the ground. "*Là, elle est fâché.*"

"She's mad," Zack whispers. "Come over this side."

"Are you scared of her?" Emer asks.

"Nah. My mother, she has big voice. Always she sound mad."

"Come see my chessmen." Emer was proud of the hand-carved pieces the San had given her before she left. Sounds of crashing cutlery and crying babies made them move.

"Hokay." Poupoune threw her long legs over the fence and was over in a second. She stood on her spindly legs, legs as round as the legs of a kitchen chair, only wavering uncertainly. "Oh." She took in the clumps of tufted grass and the one tree at the back. *"C'est différent ici."* And she added, *"C'est nette."*

"Clean?" Hmmm. Never thought of it that way.

Poupoune grimaced as if she had a sour lump in her mouth.

"Let's go in. Go in, Emer," Zack said, waddling ahead of them.

"I have to get my chessboard, anyways." She disappeared into the house.

Poupoune doesn't move, but scans the whole yard with her eyes.

She's been in it before. It's better kept than her own. Even has a vegetable garden. *Avec des fleurs aussi!* She feasts her eyes on the flowers. Her heels firmly dig two small holes in the earth. The house would be better than her own too. She does not care to see that. Her pride tells her it's best to wait in the yard.

Emer called back, "Aren't you coming?"

"Non. I wait here."

Zack opened the inner screen door. "C'mon!"

"C'mon!" Emer said. "Then I'll go to your place."

Poupoune stood rigidly in the two holes she made for her feet, and shook her head violently that she won't, and that she certainly won't let the English girl come into her house.

"But why?" Emer strained to see her in the dusk.

Zack slammed the screen door.

Poupoune stared at her shoeless feet. When she became aware of the length of her black dress, with its uneven hemline, she raised her head, and, mustering all of her pride together, haughtily walked down the Maguire laneway toward the street.

Emer ran and tried to grab her long bony arm. She hadn't made any friends since she had come out of the San; she wasn't going to let this prospect get away so fast. They struggled quietly on the sidewalk.

Poupoune, her lips sucked tensely inside her mouth, tried to unglue the tentacle-like hold on her arm. Defiantly, the words clipped out of her mouth. "You want see *my* house?" The street lights had not come on yet.

Emer nodded yes. Her eyes fell to Poupoune's shoeless feet on the hot cement.

Poupoune ran straight past her house to the corner of Prospect and King Edward.

Emer ran after her. She again tried to grab hold of her arm, but Poupoune would not be touched.

At the edge of the sidewalk she pointed to the corner store, "*C'est l'épicier.*" She was waiting for darkness to enshroud her house.

Emer read it out loud. The sign says, "Routhier's Groceries."

"*C'est ça.*" They crossed the street at the corner, with Poupoune giving her the grand tour. Biding her time, she pointed to a two-storey brown house. They were all out on the front porch sitting on some old trunks.

Emer saw that the father had a long beard and a black beanie on his head. She was wide-eyed.

"I don't understand what they're saying." She thought everyone in the world spoke English.

Poupoune nodded in agreement. "*Moi non plus. Ce sont des Polonais.*"

Next door to them is a duplex. On the front lawn sat a howling baby. His eyes seemed glued shut with green stuff. His mother ran in and out with heavy boxes.

"I think the baby's sick." Emer clutched her stomach and let her tongue hang out. "Yuck!"

Poupoune shrugged. She had lived on the street all her life. She had seen it all. New people moving in, old people moving out. Pointing to the duplex next to it and the man in the rocker, she said, "*C'est Monsieur Chapelle.* Saturday nights they have big fight. Him and Madame. Police come. Lots of fun."

Emer swallowed hard. Grown-ups fighting? Police coming? Wow!

Her attention was drawn to some furniture in a moving truck parked next to the Chapelles' house. "Gee, look at this polished table. You can see your face in it," she said, distracting herself from the rawness.

Michael came out on the porch. He beckoned her in for supper.

"They move into apartment house. They are rich people. Only rich people, they go there. They have big radio too. Sometimes they play loud. I hear." The girl looked wistful. "But they very quiet. Not so much fun as Chapelles' house."

"My father's calling. I have to go home." She quickly scanned the gold plaque on the stone gate. "Truro Apartments."

Poupoune continued, "I am glad I am not you."

"Why?"

"Because you live next door to crazy woman."

"Oh?" She imagined a witch with stringy long black hair and laughed. But as she faced her house from the opposite side of the street, she saw a woman on the other side of their duplex sitting in a nursing rocker, bolt upright.

Poupoune whispered confidentially, "Monsieur Larocque's

wife she stare all the time," and added, like a little old lady, "Monsieur Larocque, he is very nice though. He has no job and he give me candy."

Emer remembered the thin man who had given them the sunflower seeds. "Yes, I know."

The two girls tiptoed closer to the rocker. "Why does she stare?"

Poupoune giggled behind cupped hands. "Because she crazy."

Emer was puzzled. Craziness and staring just didn't seem to fit, and she's ramrod straight too. How strange.

Flushing with embarrassment she pointed. "Me, I live there," she said, indicating the only free-standing shack on Prospect Street. It was a brick house to the right of the Larocques'. At that moment the street lights came on.

Emer had difficulty taking her eyes away from the painful sight of the old lady to the painful state of Poupoune's house. The front door hung at a slant. A greasy windowpane glimmered dully in the fading light. Loose bricks were scattered all over the alleyway at the side of the house, leaving patches of emptiness where she could see straight through to the plaster of the inner walls. The parlour window was cracked. A piece of cardboard kept the draft out. Emer looked up and down the street at the houses on either side. She saw the street now as if for the first time.

It had seemed a pretty street when they first moved in, with its people and tall trees. But looking closely at all the funny crooked houses jammed one on the other, it looked sad somehow. The people in rockers on their porches seemed lonely and forgotten. Emer's heart throbbed in her head at her new-found sight. It was a sorry street. Where there was no future. Waller Street would have been better to live on. At least there were no sorry sights to see. She wondered why her father had moved them here. People seemed so poor. She stared at the smashed parlour window. It wasn't the poorness she minded so much as the shame that went with it. Poupoune was ashamed to be poor; Emer knew that much and that she minded. Suddenly the door of Poupoune's house opened. It fell back against the wall with such force that the few remaining pieces in the front windowpane fell out and shattered into the hallway. A fat woman with pitch black hair appeared in the doorway.

"Where is that bitch?" she shouted, and slapped her fat thigh with a switch. Her eyes fell upon Emer. "Hey you, you seen my girl?"

A heavy smell of grease and urine drift out the open door. Emer nodded and whispered in fright that Poupoune must be in the back.

"Hah." The woman snorted a heavy lump of phlegm back into her throat and hurled it with a curled tongue onto the damp earth. "She is never around when I want her, that one."

A streak of lightning illuminated the woman's body with grotesque clarity. Involuntarily Emer stepped back. She could hear the squalling of babies in the back kitchen but her eyes were glued in fascination on the woman's swollen belly.

Madame Sarrazin was used to being stared at in that way. "How old you?"

"Thirteen," she lied in fright.

"You speak English. You must be Protest-ant."

That was final.

Somewhere a phone started ringing. Emer didn't hear. She stared at the woman's middle part, wondering what it was she was protesting about.

"*Mais mon Dieu*, what is the matter?" The stomach swung around.

"The cat, she has your tongue?"

The door slammed shut. The bricks danced.

Emer stood still in the silence.

CHAPTER THREE

Michael

AS SOON AS MICHAEL establishes his family in the little house on Prospect Street, he walks over to the University in search of Father Bruneau. Mid-afternoon. A good time to catch him, in between classes. At King Edward and Rideau, rain starts to come down in hard, driving drops. He steps inside the doorway to Leo's Snug Café. The store-front looks like a waterfall. Through it he sees an old colleague. Michael sits down in the booth opposite Bert Buckingham.

For a full instant Bert looks at him in disbelief. "Well, for God's sake!" He lowers his newspaper. "What a surprise! Michael Maguire! God's sake! I don't believe it!" He touches Michael's arm to make sure he's real. "Who would have believed it?" he shouts. "Good to see you! How are you?"

Michael laughs at his friend's spontaneity and shakes the rain out of his jacket. "Wonderful. Never felt better."

Bert's massive body stands up and they shake hands. "So, you're out! Back in the land of the living! To think that three years ago I thought you were for it." He starts. "My God, has it really been three?"

"All of three years." There was an embarrassed pause.

The waitress slaps a wet rag across the marble surface.

Bert orders two coffees and shifts his weight uncomfortably. "I'm sorry I couldn't get out to see you, Mike."

"Forget it. I wasn't much interested in seeing anyone anyway."

THE WORLD'S FAIR

"I did think of you though. I really did."

"Sure."

Self-consciously Bert offers him a cigarette. Michael refuses.

"Did you ever complete your Master's?"

"No. Not quite."

"Still working on Fermat's last theorem?"

Michael stretches out his fingers on the tabletop. Pierre de Fermat was a lawyer and amateur mathematician who, in about the year 1637, annotated his copy of Bachet's translation of Diophantus's *Arithmetika*. "There are no positive integers such that $x^n + y^n = z^n$ for $n>2$." The equation both rankled and excited him. He seemed to be always on the verge of solving it.

"How did you guess?"

"How could I not guess? Been working on it since I've known you."

Father Bruneau had been math professor in Michael's fourth year, before his appointment as dean. He'd been inspired by the precision of Bruneau's presentation of Fermat's work. It was beautiful. His low-key comment at the end of the seminar clinched it for Michael: "If it could be solved, it would open many doors in the world of mathematics."

Aside from the prize money involved, it appealed to Michael's pioneering spirit of problem-solving.

"If I can crack it, it's not only my Master's—it could mean a doctoral." He'd promised Emer life in eternal sunshine if they got out of the San. It was a promise. "Peru, here we all come," was one of his all-time chants.

The silence is broken only by the hard, pelting rain against the plate glass. Someone puts a nickel in the nickelodeon. Bert exhales smoke from his bulbous nose. "How is Bella?"

MICHAEL

"Why?" he asks suspiciously, aware that his suspicion is an old habit. It comes from their school days, when they competed with each other for women. Him and Rex Manners. Old buddy-boy. From the flatlands. Sas-cat-chew-awn.

"Just asking."

Bella. Beautiful, enigmatic Bella. Daughter of beautiful Anna. *La fille d'Anna. De la Pointe Gatineau.* It was what attracted him to her, the enigma. She inspired him to restore clarity in her life. He loved trying to sort her out. Reminded him of the young girls sitting around his grandmother's table, asking him what they should do with their lives. He felt badly for them, but attracted at the same time. All of ten years old, giving them advice made him feel needed.

"Fine," he says.

"Where's she living now?"

"We're living on Prospect Street."

Bert arches his brows. He lives in Sandy Hill.

"Downtown, eh? The kids too?"

Michael swallows the hot coffee, nodding the class difference into his cup. Not being married had its drawbacks. It was called keeping a low profile in Lowertown.

"Do you love her?"

"Love? What do I know? I married her before I went into the Sanatorium. Didn't think I'd make it. I married her so she'd get the Relief money for the kids."

"So you finally got the dispensation from the Bishop?"

Two months after the TB diagnosis, Michael had lived in the Bishop's Palace. He sweated it out in the dark lobby on a hard wooden bench in front of the enormous, bleeding Christ. For days he waited for His Eminence to make an appearance. When he finally did, Michael asked the Bishop for an annulment of Bella's first marriage. He wanted to marry her. Her first marriage had never been consummated. Before the marriage, yes, but not after the ceremony. The Bishop raised his bushy eyebrows.

"That can't be proven."

"I have two children. I have TB. I might die. I want to marry her. I want to provide for them now, in that eventuality."

"They're illegitimate and you shall die in mortal sin." The Bishop's cheek twitched.

Michael fell out of the marble palace. *Mea culpa, mea culpa, mea maxima culpa.*

"I married her in the United Church."

Bert chuckles. "You're living in mortal sin, then."

"How'd you guess?"

"He wouldn't annul it?"

"No." Live with or without her. It's all too late. Two children and ten years too late. "You must live together as brother and sister," the Bishop intoned. Michael's immortal soul is condemned, any way he slices it. Shouldn't have followed her home on the Rockcliffe streetcar. He'd played violin in the orchestra at the Standish and was trying to out-Venuti Joe, in a self-styled Paul Whiteman orchestra. Bella appears one night. They sip wine between sets. He walks her through the tall maples of Rockcliffe Park to the little dock on her way home to the Pointe. Heard her story. His heart opened.

"Red Lips, kiss my blues away." Who was kissing whose blues away? Stay together because of the kids. Yippee! The very day he went into the San, Equapoise set a new track record and Bert made a royal flush.

"Remember that royal flush you got?"

Bert laughs. "Yeah, that was unforgettable. In fact that was

MICHAEL

the day your Dad and I drove you out to the hospital. Afterwards he took out an insurance policy on you."

"What?"

"He figured you were finished."

"Fucker."

"I wasn't with him. Your mother told me."

"Bitch."

Bert clears his throat. "Well, it suited the two of them, wouldn't you say?" He stands up. "Look, have to disappear into the kitchen for about ten minutes. Hang loose. I'll be back."

"The kitchen?"

"Yes. I have half-ownership of this place now."

"Congratulations!"

"Just checking on staff. Be back in a flash."

"Right. A new chapter for you, huh?"

Michael recalls that talking with his old friend is like talking to himself. Past experience of their friendship always has beneficial results. Bert and he had always been privy to each other's personal lives. Presently it inspires Michael to re-examine family history afresh. Now that he's out, processing is the order of the day. It hastens, he hopes, an arrival at closure.

Michael winces at the inflow of his mother's family folklore, her unfinished history. Her paternal side came from France. One of the Louis gave her great-great-grandfather a rectangular piece of land in Papineauville. A piece of land on the St. Lawrence River that thrust its way into the wild interior. A seigneury southeast of Quebec City. Ancient history dead and gone.... But *not*. He corrects himself. History living itself out in other forms, in the present.

THE WORLD'S FAIR

Curbing his uneasiness about French history, he reminds himself that he's Irish. Nothing to do with me. Pure historical facts. Nonetheless, he's assaulted with a flood of unbridled thoughts of Papineau ... Louis Joseph. The brilliant mind.

The only Frenchman seated in the then British Parliament ... 1795. Michael muses. Anyone thereafter who displays a creative intelligence inherits the title of having "*la tete de Papineau*." Papineau's head. A phrase that his mother often uses on him. His knowledge of French history was as seen from her perspective.

The history of Papineau is the history of a nationalism that was born out of Wolfe's attack upon Montcalm's back. There was no battle as such. Montcalm's cannons were fixed on the Island of Orléans, where Wolfe had encamped his men for several weeks in the summer of 1759. French cannons fixed on the English base at Montmorency Falls.

Redcoats, flat on their bellies in the dark, sail south up the St. Lawrence. Barely dawn, Wolfe sees a goat path on the side of the cliff.

To turn the cannons around would take six workhorses and many days; according to his mother this was spoken from mouth to mouth among the people. The whispered tradition. It ran deeper than legislation, searing itself into memory, Michael observes.

Reviewing the fragments of available information, he knew that the criteria for winning a battle in those days was that the leader of one side had to be killed by a member of the opposing force. Wolfe went down first on the Plains outside the walls ... Montcalm a very short time later. Not, according to the book, a clean win.

Historically, France was too involved in the upcoming revolution to send support. The British mandate at that time was to win for the sake of bolstering the weak British economy. Quebec fell.

MICHAEL

All heads lowered in grief. Up went the Union Jack. Commerce began. Game over. The aftershock continues. That was his mother's take on Canadian history.

― ⁕ ―

His father, on the other hand, was another story. John Maguire's family came over in the "coffin boats" from the parish of Ballybruck during the potato famine in the mid-1800s. Michael can hear his mother now. "He's a johnny-come-lately straight out of bog country." She snorts mockingly. *Her* lineage was French aristocracy. "Harrumph!"

As for Silvy's side of the family, the maternal side, a wobbly fishing shack perched on the Gaspé rocks on the edge of the tumultuous Atlantic told the story. It housed a family of twelve boys.

Silvy's grandmother died while giving birth to the thirteenth child, her mother, Alma Couture.

"Another dynamite couple," Michael ruminates sardonically.

His mother married John at fourteen. Six months later Michael was born. His half-sister, Andrea, was two years old at the time. Three months after his birth Silvy takes off for the circus. She places Andrea with grandmother Alma and Michael with Aunt Maura, John Maguire's sister.

Billed as Leontine the Lion Tamer, she tours small towns in the northern States. How she reconciles her aristocracy with the circus, God only knows. Perhaps her flightiness came to her from her mother's side. He couldn't figure it. Finally Michael decides it's best to leave sleeping dogs lie.

He phoned Silvy the day he got out of the San. His disturbing dreams had followed him into the hospital. He wanted an end to the silence.

"When can we meet?" he asks her. No response.

He was about to repeat the question when she said, "Look, I'm relieved that you're better, but I don't want any more discussions on the subject of your father. I'll talk to you about anything else, but not about that. It has no bearing on anything."

No bearing? Where did she come up with her vocabulary? In spite of himself his jaw drops open on the other end of the line. "Are you still there?" she asks.

His mouth is parched. "I'll go elsewhere then. I'll find out from someone else."

"Do as you please. You can come pick up your books, but I won't answer any more of your crazy questions." The phone line hums. End of interview.

As for John Maguire, his "father" left for the First World War when Michael was five. Michael remembers a man in a rough khaki uniform picking him up and hugging his good-byes in Maura's backyard.

The only other time he'd seen him was when he needed two hundred dollars to go to university.

Silvy said it would be a good idea, seeing as she didn't have the money.

They met in the boiler room of a factory. His father was up to his elbows in black grease.

When the old man refused, Michael said, "You are my father aren't you?"

"Sure, 'tis a wise man that knows his own father."

Ouch! Duck! "What barrel did that one come out of?"

The old man had replied in true W.C. Fields fashion. "Gunsmoke to mystify the victim, m'boy. Money, you say? For university, you say? Unh-unh, nothing doing." He throws him a hard look over

MICHAEL

the flapping towel that says I know who you are, but I'm not going to hurt you with that.

Michael feels the look. Reads it correctly and, at fourteen, reels.

"Shit, what else am I supposed to say? You bounce in on me here, unannounced. I never had an education and look at me. I'm one of the few people in Ottawa—bejasus," he sputters, "in this *country*—with a job. What do you need an education for? What's an education got to do with it?" And then, as an afterthought, "Try your mother. She's always got a buck in the bottom of her bag."

Michael felt a gagging lump.

Maguire was high on humour. It was his Irish trump even when it was tragic.

Michael fell out of the factory.

"'Tis a good *bouche-trou*," Maguire shouts after him. To himself he adds, "It stops the truth from leaking through."

Michael leans against the factory wall in shock. He can hear the old man ranting disjointedly above the screaming machinery. "For a while, anyway. It kills the pain. All 'round. The First World War was rough, but this is the roughest yet. Straight-shooting is straight-shooting, but this is open massacre. Don't care for it one bit. Shit, why didn't I listen to my sister? She told me the Longprés were rotten to the core. I didn't believe Silvy would screw me around like that. Me a regular soldier in the British Army. I was had."

Michael heard the rafters echoing his rage as, alone, he raved at the sweating walls in the boiler room. "That bitch! That bitch sending him after me for money! I'll get her back! I'll pay her back. One way or two others. The fuck I won't. That cheap, two-timing, demented cunt! Never fear, Maguire's here. I've been shivied by a fuckin' question. I'll kill the cheap tart with my bare hands."

The damage was already done. Michael had been shivied by the answer.

Bella, however, felt that the old man's story of not being Michael's father was pure defence of his pocketbook. Nothing else. It was she who, in her wit, forever afterwards called old man Maguire "Long pockets, short arms."

The recent news that his father had taken out an insurance policy on him before he went into hospital confirmed his feeling that Maguire was not, in fact, his father.

❦

"Sorry, Michael. Things in the kitchen need attending to."

Michael readjusts himself in the booth. "Congratulations! It's certainly a big step away from teaching."

"One has to do what one has to do. Particularly these days when even the teaching jobs are at a minimum."

"You're still at the university, aren't you, Bert?"

"Sure." Bert shrugs as if the job bores him. He teaches English to a bunch of what he calls "uninspired lunkheads." "I have a really hot idea, though. Fortuitous as hell that you walked in. How would you like to come in on it with me?"

"What is it?" Three years hadn't changed Bert. Yet another "million dollar" idea.

"How about being your own boss?" Bert's child-like enthusiasms haven't changed.

Remembering past plans with Bert that had failed, Michael declined. "Think I'll see Bruneau first." The waitress fills a second cup. He watches her disappear into the kitchen.

"What happened to Ruth?" Michael asks. Had the legs of a thoroughbred, that girl. All warmth and soul; moved gently. A

MICHAEL

ballet dancer could not have improved on her. Head bent over his chest, sucking his nipples. Lightly skimming his thigh with the inside of her arm. Her warm fluid spirit moving over, under, on all sides engulfing him within her.

"Seriously, Mike, you could make a real mint if you came in on this with me."

Michael had lost too much time and money on the last "deal." "I told you, I'm not interested. Anyhow, I haven't got the money you'd probably need to get started. As a matter of fact, right now I'm looking for a teaching job."

The nickelodeon played.

"I'm no millionaire,

And I'm not a one to care.

I've got a pocketful of dreams."

"God, Michael, I've got a bushelful. Do you think that's too much? A bushelful?"

"What's become of Ruth?"

Bert rubs his palms together. "That's just it, though. You don't need cash for this deal. That's the beauty of it."

His evasiveness annoys Michael. "What happened to her, Bert?"

"How should I know?" he replies impatiently. "Waitressed here for a year after you left. Picked up a job at the Regal Hotel in Hull. Had a kid."

"Yours?"

Bert looks around the restaurant as if he were searching her out. "Don't think so. She died two months ago."

Snap.

"What of?"

"Gonorrhea."

Snap some more. "C'mon, people don't die of that anymore."

"Don't they, though?" Bert stomps his cigarette until the paper splits and the loose tobacco forms a little mound in the middle of the ashtray.

"What's the matter with you? You always used to be so game to make good money quick. What's changed you?"

Hardcore Ruth always said, "Time, that's what changes you, my boy." She was right of course. Thirty was a pretty sobering thought.

Bert flicks his cigarette in the ashtray. "C'mon, Michael. What do you say?"

The glint of his gold wedding band flickers in his eyes. "I'll come straight to the point, Bert. I didn't come in here to discuss ways of making fast money." He sucks in some air.

"What are the chances of getting my old job back?"

"Teaching Maths?"

"That. Or anything."

"You have changed."

Dance with the fucking reaper for three years and see which way you swing, baby. "Let's just say that for the time being I'm not sticking my neck out on any uncertain projects. What are the prospects for the summer session?"

Bert pulls at his earlobe and squirms in the booth uncomfortably. "To tell the truth, Mike, there aren't any jobs going. Bruneau just rehired all of the old staff. Didn't take on any new people at all." He thinks for a moment. "No, that's not quite true. He took ol' Rex-buddy-boy back into the History Department part-time, because he went down to Mexico to study the Aztecs. The old man found that impressive." Flipping the newspaper to the front page, he said, "Everyone's having a hard time. Geez, even Chamberlain's getting it. None of us know where we're headed."

"But I'm not new. I started teaching right after my degree."

MICHAEL

Michael was proud of that. "By what stretch of your imagination could you call me new?"

"I never said you were. I only said Bruneau wasn't … "

"I don't care what you said; you were implying."

"You've been out of circulation for a few years, know what I mean?"

"That has nothing to do with it. I was the best Math teacher that department ever had. In spite of everything else, Bruneau would acknowledge that much. I worked with those kids and I got results, by God!"

"Take it easy. Don't be so touchy. He's a lot mellower now. He may have forgotten what's past." Bert's reassuring words did not reassure Bert. He rolled his body from side to side searching out a comfortable spot. He studied the dark intensity of Michael's eyes. "He's sowing the seeds of his own destruction," Bruneau pontificated. A trite saying that's true of most everyone's condition. Bert shifted. The bench creaked under his weight. The Bishop's refusal to annul Bella's first marriage was a non-issue for Bert, as it was for Michael. However, he wasn't so sure that the Jesuit would look the other way on this one. This one being Michael's marriage to Bella in the United Church.

"Sure. Sure." Michael watches the rain slowly drizzling down the window. "I'm just on my way to see the old man now. Work something out." Bruneau had always been impressed with his teaching methods. The good results he got from his students were the envy of the faculty. Once or twice a few students complained of Michael's rigid discipline; the old man gave him a reprimand. Michael felt that overall his record as a teacher was one to be proud of. He was certain that the Dean would reconsider him simply on the strength of his teaching ability.

Bert whispers. "Let me give you a piece of advice. Steer clear of him."

Michael slowly wipes a circle in the steamed-up windowpane, wondering about his friend's concern. "Easy for you to say. I've had time to think these past few years. I know now what I must do. Father Bruneau or not, I've got to get back. Teaching and my thesis are my ticket." His ticket to the peace of mind that comes from working at what he loved. Out of it, he felt sure would come a ticket to a better climate in Peru. Out loud he said nothing. Best not to. Best to aim his arrow at the bull's eye silently.

Three months before he went into the San, before the diagnosis brought his life to a crashing halt, there had been a front-page picture and an article about Bella's civil divorce in the *Ottawa Citizen*. Later, in the receiving line at a faculty social gathering, she was introduced as his wife. In consequence, the priest had forced Michael to resign. Father Bruneau had not wanted a "scandal" hovering over one of his staff. The present reason for their downtown living quarters.

"What does Bella say to all this?" Bert asks.

What does Bella say? What does Bella feel? What does Bella think? He could see the casually arranged upswept blond curls caressing her tightly drawn translucent complexion in the window glass. Bella, the reason for it all, had not two thoughts to rub one against the other, or so his mother always said. His mother was certainly no illumination herself. Bella's saving grace was her natural wit. By the time he met her she was divorced. A divorcée in 1929! A "Scarlet Lady" at eighteen! She'd already had a full life with no discernible future. Her history intrigued him. The difference between her and the girls at his grandmother's was that she smiled through it all. That and her vivacious dancing style were what had

MICHAEL

attracted him to her. When he came to think of it, she had a great natural beauty with a generosity of spirit that he had never met before. When he walked her home as far as the Rockcliffe Lookout, she had looked directly up at him just before he kissed her. "You have the most beautiful feather in your hat," she said with an impish smile. "It stands straight up."

He grinned. What an irresistible line. He thought that he'd heard them all. "Is that right?"

"Mmm ... that's right," she says as they kiss. She had the taste of promiscuity ... of the forbidden fruit of his youth. He had to have her.

They undressed each other in the shelter of the Lookout. Her full, round breasts shone with a pearly sheen in the moonlight. He gently kissed her nipples and felt her heavy breathing demanding more and yet more. They revelled in the exquisiteness of their nude bodies pressed one on the other, diamond upon diamond. The earth seemed to exhume aromas of pine trees, oak leaves, and freshly cut grass into his very mouth as the moonbeams scattered over the earth in a shower of nectar bliss.

At dawn they fell asleep in exhaustion. As the sun peeked through the balustrades in the clear light they sat up silently, looked at each other, and knew that they had just committed themselves to each other for a lifetime. This desire never waned. It remained strong and held their marriage together. They continued to fulfill each other's desire for sexual expression.

Bella's sexual come-ons were straight from the heart. He wondered about that. During their courtship he'd felt sorry for her. His feelings were like those he'd had for the girls around his grandmother's kitchen table. Life hadn't given them much of a chance, either. But Bella was different somehow. She just kept smiling through. Even while he was in the San. She came visiting every day for three years.

Michael murmurs, struggling to disengage his attention from the glass. "Well you know Bella. Nothing is very important to her unless she is immediately concerned." As long as the rent and groceries were paid, Bella never asked questions. Not the ideal relationship, but for the sake of the children, worthwhile in itself.... Was that dishonest? He wasn't sure.

Bert cups a lighted match to his cigarette. "I would have thought that in this case she was."

"Yes of course she is, but she never said anything about my returning to the university. So I presume she doesn't feel involved and hasn't given it any thought."

"Well then, all I can say is, if Bruneau says no, you can come in on this plan of mine any time you want."

"What plan are you talking about?"

"I've been thinking about it for a long time, but as soon as I saw you everything fell into place."

"Go on."

"How would you feel about running a private school all your own? You teaching Math in the mornings, me teaching English, and Rex teaching History the rest of the day?"

Michael smiled. "Old buddy-boy too, huh?" Rex was one of his favourite Damon Runyon characters. A history professor with a penchant for the racetrack. A character straight out of his grandmother's back kitchen. A devil-may-care cowboy from Canada's flatlands. A take-off-your-ten-gallon-hat-slap-it-on-the-earth-and-shout-YAHOO! as far as the horizon could take it. His mere presence invited Michael into it, every time. A freeing experience. "What does Rex say about it?"

MICHAEL

"Can't get a hold of him. Must be in Peru again."

"Ahhh....Yes Peru. Machu Piccu. 15th Century. Amazing history."

Bert's voice droned on about his teaching plan.

After a restless pause, Michael said, "That idea's old hat, anyway. I suggested it to you five years ago and you weren't interested."

"Yes, but the situation has changed. The staff cutbacks are enormous. The workload is more than one teacher can carry, with forty to fifty in a class. Students are screaming for extra attention. Private schools are in demand. And the beauty of it is, you don't need any investment to get started."

"Except rent money for a couple of classrooms, desks, chairs, blackboards.... No, Bert. I've been through it all before. There was never a spot cheap enough or local enough."

"Well, think about it, think about it. That's all I ask."

Michael glances around the cafe, suddenly hating the smell of acrid-cooked bacon. "This place has deteriorated. C'mon, let's get out of this greasy spoon. Don't know why we ever used to come here to begin with."

Bert slams his coffee mug. "Ruth!"

Her name stops Michael at the door.

After a moment of thought, he shrugs his acknowledgement and smiles at Bert. "All right, so I haven't forgotten her." Those never-to-be-forgotten "Jelly Roll Morton times." Her favourite tunes as well. How could he? Had it been love? Or lust? Not sure. It certainly felt like it could have been love.

The two men walk in the steaming summer rain. Up the slope, they pass the austere grey-stone walls of the Grey Nuns' convent. Bert mutters morosely. "They own half of Ottawa. Smart cookies."

"Speaking of smart cookies, how did Rex get to Peru?"

"Ol' buddy-boy won two hundred dollars at the track. Where else?"

"Still at it, eh?"

Bert nods. "Addicted."

Michael wonders if his friend is simply addicted to Machu Piccu studies. "I wouldn't mind seeing him again."

At the corner Bert asks him to his place for a game of chess. Old habits die hard. But not this time. "I'm on my way to see Father Bruneau."

They walk on in silence up Rideau Street. Most of the stores are closing. People are hustling home with their sodden paper bags. Every now and again the sky lights up with a sheet of summer lightning. The two men lean on the cement balustrade by the Château Laurier and watch a skiff work its way through the locks. Bert wipes the drops of rain streaming down his face with a white handkerchief.

Michael observes the civil servants in the square. They swarm like slugs after a rainfall. The Parliament Tower chimes the hour of six. Michael listens to the familiar sound. As always, the chiming bounces against the side wall of the Château. The notes seem to shatter themselves on the asphalt wall, shivering their separate ways into the Rideau Canal, vibrating against the blue steel locks below. The delicate tinkling reminds him of Maura.

"Listen, Michael, it's fairy-tale music. T'would make a harpsichordist proud," she said, lapsing, as she sometimes did, into her Irish brogue. His appreciation for music began at the side of the Rideau. It originated with the mysterious orchestration of the myriad bells in the Bell Tower on Parliament Hill. From the age of six she paid for his music lessons. Harpsichords and Maura went together. The steady diet of boiled navy beans flavoured with fatty chunks of salt pork gave him no indication of where she got the

MICHAEL

twenty-five cents to pay for his weekly tuition. He thought of his own children. Of their future.

He admired Maura's expertise with money. She had been a good provider. Nickel and diming it! Remembering with pride the Irish immigrants who came as workers to dig the canal, Maura's father among them. He smiled.

He hunches his shoulders over the cement railing to better hear the notes. A train whistles across the inter-provincial bridge, and can be seen zooming into Hull and beyond. To an outsider, Michael looks as if he were about to jump. Bert's low monotonous voice drones into his consciousness.

" ... and if it happens Bruneau doesn't give you a job, I can lend you some money to tide you over 'til you do find what you want."

"Thanks, but no thanks."

The warning cry of a train hoots under them.

They follow the locomotive's trail of smoke until it becomes white puffs in the distance. "I never realized how difficult Bruneau's sanction made it for you."

Quebec blinks across the river at him. He blinks back. "I'll speak with him tomorrow," he said, hoping that the Dean of Studies had loosened up about the rules on morality.

A streak of lightning rends the sky from one end of the river to the other.

"Looks like a real storm is mounting, and we're right in the middle of it."

Michael, wet to his skin, laughs. "We've been in the middle of it for a long time."

The rain bounces stinging ice-pellets on their grinning faces. They leave the railing reluctantly and walk slowly, in counterpoint to the pelting drops.

CHAPTER FOUR

Maura

MONDAY MORNING IT WAS, and the sound of screeching clotheslines assail the air like so many thrush come to find a place in the sun. The view from above finds row upon row of flapping laundry from one end of the street to the other. The vivid blues, whites, blacks, pinks, and greens wave like banners proclaiming Monday morning in Clarkstown.

 In one yard, almost buried alive in flapping laundry, a slight wisp of a woman is surrounded on all sides by clothes, clothes, and more clothes. Wet clothes. Clothes belonging to her older sister Meg and her four grown sons, and, of course, to herself, Maura. The sheets blow about her, almost winding her in their grasp. Her white hair blows this way and that. She can scarcely breathe. No oxygen at all, at all. She struggles to control the billowing clothes. The breeze rises slightly. She pinches a clothespin open. Ah, she breathes; there's air. Her clothesline whines resentfully as she pushes it further into the open. Stooping low into a hamper, she pulls out a pale green chenille bedspread. "Drat the hand-wringer. Doesn't do the job anymore." Maura heaves its heaviness with all her might over the taut wire. Daintily she shakes out another small bundle. A cluster of delicate lace handkerchiefs emerges along with several antimacassars and a needlepoint cushion cover. She shakes the cushion cover vigorously, examining it with the eye of an expert. "Hmm, the handwashing saved it. Good, she'll be pleased." She casts an eye toward Meg in the summer kitchen thumping a rolling pin. Maura tugs at the sharp wire and the clothes waltz out to the end of the line, joining the anonymity of the rest of Clarkstown's laundry.

She wipes her thin hands on the front of her flowered dress.

"Well, there's another job done." She presses her hands to the small of her back and arches her forty-four years slightly to relieve the stiffness. "They'll smell real fresh when I take them in tonight." She gazes directly into the sun, breathing in its rays. "My, but it's a beautiful day." She sighs and picks up the hamper. "Lovely day for clothes to dry…. And," she adds, "for my garden to grow in." She places the basket inside the door to the summer kitchen. "I think I'll have a look at what's going on out here."

Meg doesn't answer. The pounding of the roller on the pastry board drowns everything out.

The warm breeze wafts Maura gracefully down the three porch steps. She glides to the foot of the garden like a swan on a calm surface, and comes to rest at a bed of fragile violets. Her white head turns slowly, this way, then that, surveying the kingdom she has lately created. She bends down to inspect the violets more closely. "They're coming along nicely." The delicate blossoms seem to nod back at her in agreement. She smiles with the inner satisfaction that comes with achievement. Gently she examines the frail leaves with pale, tapered fingers. This is the first garden she has ever created. Her glance rests on a small plot of cucumber plants. Their leaves cling pathetically to the earth as if they are trying to support their own weight. They rest limply in her hand as she tries to support them into a growing position. "Poor things. I planted you too close, an' now you're choking yourselves for air. There wasn't too much room to plant you. Next year it'll be better, though," she says apologetically. "Had to choose a spot out of the way of the children. Maybe if I pack the earth tighter about you, it'll give better support." As Maura works to the end of the furrow, she notices small footprints. She smiles. "Let's see now. Whose footprints were those? They can't be the babies'; they're too big. They're not Gerry's … ah, they must be young Sheilah's." Meg's grandchildren had lived with them for nine years at Maura's invitation, because the son-in-law had been without work. Burroughs had finally landed a job with the City that May and they moved out. Maura gently rearranged the earth where it had been disturbed.

The cold light of the early morning sun beamed down almost harshly on the soft white swirls of hair nearly buried in purple flowers. Her first garden since she was given ownership of the house by her father, fifteen years ago, and it gave her great joy. Not the same kind of joy it gave her to raise Meg's children or her brother John's boy, but certainly as great a joy. So it's not a garden like most other gardens because there is no grass. Soft green grass that makes a garden a garden. No, there is none of that here. Not this year anyway. Because of the children and their footprints. So there is no soft green grass in the garden, … but there are plants. Yes, there are plants.

They grow beside the fence in the centre of the divided yard. And the plants have given her comfort since the children left.

A man's voice speaks cheerfully over the fence. "Good morning, Miss Maguire."

Maura looks up and hastily rises to her feet, brushing the dirt from her dress. "Good morning, Monsieur Latouche."

"Oh, do go on with your work. Please don't let me interrupt you." He leans over the picket fence.

"No, no. I'm finished." She holds both her hands stiffly away from her dress, her arms bent at the elbows.

He peers over at the plants. "How are they coming along?"

"Not too badly."

"Are those cucumbers that you have planted there?"

"Yes, and they're not making out too well. I think I planted them too close."

He squints to see them better. A surge of sheets floats high over his head.

"Maybe it would be a better h'idea if you transplanted them over on my side. More room here."

It was sometimes difficult for him to master confrontational vowel sounds that didn't exist in his own language. It made Maura smile. "Oh, Monsieur Latouche, it's very good of you but I don't want to put you to any trouble."

"No trouble at all. You bring them over here and I'll look after them for you."

Maura looks over at her plants. She asks, "Now?"

"Sure, you may as well. Just you hand them over here to me and I'll plant them. Give them a bit of a chance. The kids nearly trampled them to death over there."

"Ah, but they didn't mean to," she says gently. She goes over to her plants to free them from their tight beds.

Monsieur Latouche gazes at her bowed head as she busily lays the plants side by side until she reaches the end of the line. She places them in his big open hands.

"There you are," she says. "I hope I'm not putting you to too much trouble."

"No trouble. No trouble at all."

"It's very considerate of you." She leans over the fence and watches as he starts shovelling up the earth with his hands.

Monsieur Latouche grunts with the exertion. "At least here there's no children to step all over them."

"Ah now, they have to play somewhere."

"Well, not all over your plants. *Sapristi!* My goodness, you were too easy on them."

Maura catches a glimpse of the blue sky through the soaring sheets, and silently wishes the children were there again. She'd always had children about her, as far back as she could remember. At first there were her sister's children, the four boys and Bessie. Then her brother John brought his son to her for safekeeping. Dear Michael, such a good, intelligent child. She caught herself pursing her lips and worrying about him. That wouldn't do at all. Of course he would get better. He'd be out of the San in no time. She consciously resumed her stream of thoughts.

When Michael left home and young Bess got married there were her children to look after. Now, there were none. Still, Bess did promise to visit on weekends. Small compensation. For a month the house has been emptied of children and her life emptied of joy. Except of course for the plants.

Monsieur Latouche's voice droned vaguely in a distant fog.

"You've been raising other people's children as far back as I can remember. You let other people take advantage of you. That's your trouble. Look at Bessie now. It's none of my business, but you'd think her husband would have had more sense. Poaching. I can say it now they're gone. That's what it was, poaching. It's a wonder to me that they didn't find a house of their own long ago."

Maura sighed heavily. Babies peopled her mind as naturally as water a duck's. They were part of her. And now it was all over. It goes by so fast. She wonders if any of them remember her as clearly as she them. Probably not. Children are more fascinating to adults than adults are to children.

"Yes," he says with a nod, "you're too easy. And people walk all over you when you're too easy. That's my experience."

Maura gazes unseeing at the blur that is his face. "What's that you say, Monsieur Latouche?"

He looks into the pale, washed-out eyes and sees that she's not been listening. He shrugs. What's the use of feeling protective toward a woman who isn't protective toward herself? "I'm just saying," he says with infinite patience, "that we forget. Maybe I won't be living here in another three weeks. Your plants might be stuck over here with no one to water them."

"Oh," she says. "I forgot about that." Monsieur Latouche was her tenant. Had been for ten years. In all that time he had never left the house. Not even on a holiday. Maura finds it difficult to believe that he might have to move out at the end of the month. Meg insisted that they'd have to ask him to leave. Interest rates on the mortgage had gone up and he'd never be able to afford the adjustment. They would simply have to find a new tenant.

He stood up, brushing the dirt from his trousers. "I guess things are pretty well settled now."

"Well, as a matter of fact…." Her mind raced, trying to readjust her thoughts to the problem of the house. Her younger brother, John, had been in. When was it now? A week ago? Yes, a week ago. John had been in to go over the mortgage renewal and the new interest rates. It didn't seem possible that the Royal Trust could do something as nasty as turn her out onto the street. Surely they'd wait until things fell into place.

Monsieur Latouche's rent money had paid for the mortgage over the years. Two thousand dollars was left to pay on it. Though Maura was the youngest of the Maguires, her father left her the house when he died because he knew she'd never marry. Also, she was the cleverest in simple arithmetic.

"Yes?" Monsieur Latouche says a trifle impatiently.

The word made her jump out of her thoughts. "Yes, well, as you know, John was in to see us last week. He said he'd raise the money for us, an' we have yet to hear from him."

He toes the ground. "I see. Too bad I'm not in a position to help you out."

"Ah now, don't you worry yourself. Things always have a way of working themselves out. Goodness me!" She claps her hands to her bosom. "John is a boilermaker, you know, an' it's a good job, too. If we can arrange a loan from him, you'll be staying on an' there's just no two ways about it." She moves to go in, as if the matter's finished. "There now. That's settled."

"But what about Mrs. Vance? She's the one wanted me to move in the first place."

She smiles at him. "This house is in my name, not in my sister's. I have the final say."

Henri Latouche is not in the least reassured. He has talked to this woman over the back fence every day since he moved in. He knows her. He knows her sweet, naive gentleness. It always inspired in him an infuriating desire to protect her. He knows her deep love of children, her good nature, her warmth, her laughter, and the sweet smell of her skin. He knows her. He knows her vulnerabilities. And so he is not reassured.

"If only I could pay more than the twenty dollars a month. Then you could pay off the interest."

"Yes, that's right."

"But I always understood that my side of the house was your only source of income. If it's all used on the mortgage, how will you make out?"

"Now don't you worry your head about it. It's not your problem."

MAURA

But he persisted: "How are you going to manage?"

"I'll manage. Somehow I'll manage."

He shrugs. Why does he bother himself with her when she is so independent? "Anyway, Miss Maguire, don't want you to think that I haven't appreciated living here all these years at such a low rent."

"Oh, now, now." She taps his arm. "You've always been a very good tenant."

"The way you'd wait for the rent sometimes when I was late with it. And never say a word. I'll always remember that. The hard time I had after Madame died and you waited on the money without ever complaining."

"Ah sure, I knew I had nothing to worry from you." She puts her hands on her hips and takes a step backwards to look at him better. "Besides now, stop talking as if you're going to leave tomorrow, because you're not, you know. As I said before, if I have any say in the matter, you won't be leaving at all."

Monsieur Latouche toed the ground and smiled. My goodness, what charm!

She waggled her finger under his nose. "And stop smiling! What I say is true or my name isn't Maura Maguire from Ballybruck! So you can stop this ... this farewell speeching of yours."

He had worked all the years of his life as a civil servant and now his government pension wasn't enough to live on. He could taste the bitterness in his mouth. What to do? Where to go? And then, too, he loved this woman in a way he couldn't put a name to. Staring at the ground, he felt powerless. The earth was black and damp under his feet.

She fell to staring at the same spot on the ground, respecting his silence.

Maura stood on a revolving ball of a star, staring at an infinitesimal speck of a speck at a moment in time that no longer was, trying to gather her earthbound thoughts enough to communicate.

She finally looked up and whispered very low, "Don't worry about me. I'm not destitute. I have relatives. Goodness me, I have Meg. I'll never be wanting for anything. Please don't worry."

A screen door slammed resoundingly and they both looked up.

Meg stood stiffly on the porch, impatiently clutching and releasing the apron that hung from her shapeless middle. Her finger-waved white hair clung to her skull like a cap.

"Good morning, Monsieur Latouche."

Her thick glasses reflected the light in his direction, causing him to shield his eyes. The warm smell of cinnamon and baked apples permeated the fresh morning air.

"Maura, dear, could you come in and give me a hand with the pies before the boys descend on us for dinner."

"The boys, indeed!" Monsieur Latouche muttered under his breath.

Maura excused herself and hastened into the dark summer kitchen.

He nodded in what he assumed to be Meg's direction. "Good morning, Mrs. Vance."

She asked politely, "How's your rheumatism, Monsieur Latouche?"

"It's much better, thank you. Especially being out in the sun."

She rasped, "Yes, you've been out here long enough, haven't you?"

Meg could be a tartar when she wanted to and that was most of the time. To her, other people always had a better life than she did.

He shaded his eyes from her glasses and decided not to answer that one. Her sourness always amused him for some reason.

"I think I'll sit out in the sun myself this afternoon and rest my legs."

"The sun will do them good," he said. "It seems to draw out the pain."

"That's right. Draws out the pain. Ahh, it's a terrible thing to grow old," she said with a sigh as she shuffled along the porch to the door. "It's a beautiful day. Not a cloud in the sky. Lovely ... lovely...."

Monsieur Latouche looked down at the delicate petals of the wild phlox along the low, dividing fence, and was astonished that two sisters could be so different. *Why does she put up such a front? She hates the outdoors. In all these years I've never once seen her sit on the porch.*

Meg stood inside the dark kitchen, trying to blink away the sunspots.

Maura leaned over the wood stove, stirring the bubbling apple compote.

Meg swallowed the mouth-watering aroma of the cooking apples and rubbed her eyes, trying to stamp out the burning heat. "Did you have to stand there and tell him all our business?"

"Ah now, Meg, I didn't tell him anything that he didn't already know." She measured a teaspoon of cinnamon into the sauce.

"Well, our affairs are none of his." She yanked her glasses off, exhaled on the thick lens, polished them on her apron, and placed them on her nose.

She never gave up being the "elder" sister.

"Just you stop being so loose with your tongue or the whole street will know our business."

"You know very well Monsieur Latouche can be trusted. He's a good man." Maura brought the pot over to the table and sat down opposite her sister. "He's kind and thoughtful and he doesn't gossip."

Brusquely Meg rolls out her dough to the full size of the board. "Well, I don't care. I don't want it known up and down the block that we're having trouble with the new rates."

"But he's known that right along. Ever since I told him I was raising his rent. He knows it's to cover it. I never told him anything new."

"All the same, I don't want you standing out there talking."

She arranged the paper-thin dough into the pie plates. "All these years standing out there talking. It just doesn't look good either. I'll be glad when he's gone an' that's no lie." She nodded her head and clucked her tongue. "Whatever will the neighbours think?"

Maura stared down into the brown lumpy applesauce. "I don't care what the neighbours think." Her assertiveness surprised her. She noted that she felt good saying it.

"All these years," Meg went on, "talking over that back fence every morning as if your life depended on it."

"We were talking about the garden."

"If he'd only get himself a job instead of living off her insurance money. Can't be much left of it now."

"He's living on his government pension."

"Some people are natural-born fools though," Meg continued. "Can't use the same yardstick on them as we use on ourselves." She snorted. "Ah, I'll be glad when he's gone."

Maura looked at her sister. "I won't." She looked forward to those daily morning encounters. They were refreshing. There, now, she had finally said it, after all this time.

Meg pressed the dough firmly into the corners of the tin plates. Her wrinkled face swirled downwards, seemingly at rest. Impassive. No flicker. No twitch.

Maura waited for her sister to react, as she usually did whenever she took a stand. No response. Nothing happened. Meg shut down.

MAURA

Though she was only three years older than Maura, she hadn't aged nearly as well. Bitterness had left its mark on her face. Raising five children on Tom Vance's miserable salary in the stables had been a hardship. And when he died he'd left her nothing.

The Maguires had left County Limerick when both girls were in Grade Seven. Meg's eyesight had always been a problem in school. Her father defended it by saying, "She can't count because she can't see the board."

Maura remembered her father exploding as they ran down the gangplank in Quebec City, "We're damn lucky to be alive after that trip." They were just plain lucky that they hadn't boarded a "coffin boat." Her father had called it "divine protection." Then they all got jobs in Ottawa, including the two young girls. They charred in the rich houses in Sandy Hill.

Young brother John started work at 14 in a boiler factory. He picked it up again after he came back from the 1914–18 War.

The challenging trip over the Atlantic had taught Maura never to begrudge the universe for its shortcomings. It taught her to live every moment as if it were her last. And so she did what she loved most; she raised other people's children, to hide the ache that she'd never had children of her own. When she'd started caring for them at St. Brigid's Orphanage, she was astonished to be paid for work that she loved doing. She survived on that and the rent money from the duplex. And took pleasure in knowing how to make a nickel stretch.

She was so loved by the children that the nuns let her take children home with her on holidays and long weekends.

They even gave her Jesse. Her adored Jesse. Whenever she thought of Jesse and her father, the man she had loved, the pain welled within her. It never went away. When the baby died in the diphtheria epidemic, her heart broke, but she continued to tend her miniature crèche. In time, they sent her more babies to look after.

After his death she never thought of marriage as being an option for her. She thought of her work as a "calling." In her view she had been called, and she carried it as far forward as she was permitted. There was no other man after that, though there had been several suitors.

In any case, observing her older sister's marriage at close range, she had grown to prefer the freedom of the single state.

Her "true" marriage had become the raising of children.

She was married to her sister in the sense of being devoted to their relationship, such as it was.

When old man Maguire left the house to her and not to Meg, her sister was angry and remained so. Meg felt that life was not fair. Other people always had it easier.

Meg's neat white head was well bowed into the dough while a fly, just as busy, buzzed over her.

Maura knew the signs. Her sister had retreated by clicking herself off. Back to her room of pain. Ah, well. What's the use of trying to bring things out into the open? She would never discuss a thing reasonably. The most important things never got said. Meg was too concerned with what the neighbours thought about her and Monsieur Latouche—and it was ever thus, she thought.

Whatever would Meg have made of her secret engagement in her twenties? What would she have made of that, she wondered?

She watched a fly settle on Meg's head and whooshed it away with her hand, out the open door. "Ah, well," she sighed, "Kelly for bikes." An old Gaelic expression that she used when she was at a loss for a response.

"What's that you say?"

MAURA

"Nothing. Nothing at all."

"Pull up your socks then and pour the sauce into the pies. Can't be sittin' here 'til the cows come home."

"It's funny," Maura said as she poured, ignoring the platitudes, "that Johnny hasn't been in touch with us."

"What's so funny about it?"

"Well, he did say something about trying to raise the money. It's funny he hasn't been in touch. He might've let us know, either way, before this."

"I never did place any faith in that one. Never will. He's let us down before this, and well you know, there's nothing funny about it."

"It would be grand if he could raise it, though, wouldn't it?"

"Yes, grand for your Monsieur Latouche."

Maura placed the empty pot on the table. "That was unnecessary."

"In any case"—Meg scraped the old dough from the table with a knife—"it's best to carry on as we planned at the start. Find a new tenant, raise the rent, and start catching up with the backlog."

Maura suddenly had an idea. "Maybe when Michael gets better, he and Bella could move next door with Emer and Zack."

"Oh, that reminds me. I forgot to tell you. He phoned while you were in the back. Said he was out. They let him out a week ago."

Maura sat down slowly. "They let him out?" she whispered. "He's better! Emer too?"

"Yes."

She was barely able to contain herself. "My, but that's good news, isn't it! He must've sounded happy," she mused. "Did he sound happy?" She leaned forward on the table like a child. "Goodness, why didn't you tell me this before?"

"Said he'd come over to see us as soon as he's settled in. They're moving to Prospect Street."

"Where's that?"

"Somewhere downtown. Four blocks east of Rideau Street," she snorted. "Where else can he live, given the circumstances?"

The shadow of a frown passed over Maura's face. "He probably hasn't the money to live anywhere else." She wished she could help him out. It upset her to think of him being strapped for money. "He's starting out all over again," she said in awe.

"Not married in the Catholic Church, indeed!" said Meg as she slapped some fresh pastry on the board. She spoke to the rolling-pin. "The United Church, hmph! If the Bishop refused to annul Bella's first marriage, then the answer was 'No' and that's that. All the parishioners out here thought so too! But then there were the children to consider and he had to do something and it was just an all-'round sticky affair." She flipped the pastry into a pie tin. "I suppose he's chosen to live downtown in the hopes of achieving a low profile with the parish."

Ignoring her comments, Maura said, "Well, did he sound happy?"

"Couldn't tell," said Meg as she resumed scraping.

"Did he say if he'd go back to teaching?"

"Didn't say."

"Bella and the children must be very happy."

"They should be. He's lucky to be healed at all with all the running around he did before he went in. Always consorted with the wrong kind, that one. Marrying a divorced woman, indeed!" she sniffed. "A movie starlet!"

"What's the matter with you, Meg? Aren't you happy to hear he's alive?" She shook out the flowered oilcloth.

"He's your boy. You raised him. He's no concern of mine, that's all."

"All the same he is your nephew."

Meg winced. "I'm not even so sure about that." She had never approved of John's shotgun marriage to Silvy Longpré. "She was a run-around," she said as she scraped the table clean. "And her mother, her very own mother, Alma Longpré, ran a whorehouse. Everyone in the parish knew it. And who was our Johnny seeing, anyways? Was it Alma or was it Silvy? He was twenty-two when Silvy was thirteen and pregnant by God-knows-who. Alma was twenty-eight. Or so she said. More thirty-eight, I'd say! Anyway, right smack in the middle he was, age-wise." Meg heaves a heavy sigh into the confusion of it. "And then he marries Silvy when she's fourteen years of age! Michael is born a few months after the wedding. And she hands the baby over to John, so's she can take off for the circus, no less! There'd been so much coming and going in that house, I doubt our Johnny was the father."

Maura looked out the window. She frowned, as she always did when the subject of Michael's paternity came up.

"She fobbed him off on John, God only knows," Meg continued.

"My goodness. You've been resurrecting that one for years. Can't you let it go? You can't take that out on the boy—on Michael, I mean. If that is so, it's no fault of his own," Maura protested. He was more sinned against than sinning, she was about to say, but then that would only add more fuel to the fire.

"I can't put it down to anything. I just don't feel he's our flesh and blood. You know what I mean? And please stop calling him a boy. Michael is a married man now with two children." Meg sees no discrepancy in calling her own grown sons "boys." Or even saying that Michael is married when she doesn't believe that he is.

THE WORLD'S FAIR

The front door creaks open. They look at one another in panic.

Maura throws the thick oilcloth down. "My goodness, it must be noon already and the pies aren't even in the oven yet."

"Ma?" Louie calls from the vestibule. "'Severything all right, Ma?"

"Yes, dear," Meg says cheerfully, her bitterness evaporating into a thin smile. "Things'll be ready in a very little while."

Louie came into the kitchen and fell into a chair. He pushed his cap back and wiped his shining forehead with the back of his hand. "God, it's hotter than Hades in here. Must be ninety at least. What's the wood stove on for?"

"It was cold this morning and we decided to bake pies with last year's apples from the cellar."

Maura threw a white linen cloth over the table. "How was your first day?"

"Not bad at all. Got four good fares this morning. All around Parliament Hill. Most of them MPs late for work."

Meg looked at her son proudly. "Do you keep all the fares, son?"

"Well of course not, Ma. I've got to pay old man Provost for the use of the car, an' then there's the gas and the oil. I don't know yet if there'll be much profit. We'll see. Stick it out for a month anyway."

"Michael's been let out of the San."

He looked at his aunt Maura, wide-eyed. "Is that so, now? Well what do you know? The old son of a bitch made it!" The word made the two women jump as if they were stung.

Meg stopped grating the cheese. "Louie, stop the language. I don't know where you picked it up. We certainly never spoke that way in the house." She eyed him suspiciously.

Maura polished the soup ladle. "Ah, he's thirty-nine. Let him be. Maybe it's us that are out of style."

He stuck his thumbs in his trouser tops. "Silvy will be plenty glad to hear about this."

Meg's lips formed a thin purple line. "I told you to stop seeing her and I mean business, Louie. Alma Longpré's the devil, and her daughter Silvy's the devil's wheels. They stole Johnny from us, and now they're working on you!"

Louie grimaced.

Meg laid the table for lunch. Her hands shook with rage. "Don't you think it's enough that they ruined the first generation of Maguires, without beginning to work on the second?"

"Ah, Ma, what's the harm of just dropping in and telling her this?"

"That place in Eastview is a brothel and you know it. They're a bunch of hoods!" she almost shrieked.

Louie looked at his mother in pretend disbelief. He knew the stories that had circulated around town about the Longprés. They were only partly true. "Ma," he said, using the most reasonable tone he could muster, "are you saying that the day Toussaint brought Baby-face home from the Byward Market …."

"That pimp!" she interrupted.

It was Maura's turn to wince.

He continued, "…. because she didn't have the fare, and Alma gave her a bowl of soup and a bed for the night, that made her house a brothel?"

Toussaint was Silvy's debonair brother. Louie had liked him. Congenial man-about-town, he was. He was a cab driver on weekends. There had been some mystery surrounding his accidental death, but nobody spoke of it in the family. Had a big heart for women. Louie remembered driving in the front seat with him when he picked "Baby-face" up. He was fifteen then. "Where're you going, kid?"

"Home," she said. She didn't look any older than Louie.

"Where's home?" She was so good-looking they couldn't take their eyes off her. "Stacked! You know what I mean?" Louie would tell his schoolmates in the schoolyard.

"Dunno."

Toussaint gave her a long hard look in the rear-view mirror.

Swerving the car around, he brought her home to his mother. Toussaint was a colourful character. Great guy! His mother would never understand that. So he kind of knew the story. He had to acknowledge that she did have a "dose" though.

"Yes, it was a brothel!" Meg pursed her lips and felt she might throw up. She looked at Maura for confirmation. "Tell me, how did that family's nightmare ever work its way into our lives?"

Maura turned away.

Louie sprinkled salt on a stalk of celery. "But you're talking years ago. When Michael was a kid. I was an older brother to him then." He reminisced. "We all slept in the attic, shared secrets. But things are much different at Silvy's house now. Sure, I remember when Michael came home one day from his grandmother's with a brand new pair of high rubber boots and when you asked where he'd got them he said, 'Baby-face bought them for me.' Remember that?"

"I forbade him to go back there. I didn't want him to be influenced by his mother's side of the family. 'Baby-face' was a known streetwalker in the parish. They're not our kind of people. I've said it before and...."

"Yes, I know, you're about to say it again," said Louie with a laugh. "What's our kind of people anyway?"

Not wanting to hear any more arguing, Maura said, "I'm sure Silvy would want to hear the good news."

"No." Meg nodded towards her son. "This one here is just using it as an excuse to see Silvy again. But I'm telling you, you pass through that door to see that woman," she said through clenched teeth, "and you need never pass through it in this direction again. You won't get within a squatter's inch of this place."

"Now, Meg," Maura whispered, "surely you see that what happened to Michael was exactly a result of this closed attitude. His secret visits walled him in against himself. The conflict made him sick." Meg was repeating the pattern with Louie. She was forcing him underground.

"I don't care. I mean what I say." Meg's glasses were fogged up. Maura slipped out the back door to see if the clothes were dry. It was hopeless to argue with her sister when she got onto the topic of Silvy Longpré. Nothing brought her back to reason. What was it that made Meg so angry? She filled her lungs with fresh air.

Michael. Dear Michael was better. When Maura thought of Michael or for that matter of any of the children that she had raised, she never thought of them as the adults they'd grown into, always only as the sweet, smiling, soft little balls of fluff that sat in her lap. In her memory she never saw Michael the adult. She saw Michael the little boy with the smiling brown eyes sitting on the back stoop eating a buttered hot muffin in one hand and spitting on his pencil with the other, doing his homework. The clever bookworm. The child who always came first in school, who never stopped asking questions, even after the books were closed. He was the only child entrusted to her care who had grown up to have, as she termed it, "a good mind." She couldn't wait to see him and Emer.

Inside, she could hear Meg's angry voice drowning out her nephew. "Alma Longpré was at the bottom of all those shenanigans that went on in that house. The whole thing made your Uncle John very unhappy. Silvy did her dirt on this family an' I won't stand by to see her do the same to you."

Maura looked up at the domed blue sky. The sun was directly over the house; the heat was mounting. It was going to be another Ottawa scorcher.

CHAPTER FIVE

Alma

ALMA COULD NOT SEE the sun. It was a year since the vague orange glow of the fiery sun had finally died and left her in a world of unending darkness. She wore the coloured glasses out of habit. Sitting on the sun porch upstairs, an old woman in a long black poplin dress, she rocks gently back and forth and strokes the livid place where the sun warms her thighs. A rope of black beads hung twisted from her neck. She was thin and worn and her hands were gnarled. Her body bore all the marks of ravage, and lately she had taken to muttering, but the spirit in her was far from broken.

Cadaverous in her rocker, she clung to what was left of life and warmth, and she plotted, seeming to munch her gums. It was an old stratagem she toyed with in her mind: how to get the next bottle smuggled into the house under her daughter Silvy's nose. Maybe Louie. He refused her once because Silvy told him to, but he wouldn't dare again. There's too much I got on him and he knows it. She cackled at her own cleverness, and the pride in that cleverness made her feel better.

She had been the youngest of twelve children. Born and raised in the Gaspé. A little wooden shack on the Atlantic.

Her mother died giving birth to her. She had learned early how to defend herself from her twelve brothers. Four in a bed. It was 1871 when her mother died.

Alma won some, she lost some. But in her own mind she won them all.

Monsieur Le Curé came visiting on Sundays after Madame Couture died. He was no better than her brothers, with his big uninvited hands. Nobody's ever stopped me, and nobody ever will either. Fought 'em off single-handedly then. Not too much different now, either, she sighed.

"Choe an' me, we got on good though." She melted at the thought of her late husband. "The heart of a true aristocrat. Big, soft-hearted Choe," she murmured. The best of the four Longpré brothers. Best of the bunch! She whispered with approval.

Maybe her life was lived, but it wasn't over yet. No siree! She had another five years more of kicking it up and she damned well would, too. Let them fight with her and try to lay down the law. She had her ways, and thinking of them made her giggle. They can't fool me; none of them can fool me, she thought.

And so in her blindness the fight refused to die, and it was a fight against the whole unseen world.

Silvy's voice broke in, followed by the rustle of her new flowered taffeta dress. "Ma, I'm going shopping. If John calls, tell him I've had enough."

"Yeh, yeh! Go to hell! She's had enough!"

"Oh, Christ, Ma. Be serious, can't you?"

Her head kept nodding. "Yeh, yeh."

"Are you still ... ?" Silvy's eyes narrowed. "Did you get some more?"

The nodding stopped. With dignity, Alma fixed her attention on the doorway. "Well, that's a fine question for my own daughter to be asking."

"Ah, Ma, quit the airs. I know you too well."

Silvy stepped onto the sun porch to look at the day. "Michael said he'd be by to pick up his old university books. He says some are very old and valuable."

"Is there any soup on the stove?" In the old days Alma always had a pot of soup on the back of the stove for anyone who came by.

"I didn't have time to buy a soup bone. Anyway, he's just coming to pay a visit and pick up those books. They're under my bed in a cardboard box. Just tell him where they are."

"An' what good are his books to do him in hospital?" She could be forgetful at times.

"Ma, if I told you once I told you ten times, Michael is out of hospital. He wants to get back to teaching and working on that theorem he's been trying to solve. He says some of the books are collector's items."

Alma groaned. "Nobody ever tells me nothing around here…. An' Emerald, my girl Emer?"

Silvy gives her girdle a tug and smoothes the dress over her hips as she surveys herself in the glass. Not bad for forty-six, she thinks. "Yes, yes, she's just fine."

After that last phone call, Silvy had become anxious about Michael showing up before she got away. She wasn't having any more of his fifth-degree questioning. She was also concerned about more important business.

"I'm off for a bit of shopping."

"Heh heh! Seems to me you're off for a bit of something else."

Silvy drew herself up at the doorway. "And just what do you mean by that?"

Alma smiled. "Ah, quit the airs. I know you too well."

The door slammed hard, making the windows rattle all around the sun porch.

THE WORLD'S FAIR

Alma rested her head against the back of the rocker and pushed her feet against the floor to get it back in motion. She smiled, and the sun was warm on her. It was a good life.

Downstairs, Silvy started an argument with her tenants. She could never quite decide which part of the duplex she preferred living in. She had tried both, and it was only two months since they had got the people to move down from the top. They had two dogs, and it seemed only reasonable that they should have the yard.

Now that her feathers were ruffled from the argument with Alma, she preened herself for another fight, dropping the hint that she wasn't altogether happy with the state of things, in particular with the barking dogs and the bones left lying around the yard.

Alma tried to listen but couldn't make out exactly what was being said. It irritated her to think of all the confusion and trouble that was visited on her every time her fool daughter got restless. It made her uneasy, because there was nothing she could do. Silvy took after Choe there. Alma never knew what Choe was going to do next either, God rest his soul. She wasn't living in her own home anymore; an old woman being shuttled back and forth between relatives had no say in any matter, even if it involved her own comfort, and she had come to dread her daughter's frequent whims and threats.

She didn't want to move anymore. It meant a long period of uncertainty and adjustment, and she wasn't up to it.

The voices gradually subsided and Alma heard her daughter's heels clicking down the boarded walk. When that sound died, she was aware of another kind of tapping. She listened for a moment, then placed it at the back of the house.

She got up and felt her way through Silvy's bedroom, lately turned into the front parlour, groped down the hallway, careful to avoid the table that Silvy had stuck there, and felt for the knob. She opened the door and was in the bathroom. Silvy had installed it herself right in the middle of the hallway, between two doors. She claimed it was handy to have it there since she was always running up and down to it, anyway.

Alma opened the second door behind the toilet, scuffled down the remainder of the hall and into the back bedroom. "Who's there?"

A man's voice called up, "C'est moi! Horace."

She hurried to unlock the back door. "Well, Jesus Christ! Where in creation have you been? You're a turd for not coming to see me before this." She felt his face and shoulders and was pleased to have one old friend remember.

She took his arm and started back for the sun porch. "Mind you don't bump into that bloody table."

"Yes, I know," he replied as he bumped into it nervously. "No one here but you?"

She laughed, having known Horace since the heydays on Nelson Street, when he'd always be lying in wait for Silvy to leave before he'd put in an appearance. "You know full bloody well she's just after leaving."

They sat down at a table on the sun porch with a potted rubber plant between them. Alma looked straight into it. "And why didn't you come to see me sooner?"

Horace leaned over to see her and made a small gesture of apology with his hand. He always spoke to her as if she could see. That's what warmed him to her. She felt that animation in him.

"Well you know, Alma, after the last time...."

His timidity made her angry. "So, she threw you out of the house. She's done that before and it never stopped you."

He smiled sadly to himself, remembering. His head was set to one side most of the time. He felt age in him and didn't say anything.

"Ah never mind her," Alma said. "She thinks her shit don't stink, but her farts give her away."

Laughter broke between them, and then as if all their problems had been dealt with fully and completely, Alma leaned so far forward her face was buried in the rubber plant. "And did you bring me a little nip?"

"I sure did. You don't think she frightens me that much, do you?"

"I'll get the glasses. What did you get?"

"Gin."

"Christ, gin. And I've even got a Pepshi." She said it that way because of the missing teeth. "It's hidden under the mattress. Goes well with gin. Hold on a minute." She disappeared down the hallway.

She came back holding the Pepsi hard to her chest. "Can't drink gin without Pepshi."

She heard Horace pour two gins and the soft drink into one of them. "Aren't you having some pep?"

"Ah, give it to me straight."

"Well, frigg you, Jake," she said—that was her toast to a good old friend. She took a swig of it.

"Hey, Alma, go easy. I don't want to get thrown out again just because you can't handle your liquor."

She tore off her dark glasses and glared at the rubber plant.

"Well, anyway," Horace said, "don't drink so fast."

"Oh, go pee up a rope."

Horace laughed and put her glasses in her hand. He settled down to his drink. "You like it better up here?"

"Up or down. I don't care much as long as it's one or the other."

"But it's nicer than downstairs," he said. "Nice porch. It's a good house all around. Fine piece of property. I don't understand how Johnnie lets her stay here and all, seeing as they're not together. He mustn't be a bad type."

"Oh, but the house is Silvy's now. Has been for six months."

"Is that a fact?"

"It sure is a fact. She conned it right away from him," she said, waving her arm.

"Go away with you." He reached for the bottle under his chair. "How'd she work that?"

"Well, she mayn't be able to read and all that, but she's not dumb. Not that one. Born in the Gaspé her, one year after Toussaint. Choe adored her. Takes … takes a bit after me." She listened a moment, then pushed her glass around the jungle plant. "Don't mind if I do."

She licked her lips and curled her fingers around the glass. "You know," she began, "you know how he got aholt of the place at the start? The old badger trick was played but good on old man Renault. Years ago he had quite a thing on for Silvy."

"Gustave Renault?" he asked incredulously.

"That's right. He was up for Mayor of Eastview. Toussaint, God rest him, used to cab him around on the Hill when he worked up there."

Alma munched her gums and smiled to herself as she reconstructed the story. "And how Johnnie broke in on them with a witness—namely Louie Vance, his own nephew—and played his tune with all the stops out."

Horace laughed. "The injured husband. The old badger trick."

Alma waved her hand. "Yeah. All that crap, played it without batting an eye, as if Silvy wasn't in on it all the time. Made it look to be something scandalous. I mean, it could have killed Gustave's career."

Horace slapped his knee. "*Sapristi!* I always wondered why I lost my vote at that election. Must'a leaked out somehow."

"But not until he'd signed over this place to Johnnie along with two thousand dollars that was later split three ways. Well, it's true that Silvy got her cut of the money, but she was always festering for being a damn fool and letting the house go in Johnnie's name. And after all these years, she figured it out. Not being one to fester for very long, she pulled a stunt on him as only she can." She snapped her fingers. "She had the house in a flash."

"No kidding."

"She started needling him and needling him, provoking him every chance she had, 'til she had him in a black rage and he beat her up. Well, it was just what she wanted. She threatened to have him jailed for assault. Well, you know, he'd been up on the count twice before. The third time would have been the last and he knew it. He knew he'd done himself. So her, who can't even read her own name in boxcar letters, she says, 'You'll sign over Gustave's house in my name for a dollar or I'll prefer charges.' What a character." Alma cackled. "It's that dollar bit that gets me. Oh, I tell you, Horace, she gets her smartness somewhere."

"Beautiful." The teacher in him loved a good story.

"Wasn't it?"

"And—and why did you never think to pull anything like that, Alma?"

"Ah, my Choe never had it in him, God rest him. We might have done quite well, Choe and me, if he'd given a bit more thought to the coming of old age, but he was from the old country."

As if that explained everything.

She reached out for Horace's arm and whispered confidentially, "Louis the Sixteenth gave his father Papineauville, named after ol' Louis Joseph," she said with a regal air. "But the seigneury dwindled once the government stepped in." She knocked her shot-glass back sardonically.

"Ahh ... Papineau," he said, as if he hadn't heard the story hundreds of times before.

"Choe's four brothers all became doctors and lawyers, but Choe took the money and opened a grocery store with me because I asked him," she said proudly.

"Later, when things got bad, he became a teamster for Molson Breweries. Drove four horses every day over the inter-provincial bridge. His run was Ottawa and Hull. They gave him a small pension out of it. Straight as an arrow, he was." As an afterthought: "Straighter. Things like pensions never bother you 'til—'til it's too ...."

Horace nodded.

"Jesus Christ!" she said. "Pour me another. I'm getting morbid."

It was a terrible thing for your own flesh and blood to go before you, she said, when they got to fingering times gone past and spoke of her son Toussaint, who fell mysteriously from the roof while he was fixing a radio antenna. Thinking about it, she drank her drink so quickly that it trickled down her chin.

"My poor boy," she said, as she always said of Toussaint. "Twenty-four was too young to go. One year older than Silvy. Big heart. Had such a big heart."

"It was a fine wake, though," he reminded her, staring off at the blue Saturday sky, remembering all the pretty women in black. There was a long, somehow comfortable silence between them, a silence palpable in its friendliness. They had shared it together before, and shared it again. With the help of God, they would share it many more times yet.

"I wonder," said Alma, "I wonder whatever happened to Mrs. Gleason. We used to have such good bats together, her and me and poor Choe."

"Ah, there was a fine person." Horace stuffed his pipe with Three Leaf tobacco. "Always good for a laugh. I believe she's still charring in the Parliament Buildings." He stood up and struck a match on the sheen of his pants, puffed, and sat down. "I always try to picture that woman with a smile on her face, but it keeps melting in my mind and she takes on that same old sour, pinched look. No sense of humour. That's what made her so bloody funny."

"Remember, at the wake … we served the pork and hot turkey, and she sat down, cut up her food and …."

Horace broke into a laugh. "Yeh, yeh!—and—and by God if she didn't keep the knife and fork both in the same hand while she ate with the fingers of the other." He choked and waved away the spicy clouds of smoke. "So cross-eyed," he said, "you thought she had both eyes in the same orb."

"That," said Alma, wheezing, "that was her cross in life!"

The laughter broke hoarse and rattling between them, and Alma wiped her eyes. "D'you think I'm in my cups yet?"

"Not yet, not yet."

"Ah well, we had fine times." Some of the liquor spilled on her dress. "Fine times...."

"Speaking of that, "Horace said, sucking the cold pipe, "I hear you tied one on last night. I hear...."

She suddenly snapped. "Where'd you get that?"

"Where? Well it was waiting for Silvy to leave. The people downstairs were bitching to her that you were out on the back porch screaming like a banshee most of the night."

She smiled. "Yeh."

"You haven't changed, Alma. You haven't changed."

"They're a pack of liars, anyways. But what did Silvy say?"

"Ah, nothing now...."

"Well, you must have heard something of it. What was said?"

"Ah well, it looks as though it could be another move. She prefers the ground floor, she says, and it seems she could let the top to much finer people than they are. That's what she said."

"Well I for one am not moving again. I've just got used to this place and...."

"Alma. Listen."

"... and ... what?"

"Alma, I hate to say it, but it seems she's preparing to pack you off to Andrea's place, and before the week is out."

"Packing me off—sick of me, is it? Well, we'll see. We'll bloody well see!!" She clutched her knee with both hands. "And ... the sonsabitches'll soon find out they can't shunt me all over the gaddamn place. Bloody irresponsible friggers. No consideration for the aged, that's what it is." She finished her drink in one gulp and wagged her finger in Horace's direction. "They'll pay, by Christ they'll pay. Silvy and Andrea both. Thank God, Choe can't see it. It'd break his heart." She folded her arms high on her chest. "Well

I'm not going! They won't budge me from here! Andrea knows I hate her husband's guts. She knows! Las' time I put the breadknife to him, the bassard. Hateful bassard!"

"Calm down, Alma. Calm down now."

"My—my daughter—and my granddaughter—and her—her husband—and the whole pack of them—hateful bassards all!"

A man's voice called from the hall. "Hey, what's all that goddamn racket?"

Horace and the old lady lunged into each other in an effort to hide the bottle and glasses. Alma dumped the glasses into the jungle plant, liquor and all, while Horace slipped the gin and soft drink bottle into his back pockets.

The old lady collapsed into her rocker.

"She says 'Go to hell.' She's had enough!"

Horace stood facing the windows with his hands clasped behind his back.

Louie came in and leaned his weight on the back of the wicker chair so that it creaked. He looked from one to the other.

"Well, what's all the racket about?"

"If it's Silvy you're looking for, she's not here."

He sniffed the air. "So I gather, and you're still at it, even after what happened last night."

Alma shook her knotted fist. "You both were happy enough to be drinking my liquor, and you think you can get rid of me that way. Bloody ingrates! Well, you'll see. It won't be so easy." She rocked in her chair violently. "You'll see."

"We'll see what, Gran?"

"Never you mind, you hypocritical bassard. You'll neither one of you get another drop out of me."

"Gran, now," said Louie in his best nephew-voice, "Silvy

feeds you and dresses you and gives you a free bed, and surely she's got a right to expect a little something in return. Christ, you've no kicks. You get Joe's pension every month. You're well off and you don't know it. That's always the way with people who have it too easy."

She heard the wicker creak as he let go of the chair and drew himself up.

"Sanctimonious bassard," she said. "You were happy enough with my company and my liquor last night, though, weren't you? Weren't you?"

He dug his hands into his pockets, took out tobacco and cigarette paper.

She leaned out of her rocker and shouted at the wicker chair. "Arsehole! Pay attention! You were happy enough las' night, weren't you?"

"That isn't the point...."

"What's the point?"

"The point is you smashed a window and then went out on the back porch and started screaming 'cause you couldn't get in again. And when we opened the door you wouldn't let us help you. There was nothing for us but to put you in a tub of warm water," he said with a sigh. "I mean, this is no life for Silvy. I mean, if every time you get pissed she's got to sit up the whole night with you and your DTs."

Alma tried to get to her feet. "Insolent bassard! Get out of my house! I won't stand for this! You're just a frigging gigolo, that's all you are. A pup trying to be a gigolo."

"First of—"

"Wait'll I tell Silvy—"

"First of all, I'm not a pup, or a gigolo, and this is not your house. And if I were you I'd remember that I was pushing seventy and make some attempt to pull up my socks and stop behaving as if each day was going to be the last."

"The hell you say!" She ripped her glasses off and glared. "And what do you know about that? Death is a decision you make, you fool. An' I'm not ready to make it yet! You got it all cockeyed," she snorted, placing her glasses firmly on her nose. "A little guy full of hot piss and nowhere to aim it but the wrong place."

"Jus—" Louie paled. "Just what are you insinuating?"

Alma quietly tapped the arm of the rocker with her fingers and bided her time.

"Well—?"

"You're aiming in the wrong place, carrying on with Silvy.... "

"What do you mean by that? I don't … " He paused for reflection."Uncle John married Silvy, so what?"

"She's … she's your own aunt!"

"So what?"

"So she's your aunt!"

"So there's nothing new about that. We're not blood."

Touché! He'd struck her down.

Alma waited. "No, there's nothing new about it."

Her voice fell to the whisper of a quiver. "No," she finally rasped, "you're not blood, but, but" — she ran for cover with words— "maybe you're not the only Johnny she's got on the string."

"Your mouth!" he said, enraged. "Your filthy mouth!"

"Think about it, Louie dear. She isn't in the house now, is she?"

She headed him off at the pass.

"Where is she?"

"She left at one o'clock this afternoon to 'go shopping,' and on a Saturday afternoon when all the shops downtown are closed."

"You're a lying bitch," he said vehemently. "It's the drink that makes you that way."

"Take my word for it, pissboy. It's the truth I'm telling you."

She smiled in the direction of Horace, savouring the sweet taste of her successful parry.

Horace's jaw dropped. The viciousness of a wildcat. He smiled, remembering her ferocious passion.

Louie took a step toward her. "Look, Gran, once and for all. Will you lay off the drink? You're driving us all nuts with your lying and needling and your carrying on." He put his hand on her arm. "Be sensible, now.... "

"Take your hands off me, you yellow pisser. Yous'll not lay a hand on me and go untouched. Now mark that well. And you can tell it that way to my daughter. Jesus, nobody's going to take advantage of Alma Longpré, by God! No sir! As long as I have life in me, I'll fight for me God-given rights. You tell her that, 'cause if you don't, I will, by Christ!"

Louie went to the table.

"Oh, well—" He took the glasses out of the rubber plant and sat down. "Oh, well. Who has the mickey?"

There was a silence.

Alma cackled softly. "Horace, pull up a chair. *On a d'la visite* ... we have a guest."

Horace twiddled the bottle nervously.

"Here y'are, Alma, and keep the rest of it for yourself. I think—I think that's Silvy coming along the street. God bless you now." And he disappeared down the hall toward the back door.

Alma rose from the rocker, found the glasses, and poured two quick shots. She clinked both glasses together. "Drink your drink, boy," she said. "Or there'll be hell to pay in the morning."

She sighed and took a swig. "Live while you're living, a long time dead," she said, "and paddle your own canoe."

⁂

"Where have you been?" Louie asked.
"Out."
"Where?"
"Out." He irritated her sometimes with his nowhere questions. "Where's Ma?"
"In her room resting."
"She been at it again?"
"Yah."
"I could smell pipe tobacco at the door. Horace, was it?"
"Yah, yah. D'go shopping, Silvy?"
"I ordered a few beers at the corner."
"Stores are closed Saturday."
"I know that."
"Well, I thought…."
"What?"
"I dunno…."
"Go on. Say it. What's on your mind?"
"Nothing, Silvy. I just thought—"
"Ma's been needling you again?"
"Nah."
"Yes she has. I can always tell when she's up to her old game. Playing one against the other. What'd she say?"
"Nothing. Not a thing."
"She said I was playing patty cakes with someone."
Louie shifted uncomfortably in his chair. He was sorry he had brought it up. "Well, it could be true."

"Says who?"

"Ah, Silvy, come off it. Everybody in the parish knows."

"Look," she said, "if you don't trust me, now's the time to pull out."

"People talk. I can't help wondering, can I?"

"That venomous bitch in there. I don't know where she gets all her spite. But I'm taking no more of it. If you want to know where I've been, I was over at Andrea's, fixing up for her to take the old woman off my hands. I'm fed up. I'm packing her things this afternoon. It's all settled."

"Ah, don't do that. You know how unhappy the old girl'd be over there—Gerry bickering with her all the time." Gerry was Andrea's "race-track-happy husband."

"She'll just have to put up with it."

"But there's no one at home all day. Who'll look after her?"

"She'll be able to manage. She can cook for herself."

"It's not right, Silvy. Pushing the old lady back on them. Gerry's not working. There can't be much coming in from the hairdressing parlour. How—?"

"Andrea said she'd take her. So she's going. It's final. I know she hates it, but it's too bad about her. I've got my crop full. She won't stop the drinking."

"What makes you think she'll stop over there?"

"I've fixed it. We went to Rivard's grocery store together. He understands the problem. Andrea'll pick up the pension cheque from the Post Office on the last day of the month and Monsieur Rivard will cash it at the store. That way the money won't go on liquor."

Mr. Rivard was a bit of a social worker with a discerning eye for his grocery business.

"Ah, that's a dirty trick."

"'Tisn't either. Andrea can get her clothes and her toothpowder and soap out of it. The necessaries."

"The old lady won't buy it. She'll get around it somehow."

"How can she?"

"Oh, she'll get Horace or somebody to smuggle the stuff in. Any one of her own cronies would gladly do it."

"They're all dead. All except Horace, and he can't keep her supplied out of his own pocket. And just as well, too, because this is her last chance. If she tries anything over there, it'll be the street for her. I won't put myself out."

"Ah, Silvy, you wouldn't do that."

"Wouldn't I though? You stick around and see."

"Your own?… "

"Yes. My own mother."

Alma's thin body sank into the feathered softness of the mattress. "An' paddle your own canoe," she muttered to the wall.

Her mouth fell open and she started to snore. The wind flapped the green blind. It stirred gently through the room, which was heavy with the scent of the Florida Water that Alma had hastily sprinkled about. In case Silvy should come in. The bottle of scent stood open on her old oakwood dresser, next to two framed pictures of Joe and Toussaint. She touched them every morning for reassurance. The doily on which the bottle rested was saturated with scent. "… A long time dead," she muttered in her sleep, "an' paddle your own canoe …."

She gave a start at the sound of her own voice.

Christ, talkin' in me cups again, in me sleep. The lot o' the aged an' the troubled. Yes, an' the infirm, too. Where's me flask?

Let's see. Wish I could. Where'd I put it? Ah, 'tslipped right under me. Must a been sleepin' the sleep o' the ... No. Not yet, by God! I'm not ready for that yet. Said so. An' I meant it too!

She glugged sweet liquid from the bottle and munched her gums with the taste of it, then carefully lowered her head back on the pillow. The intricately worked silver flask fit neatly in her pocket.

The whistle's wet, anyway. Feel better. Like a million. Paddle me own bloody canoe still, I will. Always have. Old Horace's a bloody good turd to leave me the bottle. Kinder to me than me own flesh an' blood. Hope Silvy doesn't find out. Ah, hell with her. Oh, there's still a heap o' piss left in the old lady yet, by God. They'll see I'm not just baggage to be shifted around. Fight 'em off single-handed, as I did in the old days on the peninsula. Bloody brothers. Couldn't keep their hands off me. I was a tiger then. Had to be. No choice.

She'd won some, lost some.

"Good days, those," she muttered to herself.

She chose to think of those hard early years as the "good ol' days."

"You're a long time dead," an' it passes so fast. So fast. All fightin' an' arguin'. That's all there is now. No way for a body to live. Good times those days, an' ain't nuthin' as good happens now. Don't know what I done t'deserve it. Always good t'Silvy, I was. Loaned her money when Johnnie left for the War. Not even a thank-you for it. Even took Andrea off her hands th'time she went off to the United States with that ... Tremblay, was it? Well, more fool you, Alma. Ah, well, tha's life. I raised that Andrea while she was off gallivantin' half over Christ knows where, and little Michael bunged over to Maura's and Meg's. Said she was no fittin' mother t'be raisin' kids, an' ... an' she weren't neither. She's me own daughter but must have been true if even the lawyer said it. Anyways tha's life an' it's over an' done with. Her, I mean, not life; no. Oh, how'd she have no heart for her own kids, that Silvy? Pregnant with Andrea at thirteen. My God! Couldn't stop her. Didn't know who the father was. Didn't matter much either way. They were all kids anyways. An' Toussaint was no different. God rest him. I had a handful. Two handfuls. Who's she take after?

Well maybe fourteen was no age to be married, but I didn't push her into it. Never pushed her into anything, never. An'—an'—an' she'll not be pushin' me into anything, the bitch. Wha's the world comin' to when you bring up your children as best you know an' for your goodness you get nothin'? Ah, Jesus, Mary, and Joseph, wha's the world—?

She sat up in bed and was careful not to jar the peace in her body as she let her feet touch the floor. She felt in the top drawer of her dresser for a clean handkerchief and the little gold snuff box. She took a pinch and sniffed. After the sneeze she lay back.

Ah, tha's what I needed. Clears the head. Snuff an' gin make life worthwhile. Life worth the candle. I'll hang on. Wha's that bit o' po'try Michael used to say?

'My candle burns at both ends,
It burns both day and night,
But ah, my friends and ah, my foes,
It has a lovely light.'

No one'll snuff out the candle, by gin! Heh, heh. Favourite grandson, Michael. If she pushes me off to Andrea I'll go to Michael's. Michael will look after me. The light of my life.

As an afterthought she added—and Emer. Bless the child! The two o' them make my life worth living.

She swiftly took a swig from the flask. Her tongue blocked the mouth while she swallowed and winced.

Michael! My God, Michael. Michael is a good man…. And little Emer! She swallowed a sob and took a second gulp that was cut off short. She shook the flask in surprise, wiping her mouth with the back of her hand. Well, tha's that. Another man dead. Chris', but this place is a morgue! Where'd they all go to? Funny, can't be more'n four o'clock—Oh, oh, them two is whoopin' it, now that Horace is gone. They've gone to …. She giggled wickedly. Might'a known. Might'a known. Oh, there's lot's a piss lef' in them two—an' him with nowheres at all to aim but the wrong place…. Well, let 'em live while they're livin', a long-time dead and paddle their own friggin' canoe. Ah, it's lovely. Lovely. S'worth it, every minute….

CHAPTER SIX

Two Visits

EMERALD FOLLOWS THE STREETCAR tracks along Patrick Street.

It's eight o'clock in the morning and there's been nothing to do in the old backyard. Her mother and Zack are still in bed and her father left for the University to see Father Bruneau.

"I'm going to prepare my teaching curriculum for September," he said as he rushed out the door after breakfast.

Later she saw Poupoune hustling to the corner with a basket on her arm. "Where are you going?" Emer shouted as Poupoune disappeared around the corner.

She doesn't know how to get to Aunt Maura's, but she's been on the streetcar before she went into the San and she knows that the front of the car spelled Lindenlea and that they got off at the end of the line.

She's a little nervous, but a flicker of excitement spurs her on. As long as I follow the tracks I'm OK.

She'd run away from home once before. But that was different. Quite!

Her grandmother and stepgrandfather, "Memère" and "Pepère" as Emer called them, lived in Gatineau Mills, and when she first got out of the San her mother brought her there to live with them. They ran a café restaurant across the road from the local paper mill..

TWO VISITS

"You need to be out in the fresh air," Doctor Carmichael had said.

And so, out of the city, and fresh air it was! Or nearly so. The paper mill had fumes billowing from its stacks when the wind blew, but it was as close as she could get to the country. However, worse than the fumes, there was Pepère.

Fumes of a different nature.

One morning, a week after her arrival, he sat next to her in the mahogany snug. "Here," he said, "hold it for me."

When she glimpsed the tallow-coloured piece of flesh dangling from his unbuttoned pants she thought she was going to upchuck her breakfast. The Chase and Sanborn café-au-lait and the toast neatly cut in four squares, along with the homemade marmalade that Memère went to such pains to make, scrambled to get out. The other customers in the restaurant were unconcernedly munching their breakfasts. Memère was replenishing coffee cups. She seemed too distant to call out to. Any case, the din of Emer's coffee cup rattling in its saucer plus the clanging of the silverware were stunningly deafening.

"Go on," he insisted, "hold it." He squeezed her up against the wall of the snug. She spilled her café-au-lait over the tabletop as she crawled under the table and ran to the kitchen.

He cornered her between the stove and the refrigerator.

She made a sudden break for it and ran onto the high road as fast as her legs would carry her. Not a car or horse-drawn cart in sight. Good thing, too! She mounted her trusty stallion. Heigh-Ho Silver, away...!

He reared suddenly at the sight of the village knife and scissor sharpener. The old *clochard* rang his bell, chanting, "Bring out your knives, your scissors!"

The highway for out! Let's get out of here! Emer scooted into a dried-out ditch and vomited her breakfast. Wiping her mouth with the back of her hands and cleaning them on the dew-drenched shrubs, she surveyed the ground ahead of her. The ditch was deep enough for her to walk in without being seen. There was wild sorrel everywhere she looked. She recognized the tasty sour leaves from the walks with her father while they were in the hospital. She stopped for a moment to savour their cleansing tartness and then slowly, step by hesitant step, proceeded with her escape to her cousins' house in Gatineau Pointe. Ten miles and a few hours straight ... as the crow flies. She knew that much from her mother.

Emer ducked her head whenever a car went by. Mother had told her, "Never talk to strangers, and above all, never to a stranger in a car."

That was supposedly dangerous! She'd never been told of the dangers of relatives, though. Luck was with her; only three cars and an old hay cart passed her on the highway. She crouched down and waited until they passed by, watching them intently from the underbrush at the edge of the trench. Nobody could see her because she was so small. It was a long walk on bumpy ground, but she didn't mind. The trench was cool and fresh-smelling. The sun wasn't high in the sky yet. There was a great deal more freedom out on the highway. She could pick and choose her friends here. She could say "hello" or not say it, as she chose. Apparently not so with family. If some family member took a notion to impose his wish on her there was not much she could do except walk out. Leave it behind her.

As she walked along, head down, she shook with fear and rage at the recurring image seared into her mind.

She'd tell her mother when she got home, see what she said.

TWO VISITS

Emer passed *ma tante* Julie's house on the way, but didn't bother to visit. She was one of her grandmother's many sisters. Unimaginably dulled out. Memories of all the same old *"Bonjours, comment ça va...."* were deadening in any language. Nice clutch of colourful hollyhocks at the side of the house, though. As she passed the kitchen door she heard *ma tante*'s parakeet warbling morosely in his cage. Why don't people really see what a cage does to life in any form? She wondered about that for a while.

Anyway, she was feeling pretty shook-up and didn't want her aunt to see it. Not much point in that. It would only get back to *Memère*.

Emer nevertheless waved at the old lady. Waste of time, though, because all she did was gape at her, with her jaw hanging down to her chest.

Maybe, on second thought, she's surprised to see me appear from out of the ditch. Emer shrugged. "Maybe she knows all about Pepère. Oh well, whatever...." All Emer knew was that he'd been raised in an orphanage when he arrived in the Gatineau from the old country and that he was Belgian French. *Pepère* was her step-grandfather. She never thought to ask what happened to her real grandfather. She promised herself to ask her mother.

Her cousins and aunt were shocked when saw her strolling through the village square, and they ran to the local épicerie to place long-distance telephone calls to *Memère* in Gatineau Mills and Bella in Ottawa.

"Wow," she thought, "such a hullabaloo!" If she'd known her unexpected arrival was going to create such a furor she would have walked straight through the village and over the bridge, into Hull, Ottawa, and home.

The grocery store, the doctor's house, and the two hotels

were the only places with telephones. The villagers stood around clucking their tongues, shaking their heads at Emer in disapproval.

Emer hitched herself up on the grocery counter while *ma tante* Fillette shouted hysterically into the mouthpiece jutting from the wall, "*T'inquiete pas! Elle est ici!*" Don't worry! She's here! From the counter she heard Memère's hurt response, "*Elle a déserté, elle a déserté!*" Deserted indeed! Rather look at *Pepère*'s deserted senses.

They all made such a fuss. Her cousins, her aunt, Memère. It was just incredible! The biggest thing to get all fussed up about, really, was *Pepère*. They didn't know that. She didn't tell anybody about that. She figured it out. On her own.

She told her mother as soon as she walked in the door after her cab ride across the provincial bridge. Her mother merely put her fingers to her lips and said, "Shhh, don't tell your father."

That had been a double whammy! "Why not?"

"He'd be angry," was her response.

Well I guess so! Emer thought. So she kept the secret locked. And that was the first one of all the other "secrets" that were to follow.

Considering this as she bounced along following the tracks to Aunt Maura's, she thinks that maybe strangers on the road are far less dangerous than some members of her family.

But leaving home this time is different. There's nothing to do around the house and so she left. She felt called to see Aunt Maura. Hadn't seen her since her last visit to the San and it was time to see her again. Nothing more than that. Time to see her again. That simple. Well, maybe not that simple. Her father had such a pained expression on his face after Granny Silvy had hung up on him again. She just would not talk to him. Wonder what the problem is?

If I can I'll mention it to Aunt Maura. See what she says. Anyway, I hope I can find the words to ask the question. If not, the

TWO VISITS

reward will be in seeing her in any case. Aside from anything else it's about time for another game of chess.

"Clang! Clang! Clang!" The trolley breezes past her. She waves at the passengers. They all waved back through open windows. She walks with self-assurance. She knows how to do it. With one eye on the tracks. You do it that way so that no one will stop you and ask, "Where are you going, little girl?"

No snoopers in my private affairs, please! And period!

She studies the passersby and mimics their confident steps. That, she figures, is the best way to let the world know that she knows where she's going.

The front door opens just as she's about to knock.

Aunt Maura stands in the doorway. "My goodness, child, what…? What are you doing here?"

"I came to visit."

She steps out on the porch and looks around. "Where's your mother?"

"Home."

She's visibly surprised. "You came here alone?"

"Yes."

Maura waits until the rattling streetcar passes the house; then, "By trolley?"

"No, I walked."

She hugs her. "Sure now, aren't you the one!"

Emer enjoys letting her do that, even if the old doctor had said, "No physical contact of any kind for a year."

Just as an experiment she returns the hug. It feels good.

Maura draws back to get a better look, "You look wonderful! Are you feeling better?"

She grins in affirmation.

103

Maura scurries into the house. "I'll call your mother right away and tell her you're here."

"Do you have to?"

"I think it would be a good idea, Emer."

Emer considered for a moment and decided that perhaps,… maybe,… yes. "Go ahead, then." She juts her lower lip into a slight pout. Her mother would not be too happy. Oh well. So be it!

Maura continued, "Your Aunt Meg's gone to the corner grocer."

She says it as if everything's just peachy-keen, which is what Emer loves best about her. She isn't about to start questioning or judging her for having left home and arriving unannounced. The smell of brown bread wafts past Emer as she steps inside.

"Make yourself comfortable."

With butterflies of excitement in her stomach, she follows Maura down the long, narrow hallway.

She listens to the burring ring of the telephone as Maura cranks the lever, and peers into the front parlour at her.

She'd been in the house once before, but could hardly remember it. A photograph hangs over the overstuffed chesterfield. An oval picture from which four boys in uniform stare at her through a domed glass. A lemon-oiled Victrola shines in the corner. The bare wood floors gleam warmly. Emer breathes in the smell of the unpainted wood everywhere, the wainscotting, the beams in the ceiling, and the pine staircase to the bedrooms.

In the dining room her attention is drawn to a painting over the sideboard.

"Yes, Bella, she's here with me," she shouts into the goose-necked mouthpiece. "She's just fine. I'll bring her back myself."

Aunt Maura followed her gaze as she hung up. "It's an oil painting."

TWO VISITS

Emer can't help gawking. "Someone painted that?"

She smiles. "Yes, from a picture."

"What is it?"

"It's the Memorial to Vimy Ridge. The 1914-1918 War. All Meg's boys were in it. They were older than your Dad at the time. "Sixteen, seventeen, eighteen, and nineteen."

Emer stares at the huge cement-looking archway. She remembers her father mentioning it. "They all came back, didn't they?"

Maura nods. "That's right."

"What does it mean?"

"It's a monument, a huge tombstone to all the Canadian soldiers who died in that battle." Aunt Maura is silent. "Over three thousand of them."

"Where?"

"Near the town of Arras. In Northern France."

"When?"

"The battle began April 9th, 1917, and they took the ridge five days later, on the 14th."

"And those four in the parlour came back," Emer whispers.

Maura nods.

She scrutinizes it more closely. "It appears to be two hands clasped in prayer, somehow."

Maura stands closer to her. Her face glows. "It is a prayer that it will never happen again."

"You painted this, didn't you?"

Maura nods and goes to the kitchen to check the oven.

There was a picture of Aunt Maura's front porch on one side of the Vimy memorial. On the other was the small garden at the back of the house. Glowing whites and mauves of the wild phlox in the back garden mingled with roses crawling up the trellising on the decrepit grey tool shed behind it. The energy of the strokes of colour seems to stream out of its frame at her. She can't tell if they're good or not. Then again, it doesn't really matter. There had been painting classes in the San, but she doesn't know much about art other than the fact that Maura's heart is visibly present in the lines and the splashes of colour. That was enough for Emer.

She peers into the parlour again at the four stalwarts. They look stern for teenagers. Boys trying to be men, she thinks.

Old before their time. Flirting with death can do that to you.

That part of Emer that is growing into a woman sighs in sadness at everyone's loss: the loss of all those lives, and the lost youth of the boys in the photograph. She was present for her brother Zack's birth. She knows through her mother that her body is constructed by nature to give life, to nurture life. She feels the insult of war against her. Against her body.

She feels Maura's light touch on her shoulder. Her warm eyes look into hers. "It's best to forget about it. They're all home now, and all of that is well behind us. It won't happen again."

Emer struggles to swallow the hard lump of the affront.

Her father, on their Sunday walks, had told her how, long ago, man had lived in caves, and hunted for his food. Hunting for food was one thing. Hunting each other for food was another. It was scary.

Maura kneels beside her and holds her hand. "Come, I'll show you your father's library, all the books he ever read as a child."

Emer follows her up the creaking stairs and then up a ladder to the attic. The heat was stifling, even though the two small windows were open. A threadbare blue Persian carpet covers the middle of the room. The five cots for Meg's four boys and Michael are still there. A sunny dormitory, she thinks. It smells of dried wood from the huge beams and slanted roof. In one corner there is an easel and a huge picture frame with its front to the wall. Emer runs over and peeks at it. It was a strange picture of a woman and child. "Is that you?" she asks.

Maura shakes her head. "No."

"Did you paint it?"

She smiles. "No, it was done by an artist in Quebec City. A long time ago."

For the first time, Maura looks around the room and sees it through Emer's eyes. It is full of old memories. Her heart sinks into them. One day soon I shall have to clean this up.

Emer sees some dismantled bassinets in the corner. "Did Dad sleep in those too?"

"At first, yes, but then it was mostly for the children that came to me from the orphanage."

"Did Jesse sleep here?" Her father had told her about the baby that had died in the house, when he was a child.

Maura is startled for an instant. "No, she slept next to me in my room."

"You looked after orphans?" Emer asks.

"For a time, yes."

And then, an idea whose time had come.

Emer ventures another question. "Was Dad an orphan?"

Maura is caught short. She puts her hand to her heart. "Goodness no, Emer. He was your grandmother and grandfather's son. What made you ask that?"

Her tone tells her that Maura was startled by the question. She fingers some chessmen on a table. "Just wondering, that's all." She instinctively drops the subject.

She'd been wrong about the phone call between Gran and

her father. So her father had not been an orphan. Still, Gran wouldn't tell him who his father was. She wouldn't even talk to him.

Emer watches Maura place the dusty chessmen in a box. Filled with uncertainty, she takes a deep breath, preparing to ask her worrying question; but then she decides that perhaps it would be best to ask Gran directly. Whenever the moment comes up, that is.

Emer notices that there is a bookcase lining the far wall made of planks supported by red bricks. There's also a music stand and, in the corner, Michael's old violin.

The pages of the score of *The Pirates of Penzance* had turned yellow with age.

She is surprised. "You kept all of Dad's old things?"

Maura smiles. "He asked me to, before he went into the San. The books are his mementos."

Emer scans the titles with hungry eyes.

The Real Diary of a Real Boy; *Peter Pan and Wendy*; Jack London's *The Call of the Wild*; *Grimm's Fairy Tales*; *The Adventures of Buffalo Bill*; *The Chessmen of Mars*; *Tarzan of the Apes*; *Aesop's Fables*; *Gulliver's Travels*; *Alice in Wonderland*; *The Pied Piper of Hamlin*; *Peer Gynt*; *The Wind in the Willows*; *The Hobbit*; *The Yearling*; *The World is Round or A Rose is A Rose*; *O. Henry's Stories for Boys*; *Five Hundred Games and Pastimes*; *Mozart, The Wonder Boy*; *Plato*; *Aristotle*; *St. Augustine*; *Shakespeare*; and *Magic Tricks*.

On and on the feast went.

Emer gasps, "Look, he even has four volumes of *Oeuvres de Fermat*, published in Paris, 1891-1912." She squints at the fading print. "Editors were Henry and Tannery."

"A collector's item." Maura smiles proudly. "He's been working on the last theorem since he was in his teens at university."

"Can he really make a million dollars if he solves it?" she asks in awe.

"Don't know about a million, but yes, he stands to make a lot of money."

The stillness is almost palpable. The stillness of the sanctuary where her father had spent hours in his youth studying, meditating, contemplating. Question was, could he transform his contemplative energy into something of true merit? They had discussed the merits of moving the family to a sunnier climate because of their shared Sanatorium experience. Emer was not sure about the "true merit" part of it. What did that mean?

Atlantic Monthly magazines were stacked down on the lower shelves. They were dated from 1881 to 1890. *Rosicrucian Journals*, plus the full collection of Charles Dickens. There were even some French books mixed in with them. *La vie de François Villon*, and small, slender books on the poems of La Fontaine.

"My father was interested in many things."

Maura laughs. "He still is."

"Were these your books when you were a girl?"

Maura blushes. "Some were, yes." And adds, "and some were given to me, by a friend."

Emer picks up *The Yearling*. "May I have this one, Aunt Maura?"

"Yes, of course, but I have some books in my room that you may also be interested in."

She follows Maura downstairs, into her room. It doesn't have a window. Maura lights an oil lamp and shows her into a large closet.

"I prefer this to electricity; less expensive, too."

Inside the closet is her sewing machine, her easel, and more books. In fact, the closet is lined with books. Emer can barely see the titles. She finds herself whispering, because she's in the dark. "I can't see them too well."

Maura lifts the lamp higher, but it doesn't help much. "Here," she says, "I'll choose a couple for you and we'll go downstairs." Holding the lamp high, she chooses four books.

Once downstairs, she places them on the dining room table.

Emer had already read the first one, *Little Women*, in hospital.

"*Radium Woman*? What's that about?"

Maura picks it up. "It's about Madame Curie. The first person to discover radium." She puts it down pensively. "It's apparently an important discovery."

"Why?"

"We don't entirely know yet. I'm sure we will, in time."

"And these two books?"

"They're the Brontes. You may find either one of them interesting."

Emer picks them up and waves them in the air. "May I borrow both?" As she speaks, a curly swatch of dark brown hair flutters to the floor. "What was that?"

Maura picks it up. "It's a piece of hair I was saving." She smiles to herself. "I'd lost it, and you've found it for me."

Emer blurts, "It's not yours—your hair is snow white."

Maura's face flushes. "Oh, it was a long time ago." She folds the locket into her handkerchief. "Before you were born." She puts it in her pocket.

"May I see it?" says Emer. "It looks the same as mine."

Maura feels the silky softness of her young hair. She smiles at Emer. "It feels like yours, but it isn't. Here, please take it upstairs and put it on my dresser. I don't want to lose it again."

It's funny how some memories never fade. Emer's hair is

TWO VISITS

as soft as young Jesse's. She remembers stroking the baby's head. Jesse's dark, curly, tousled head.

༄

Their conversation started there.

"She has your head of hair," she said.

"Do you think so?" he asked.

"Of course she does. The resemblance is exact!"

He smiled. "Really?"

"Brown hair, brown eyes, and ... a patrician nose," she ventured.

"Gallic-patrician," he corrected.

She laughed and reached up playfully to touch his hair. "Right, then Gallic-patrician."

The tendril-curls wrapped around her fingers, demandingly pulling her toward him. She felt the heat of his body against hers. That was the beginning of her love affair with him.

Young Jesse's curly tousled head.

Shortly afterwards, he spoke with Sister Walter Marie and asked for permission to have Jesse live with Maura. The nun had granted his request.

From that point on they started seeing one another secretly.

On Sundays she wheeled the wicker carriage over to Rockcliffe, where they had picnics in good weather. When it rained they sat under the shelter of the Lookout in Rockcliffe, a stone-structured pavillion that overlooked the Gatineau River. He talked about his youth in a fishing village. "I loved it as a child. All those boats and then coming home with a fresh catch."

Maura hung on his every word. "It must've tasted good."

"Mmm." He took her hand. "Have you ever tasted fresh fish?"

"No."

"Very delicate taste, reminds me of the white meat in chicken. One day maybe we'll go there...." He looked at Jesse. "The three of us."

Maura remembered how her heart had skipped beats as she listened to him making plans for them.

His face clouded over. "There are some things I cannot bring myself to tell you. Dark things. They haunt my dreams." He shook his head as though there was a great sadness.

Maura cupped his chin in her hand. "You can tell me anything."

"Thank you. I really needed to hear you say that." He grimaced as if he was in pain. "But I don't know that I shall ever be able to share this with you."

"You are who you are today. I love you for who you are today." In the long silence she added, "Whenever you're ready, I'm here."

In time, he took her to dances with live orchestras. He gave her his Victrola and bought her a Louis Armstrong record.

They held hands and each other for a year before he asked her to take a trip to Quebec City with him.

They checked into a little *pension* on the side of the cliff, overlooking the roofs beneath them and the St. Lawrence River.

The Château Frontenac towered above them.

The cobble-stoned streets and thick grey stone walls of the houses reminded her of County Limerick.

In the square, not far from where they stayed, painters sat out in the open air with their easels. She watched them as they painted the old Ursuline Convent, the Basilica, or the St. Louis Gates.

He bought a very modern, elongated-looking Madonna and Child for her.

She remembered going to a small, privately-run restaurant, where he ordered all the courses. Their laughing waiter said, "*Vous avez de l'aplomb!*"

TWO VISITS

When she had asked what *aplomb* meant, the waiter said, "He knows what to order."

They sat and drank red wine, listening to a musette and the beat of each other's hearts. The headiness of promise and future were in the air. Their fingertips met on the tabletop.

"Brings back the old country," she remarked.

"My grandfather arrived in this country right at the foot of this cliff," he said. "I've always wanted to see that spot. To honour it."

They walked hand in hand down the side of the cliff facing the St. Lawrence River to the narrow alleys and streets. The smells of the downtown core dovetailed into musky odours of the ancient wooden pews of Notre Dame des Victoires in the cobblestone square.

Finally, they stood silently at the edge of the river.

For a long time they held each other, watching the current moving with swiftness toward the ocean. They had felt the power of its momentum, as though they were caught in its thrust.

Two in the morning found them winding their way back up the promontory to their attic room overlooking the river.

He held her close to him as he kissed the nape of her neck and ears.

With her hands she felt the hardness of his thighs and hips longing to express his love. She felt as though she was revolving, with no will of her own, spinning toward him much like the river below, flowing toward the sea.

They kissed tentatively at first, she remembered. He pressed the small of her back toward him. She dissolved into his warmth and explored his shoulders and back with her hands. He kissed the inside of her arm.

They embraced more closely. As he unbuttoned her blouse, she kissed his face and then suddenly swooned as his mouth found her breasts. He gently sucked on her nipples. They swelled up hard and firm. She lusted for him. For the first time in her life she had experienced her own lust. He had been the first … and the last with whom she would have such a freeing experience. She felt his shy lips against her face, searching for her mouth. Their passion overtook them as they joyfully rolled and tossed, happy in their mutual pleasure. Like two wild porpoises, they swam in and out of each other, giving full expression to their deep love for one another. They lost themselves in each other so completely that for one split second, at their peak, they dissolved back into the universe where bliss, in the form of nothingness, dwells. In the very second of their release, they recognized their sexual union as a gift. Thereafter, they consciously chose to return their lovemaking energies to its source, through the thanksgiving of their bodies.

There was a strength and grace in his body that was not only expressed sexually, but manifested in their daily lives.

He had been open to giving and receiving.

Though he had been her first and only love, she'd recognized it as something rare in a man. He was so completely in union with himself and the cosmos that he was able to pass on to her that lightness of spirit.

This translated itself into a relationship that was as near to perfection for Maura as purity itself. In their love-making, not even they could tell each other apart. They were one. They had a marriage.

And then, just like that, Jesse died!

And then he died.

In the snap of a finger, it was all taken from her.

Maura noticed that she was clutching the handkerchief in her pocket too tightly, and relinquished her grip.

When she looks up she finds Emer staring at her.

TWO VISITS

Her own eyes are watering some. She brushes them lightly with her fingertips. "Oh, well, Kelly for Bikes!"

"What's that, Aunt Maura?"

"It's an old Irish expression that came over with me on the boat," she says, smiling through the mist. "It means," she starts to say; then, "to me it means, all things pass."

"Are you all right Aunt Maura?"

"I will be. In a moment, A moment is all it takes."

Emer wonders why she looks so sad. "Was that Jesse's hair, Aunt Maura?"

"No, love. It wasn't. It was a very dear friend's."

She holds Emer's hand, applying the gift he'd left her. "Those were my strawberry blonde days. That was my natural colour then." She smiles pensively. "My hair wasn't always white. The whiteness was premature. But you, now, your 'salad days' are all ahead of you." Maura wipes the last of the watery past from her eyes. "I'm so happy that you have recovered. You must tell me all your plans, how your chess is coming along, and what you want to be when you grow up."

Emer is happy that they're back on familiar ground. She starts to babble with the excitement of coming out of hospital, finding Poupoune, her new friend, and their move to Prospect Street.

Maura allows herself to be carried away on the wave of Emer's enthusiasm.

He'd left her with the gift of loving. Always.

CHAPTER SEVEN
Moving On

SHE AWOKE LATER to the sound of someone stumbling against the table in the hall, and heard a mumbled curse, and thought, God there'll be hell to pay if that's Johnnie and he finds them two together, playing.

She struggles to sit up in bed, calling, "John! Hey, Johnnie-come-lately!"

Her door clicks open and his voice cries, "Be damned with you! You're shouting at me no sooner than I gets in the door." He laughs, then, "What's the matter with yez?"

"How—?" She pushes herself up. "How are you anyways?"

"I'm fine—?"

"Oh, good. Good...."

"Is that all you called me in for?"

"No, no," she says, trying to rearrange her pillows. She thinks, Jesus, I can't handle them all. Can't be always coverin' both ends against the middle, forever. Has to be a let-up. "Come in an' sit down. I was jus' thinkin' about yez."

"Well save it for later. I've come to see Silvy."

"She ain't here, Johnnie."

"Ain't here? Whaddya mean? She knows Saturday afternoon I always come."

"Yeh, but sometimes you show up and sometimes you don't, Johnnie. You can't esspect her to be hangin' around when she's got things to do now, can you?"

He shuffles his feet. "Well, she knows this is my time for comin' to see her."

"Ah, don't give me that."

He takes off his hat. "Don't give you what?"

"No time is your time, Johnnie boy. You've no more rights now you've separated from her. No rights at all."

"Well I'll be darned!" he laughs. "Gran's getting on her high horse."

"I'm just tellin' you facks, boy. And—"

"Sure, I know, facks is facks."

The sound of her little needlepoint chair creaking under the weight of him. "Don't sit too heavy on that," she says, but thinks, thank Christ he's sittin' an' not pokin' his nose about.

He takes off his tie and asks, "Where's Silvy?"

Alma munches her gums and thinks fast; he won't go for that shopping tale, not him. "Ah, she's over at Andrea's place."

"What's she doin' over there, now?"

"Christ knows. How should I?" She giggles with relief.

"You been drinking again. Bejesus, the room stinks to high heaven. You been playin' the Queen of Sheba, have you?"

"It were a time you loved that smell, Johnnie, don't forget," she says, remembering that in the old days them two hit it off well together more times than one, she being a beauty then an' looking thirty instead of forty.

In the hot Ottawa afternoons while waiting for Joe to come home from his deliveries she cooled herself off and dressed up in a white turban, draping a sheet loosely around her body. Her ever-present jade beads stood out in gleaming relief. Complementing the beads, her hard little black nipples poked demandingly through the material at John. Giving in to their fantasies, they wound their bodies around one another, steeped in smells of Florida Water and gin, while the two children silently played dolls in the downstairs summer kitchen. She was as passionate then as she was now. John had a weakness for her and she knew it.

He gets up from the chair and walks to the door. "Anyway, I wonder what Silvy's up to over there."

Alma is irritated at him for changing the subject. "Does she always have to be up to somethin'? Can she not just be visitin' someone?"

"You were always up to something, Alma, and it's you she takes after. You're both of you full of plots and strategies. But never mind. I'm wise. It's time I went out for a drink. So tell her I called."

"You'll be in again later?"

"I may that. I may that."

"Well, see that you don't come back drunk or else the door'll be locked to you."

He laughs. "The kettle callin' the pot black." He leaves without another word, stumbling again into the table in the hall.

They're getting too much for me, the lot of them, an' he's up to something, I can tell. I'm so tired of all these goings-on, being right in the middle and taking flung shit from all sides.

She yawns and snuggles down into the bed again. A moment later her jaw drops open. Snoring gently she goes off to sleep, with her glasses on.

⁂

After Louie leaves, Silvy fixes some baloney sandwiches and sits in the wicker chair on the porch, watching the sun go down. She lets the old woman go on sleeping, putting off the argument that can wait until the last minute. Ma's just trouble all the time; even napping she's mumbling and muttering, raising an uproar out of her sleep. She sighs and shifts in her chair as she takes another bite out of her sandwich. Must have really been in her cups this afternoon, ranting the way she did. Even Louie says she's getting worse. Wants attention all the time. Bumped into that bloody table twice getting up for water. She's a needler too, which makes it worse. Tries to get Louie all steamed up about me going out, and then I bet she puts a bug in Johnnie's ear about us. Wants to see the shit fly. Well, Andrea'll keep her in line. I let her get away with murder around here, but Andrea'll put up with no nonsense. She's inclined to everything being quiet and respectable. Silvy wipes the hot mustard from the corner of her mouth with a napkin. It'll do Ma good to be kept on the straight and narrow for a few months. Andrea knows how to get uppity without letting Ma make a joke out of it. She's firm with her. A good daughter to take her off my hands.

Silvy meticulously brushes the breadcrumbs from her lap and drops them in the ashtray.

The chapel on Main Street peals seven o'clock.

Johnnie hasn't come. Always comes by on a Saturday. Probably dropped into a beer parlour after he got off work. Hides behind the bottle when he can't face what's in front of him. Says he has something important to tell me, then he disappears. Can't depend on some people. She purses her fully rouged lips. I'll rest a few more minutes and then I'll go wake her. It's nice and quiet out here. Be quieter still with the old lady gone. Start to lead my own life again.

Silvy rises and tiptoes into Alma's room.

The green blinds whisper against the windowsill in the gentle breeze.

The old lady is almost indistinguishable from the mattress in the half-light.

Silvy sighs. If I'm going to get this thing done with at all, I may as well start packing her things now. She silently opens the top drawer of Alma's dresser.

Alma's body stiffens with the knowledge that someone else is in her room. She waits and listens.

Her hankies and jewellery are being shuffled around in the top drawer. "What you want? If you want something, come right out and say it, but don't go thievin' around when you think I'm not awares."

Silvy calmly opens the second drawer and takes Alma's underwear out and places it on top of the dresser.

"Get out of my drawers. Do you hear me now? If you want something say so, but don't go rummaging 'round. You upset all the order of things."

"I haven't come here to borry anything."

"Well then, an' what do you think you're doin' in me clean drawers. Get out of there at once. I'll not have it."

"You've nothin' to say about what you'll have an' what you'll not have, so just be still."

Alma sits up on the edge of the bed. "Oh an' haven't I though? I'm still your mother, you know."

Silvy continues sorting the clothes as if she hasn't heard.

"Johnnie was around."

Silvy tries to control her wavering voice. "Oh, was he? What did you tell him?"

"Told him you were out to Andrea's place."

She looks at her suspiciously. "What made you say that?"

"Had to say something. Christ, you were in the other room with Louie. Fine thing if he'd've found you there."

"What's wrong with that? We're divorced. He has no hold on me anymore."

"Be serious! You still see each other every Saturday. What kind of sense do you think that makes?"

"That's none of your damn business. Do you hear me?"

"Anyway, the Andrea story stuck good. Might be able to fool Louie on a shopping list but not old Johnnie."

"I don't care to hear your opinions on either one of them."

"Oo, la-di-da, but aren't we somebody though?"

Exasperated, Silvy picks up a bundle of clothes and lays them on the settee. "Did Michael come by at all?" she asks with studied coolness, trying to control her racing thoughts. No matter what comes out of her, it always upsets me. It's upset me since day one. Will there ever be an end to it?

She went off in search of a suitcase, as fast as her shaking legs would carry her.

Alma quickly rises from the bed and feels the interior of the drawers. Empty. Well, well, what do you know? Horace was right. Alma Longpré is on the move again. Only this time I'm not budgin', so help me God! She sits down on the end of the bed trying to figure a way out.

Silvy's muffled voice calls from the hallway closet. "Did you hear me? Did Michael come by?"

"Nnno. Michael wasn't here." The old lady munches her gums.

"That's funny. He was supposed to come." Not that she wanted to see him again. The last round on the phone, her knees ballooned up with all his questions. She couldn't walk for days afterwards. Doctors couldn't figure it out. What the hell did they know anyway? She'd have to sort that one out at some later time when she was less busy. But running hysterically to doctors for answers when she already has them somehow has to stop.

Silvy appears in the doorway without the suitcase, feeling distraught with the whole procedure but trying to sound sociable.

"That's funny. He was supposed to come."

"No, he wasn't here." Alma mutters, trying to formulate her thoughts.

Silvy says, striking a chatty note, "It appears that Michael wants to go back to teaching, now that he's better." She leans on the chest of drawers. "Takes after me, that boy. Got a lot of get up an' go. Course he's got more education than the rest of us put together, but that'll do no harm."

"What a lot o' horseshit you go on about. Trying to claim him as your own an' you never even raised him! But you'll not get rid of me that easy!"

"Ma, really! You gotta stop using that language."

"I'll use it if I wish an' no one will stop me. That boy no more takes after you than Andrea or anyone else. You never raised either o' them so you got no claim to nothin'. They're their own person, that's what! There now. Spoke me mind. Feel much better."

"How dare you say that to me! They're mine. My own flesh an' blood and you'll not take that away from me."

"Ah, they're only yours by accident. You never really wanted either one o' them. If you can remember back that far. And you never had any use for them as they grew up either. Face the facks."

Sometimes Silvy feels her mother knows. That she really basically knows her. Knows her story. Silvy stops breathing. She's coming in too close. Nobody will ever know. *J'vais mourir avec mes secrets*, she whispers. She repeats it for reassurance: I'll die with my secrets.

Diverting her attention always worked. "Well, I'll have you know I put Michael through university."

Alma sighs. "You'll have me know nothin' o' the sort. An' it was never you that paid for his university."

"Anyways, I helped out."

She shakes her head. "I jus' don't know how you can go on believing the stories you tell. *Incroyable*! Been gallivantin' round the landscape since puberty. Only ever came home when t'was time to have Andrea or Michael. You were never around when they needed you most." The old lady thinks for a moment. "It's no wonder Michael doesn't come here today. You're full o' made-up stories. Sarah Bernhardt indeed!" she snorts. "Full of histrionics!"

"It's your fault things worked out the way they did."

Alma is so used to this line of defence from her daughter that she ignores it completely.

"Maura helped Michael out, yes. But not you. Le's just keep the facks straight for the record. Did you ever go out to work? No." She twiddles the beads around her neck. "Maura took in orphans from St. Brigid's to pay for your son's upkeep."

Silvy wipes two small tears from the corner of her eye. "She snatched him away from under my nose and he was still a baby too."

"How can you forget the truth so quickly, I ask you? Maura's never snatched anything from anybody. Johnnie brought her the baby when you left for the United States with Tremblay, and you know it."

The colour in Silvy's face drains. "Why, you lying bitch! That isn't true at all. Who told you that?"

"The whole parish knew about it before the week was out." Alma shrugs matter-of-factly.

"Well anyway, it's a lie."

"Sure, sure."

"It's a damn filthy lie. Why, that man was married and had eight kids. I'd never do such a thing."

"Sure, sure."

"Jus' what kind of person do you take me for?"

Alma sighs and lies back on the bed. "God knows. Now leave me in peace. I'm tired of all this palaverin' over what's past."

Silvy stands stiffly at attention as if prepared for physical combat. "Now Ma, I don't want no fuss. I just...."

Alma's voice resonates quietly from the depths of the feather mattress. "I know what you're about to say. My answer is No. I'll not move from here. That's final."

Silvy stands in the doorway uncertainly. "Ma, I just want...."

Alma sits bolt upright in the bed. "You heard me. Get out of my room."

"Ma, I've packed your things; they're in the hallway and I ordered a cab. Now don't make it hard for me."

"Hard for you? Hard for you, is it?" Alma shrieks. "You sneak. You hypocritical sneak! Thank God Choe isn't here to see it. You'll not move me from this room. So think on that, Miss Big Turd!"

"Andrea is waiting for you at the house; now you can't let her down."

"Let her down, is it? What about me? Is there no thought given to the fack that you might be lettin' me down?" She grunts in disgust. "Pussyfootin' around the room, packin' me clothes. As if I was a child an' didn't know what was going on."

Silvy pulls her mother's suitcase out from under the bed.

"C'mon now, Ma, Andrea's expecting you."

Alma throws herself back onto the bed and clings tightly to the brass knobs of the bedstead. "I won't budge."

"Now Ma, don't be childish. As soon as I've finished packing your bag, I want you to be ready."

"You can't do this to me," she rants to Silvy in the hallway.

MOVING ON

"You can't do this to me at my age. Whatever have I done that you should turn me out of the house? You have no heart. I won't go." Alma stands up in the bed, teetering from side to side in the opulent mattress, beads swinging this way and that. Her white fuzzy hair incongruously circles her head.

"Ma, if you don't shut up I'll call Louie to come over here."

"Are you threatening your mother?" she shrieks.

Silvy stands in the doorway, hands on hips. "Yes, I am."

"You'll not get away with this, Silvy. You'll not get away with it." She gasps and sucks in air for more breath, trying to think of a way out. "Wh ... Why, I'll tell Michael, that's what. He won't allow this. I'll phone him up to hospital ... I mean at home. I'll call Bella." She clambers down the side of the bed. "Get me his number there in the book." She likes Bella. Has a soft spot for her gentleness, no matter what kind of a "deaf-mute" her fool daughter calls her.

"I'll do nothing of the kind. Bella indeed!" As if Bella could help anyone! "Now if you don't start getting ready to leave, I'll get Louie and he'll move you."

"That big son of a bitch can hardly move himself, never mind me," she pants.

"Right, then, that settles it. I'll call him. I'm sick to death of your arguing, Ma. The sooner you leave the better."

"Did you ever stop to think, Silvy, that maybe you bring out the worst in people?"

"What do you mean? Louie and I get along fine."

"Sure, because he's a big stupid lummox. That whole Vance family's the same. A whole band o' sheep. That's what they are. Tell them what to think and they think it! But I'm no sheep, gaddamm it! An' I'll have my rights as equal as you."

She hands Alma her black velvet hat. "I know. I know."

125

Alma jams it on her head. "Maura's losing the house in Lindenlea because she hasn't enough get up an' go, but by God, nobody will ever be able to tell me that I lost anything because I never fought hard enough."

"Yeah, sure, Ma." Silvy helps her into her coat. The cab was honking outside.

The dogs in the yard start barking.

Alma grabs her suitcase precisely as if she sees it sitting on the couch waiting for her.

"The trouble with you, my Miss, is that you give no warning." She rips off her glasses and eyes her, precisely as if she can see her. "You think I don't know about you and all your cavortings from day one?" She places her glasses on her nose and holds her back straight. "Hell! I'm your mother! But you have not an idea in hell of what that really means."

Silvy trembles. She opens the door and offers to hold Alma's arm going down the steep outside staircase.

Alma declines, waving her fist under Silvy's nose. "God bless poor Michael for having you as a mother, because no one else will!"

The dogs run to greet Alma at the foot of the stairs.

She shouts loud enough for the neighbours to hear. "Mark my words, you haven't heard the last of me. You're a stupid bitch with no heart an' I regret the day I ever gave birth to you. Throwin' your own mother out of the house an' I haven't done a damn thing to you." She plays it to the rafters.

Silvy sees Madame Crevier peering up at them through her frilly kitchen window. "Shhh, now, Ma. Shh. What are the neighbours going to think?"

"Since when do you care about what the neighbours think? I'll not bloody well shush for you or anybody. Let the whole goddamned world hear. I don't care." Alma laughs—a long mirthful laugh—and throws up her hand. "I don't have to live here anymore, so what do I care what they think, of you, or me for that matter, and …" she shouts "these crazy barking dogs."

The cabby holds the door open for her and with great dignity she sweeps into the black limousine, slams the door shut, and, sitting stiff as a ramrod, she waves the driver on with a white gloved hand as she cruises off into the distance.

Silvy watches from the sun porch. She bites her thumb until it bleeds, wondering if she did the right thing.

CHAPTER EIGHT

Bella

BELLA LIES ON THE CHESTERFIELD in the darkened living room. The heavy wine-coloured drapes are pinned together with all she can find—the baby's diaper pin. It's the only cool room in the stifling July heat. She needs a few minutes to gather herself before the children come downstairs for breakfast. Michael's annoying way of putting things off wears her nerves raw. She trembles with exhaustion. It seems as though, after three years of being apart, the whole pattern is beginning again. Finally he says he's going to the library.

"I'm going to work on my computations. No one has cracked it to date."

Dreams, dreams, dreams. He exasperates her sometimes with his dreams. She knows it's his way of putting off seeing Father Bruneau again.

Heaving a weary sigh she says, "First you get a job, then you work on your mathematical problems." It's so self-evident, it's enervating.

He smiles. "Let's just give it another day. In any case, I want to contact my mother, and get that issue out of the way if I can. I want to clear the air with her first."

"I don't see the importance of that, Michael. Your immediate family comes first. That's the priority."

"I know, I know." He shrugs. It isn't his priority. There's no longer any point in trying to communicate that to her.

BELLA

It infuriates Bella that his own mother is so cruelly evasive. Even on the night of his admittance to hospital, when the doctors hadn't given him much chance of recovery, she still didn't break her silence. "Silvy has never given you a straight answer on the issue."

"We've been through it before. I'll see Bruneau after I've straightened things out with my mother."

His mother, with all her secrets, she thinks, is more mother to those crazy button-eyed dolls she sews than she'd ever been to either Andrea or Michael. Voodoo-witch! She'd rather see him die than tell him the truth. An argument is in the air. She can't help jumping in with, "But straightening things with your mother will take forever, and you know that. Meanwhile, we need money to live."

Point blank. That was Bella's style. Point blank.

She's right, of course. He can't argue. Michael finishes his coffee, grabs his briefcase, and leaves.

She fears that he's starting his extra-curricular activities again. And it's all extra-curricular as far as she can make out; the library, his obsession with Fermat's theorem, questioning his mother. She feels that these are not only useless endeavours in the face of his own family's immediate needs, but life-threatening to boot. She bites her lips. His way of putting things off is exactly what made him sick in the first place. She involuntarily groans out loud in the face of these incomprehensible facts. The pattern is emerging yet again. The incessant chess tournaments, the monthly magicians' meetings, the weekends playing violin at the Standish, late nights on his mathematical problems: they all spell trouble to her. Pushes himself to the very end. Even after the night sweats and spitting blood, he drove on without seeing a doctor. His priorities are twisted around. She doesn't have a husband, she thinks bitterly. Neither do the children have a father, although maybe that last part isn't entirely true. If there's one thing he does love, it's his children.

"Putting priorities off by keeping himself busy is exactly what made him sick in the first place," she repeats aloud to the garish green jungle leaves in the wallpaper. Some ideas loop themselves around for a second or third time. She can't help it. Old thoughts come back to haunt her about the workability of their relationship. Maybe she's in the wrong relationship? A heck of a thing to think now that he's recovered. Michael has so much common sense, and yet there are times when he displays none at all, whatsoever. What makes him so scattered? she wonders, shaking her head.

Emer watches from the upstairs landing. When the coast is clear, she pads down the stairs.

Zack follows, sucking on his favourite blanket. His "Kiki," as he calls it.

When Bella sees him she worries a little. Maybe I weaned him too early. "Take that blanket away from him, Emer."

Emer tugs. "C'mon! Give over!"

Zack is not in a giving mood.

Bella smiles and goes into the kitchen to prepare breakfast.

Opening the ice box, she notes the milk is tepid. The ice is down.

As Emer spoons the cereal into her mouth, she says, "I'm wearing the pink dress that Memère gave me."

Bella stares at her daughter. Incredulously. "The pink dress?" and then,

"*Modère tes transports.*"

Emer nods as she chomps on her snap, crackle, and pop!

"No you are not and don't talk with your mouth full, please. I haven't poured your milk yet! Control yourself... I said, moderate your transports."

BELLA

Emer is given to making surprise announcements out of the clear blue. Sometimes Bella feels her daughter tries to get a rise out of her on purpose.

"Why can't I?"

"Because it's a Sunday dress. Memère gave it to you to wear on Sundays."

Emer snorts. "Pink! Yuk!"

Her daughter's candidness always shocks her. She never spoke to her own mother that way, and wonders which side of the family Emer's frankness comes from. Not hers. "Choose something else," Bella says, pouring the milk.

"Pink is yucky, too little-girlish," Emer retorts, rubbing the dirt out from between her toes.

"Don't do that at the breakfast table," Bella says, tying Zack into his high chair with a diaper.

"Well what am I supposed to wear?" Suddenly she yelps, "Ooh, the milk's sour!"

"Wear your flowered overalls. You're playing in the back, right? Your overalls," she says with finality, brushing the blonde hair out of Zack's eyes.

"Right," Emer replies. "Out with the pink, in with the flowers."

She really doesn't care either way, and dashes up the stairs, eager to begin her day.

Bella watches her go as she helps Zack finish his breakfast. A bolt of lightning energy that one, she marvels, swallowing good-hearted laughter.

After breakfast the children run out to play in the yard.

Bella supplies them with some empty coke bottles, which she fills with tap water. They'd need it. The temperature on the back shed door reads almost ninety-three degrees and it was only nine-thirty in the morning. Emer was improvising a Buck Rogers spaceship with two wooden horses and some small planks in the big shed at the back of the house. For a moment Bella stands watching them in amusement as they douse the "flaming meteors" and each other in the stifling city heat. As she walks back into the house, she remembers fetching bottles of water out in the countryside as a surprise for Maman. Fresh spring water that jolts life back into the body. Bottles of a different order. She wishes she could go back to that part of her childhood again. The part that had been full of fun and laughter.

Chipping a piece off the ice block, she notes, "The iceman better deliver today or we'll lose everything here." She rubs it across her face and neck as she goes upstairs to have a look at Emer's pink dress. It is lovely and it is for Sundays. Pink organza, almost exactly the same as the one she'd worn the day her mother brought her to the convent. She places the little dress under her chin to re-assess it as she peeks into the mirror. Her straight blonde hair, green eyes, straight nose, and open smile tells her that the dress suits her just as well now as it did then. Her body had filled out some with childbearing, but she was well-proportioned for her medium height.

"*Endimanchée!*" says her mother, beaming approvingly of her Sunday best, worn for the scrutiny of the nuns. Maman painstakingly fills an application for her entrance into St. François de Sales Convent. She wants to make a good first impression on the Mother Superior. Pink bobby socks, the organza dress, and a pink ribbon to gather up her straight blonde bobbing hair in a neat bunch: that is to be the presentation.

Before leaving on the bus, Bella runs down the promontory in front of the house to the beach on the Gatineau River.

BELLA

Her mother shouts after her, "Éloigne-toi pas!" Don't wander off now.

She liked punctuality. It came from her days of punching in at the Parliament Buildings.

Bella clutches the empty bottles to her chest with her "good" arm. "I'm just going to get some spring water before I go," she shouts back, managing to brush her long fair bangs out of her eyes. She watches for a sign of warmth from Maman. Her smile of recognition. Bella's eyes don't flicker. She hungers for it. She isn't going to miss it. It would be kept safely in her memory. It happens. Appreciation. But only in a heartbeat, almost catching her mother in the act of being real.

"Just don't you go disappearing into the back swamp! And don't get your dress dirty either," she shouts.

Maman turns her back then, half muttering to herself.

She watches her at a distance marching around the table distractedly, tapette in hand. The fly swatter whooshed the bluebottles out the screen door—or "*la porte de scream*," as she called it. The visual difference between her and a sergeant major directing traffic was minimal. To all appearances, totally in charge. She loves her mother, but sometimes she hates her too. It's hard to get her to smile. To forget the past. To openly smile.

She sees her new stepfather, Pierre, stooping over the wood stove, tasting his latest creation. Rabbit stew. He was first cousin to her blood father, but didn't resemble him in the least. He has blue eyes, thinning hair, a golden brown moustache, and is short and on the round side.

Her father had carried himself elegantly tall, although he was of medium height. She remembered seeing him through the bars of her baby crib, his flashing green eyes and a head full of long blond hair. She proudly reflected on her resemblance to him.

THE WORLD'S FAIR

She's happy to have Pierre in the house, for her mother's sake. Maman no longer has to scrub floors.

Pierre casts a glance in her direction. He smiles through the open door at her.

She waves back as best she can, juggling the bottles. He's her uncle, really, and has always been part of the family, even before Papa left them. But now he has moved in with them. Bella likes him well enough, but Maman has said, "Pierre and I want to spend some time together, get to know each other, so I have made arrangements for you to go to convent-school with the Grey Nuns. Not for long. Maybe just this year."

Bella makes out that it's all right.

Madame Duval twists Bella's flaxen hair into a bunch, then ties the ribbon firmly. Bella's mother keeps the Duval name, because Pierre is first cousin to her first husband, so his last name is also Duval. It makes it socially easier for Maman all around. *N'est ce pas?*

"He's a chef at the Tecumseh Golf Club," she tells Bella, "and I will be helping him out in the kitchen."

She doesn't add anything else, but Bella understands that her new stepfather is a better provider than her father was. "Marry a chef and you will always have a pork chop in the ice-box," she heard her mother say to the neighbour over the back fence.

Pierre has a future, as her mother often put it. "He has a good job and is generous with his earnings. We'll never be poor again. And," she adds, "you'll be able to go to convent school. Which is almost saying a private school," she says grandly. "You'll see: they really look after the girls well there."

Bella walks toward *la grande source* to give her goodbyes to her favourite spring—the place where her older sisters had carried her in their small arms, to taste its sweetness and bring good water home to Maman. They had taken turns carrying her and the bottles between them. The empty bottles had clinked with the joyful sound of small bells. The bells and the humming sounds of the cicadas made them laugh as they bounced all the way through the long grass.

Sometimes the undergrowth comes between their line of vision and the lightly-worn trail. They dart on and off the path, barely able to follow it, as they fall about in childish mirth, momentarily getting lost here and there with explosions of giggling and tinkling laughter.

Bella thumps and bumps up and down on Aurore's shoulders.

High enough to see the deep orange and black monarchs darting in and out of sight.

Faites attention! Échappez-la pas! Maman calls. Be careful. Don't drop her!

Suddenly, through the window, she catches sight of Zack high up on Emer's shoulders. "Watch out! Don't drop him!" she calls.

Her mother's exact words. Funny how things repeat themselves, she thinks. She glanced back at the pink organza in the closet.

Then she gathered up the skirt as she ambled down the narrow pathway, wending her way through the caressing grass to the river's edge, honouring the memory of her sisters. That was the day she'd left for the convent.

She placed her bottles solidly in the sand and leaned over to take a drink from the silvery gushing spring filtering through the rocks. She stopped.

For a moment she could hear her sisters' laughter coming through the rocks.

She peered hesitantly over the edge of her cupped hands as she sipped. Maybe they're in the rocks. Maybe they're in this very water that I'm drinking. It was satisfying in its wetness, and left a sweet aftertaste in her mouth. She wiped her lips dry with the back of her hand, looking up at the blue inverted dome. A rapid flutter of blackbirds speckled the sky.

She returned to filling her bottles, wondering what her life in the convent would be like.

"I'll be going into Grade Five," she says to the gurgling waters, as if she were talking to her sisters. "At least that's what my report card says. That's because I got *Bien* in everything, including Arithmetic." She holds the blue-coloured bottle up to the sunlight, her back straight and proud as she checks for débris in the water. She puts it down. It's clear.

"I'll miss you when I'm gone; I'll miss Maman too. I am going far away, where the laughter of your good waters doesn't flow." She'd miss that more than anything.

In a flash, Bella senses someone else is in the room with her.

A large eye peers at her through a coke bottle. She jumps.

Emer laughs and stands in the doorway, peeking at her with one eye magnified ten times over. "I can see you ten times bigger, Mom."

"Emer, you frightened me. Stop that! Don't do that!"

"Can Zack and I have more water for our spaceship?"

Bella quickly closes the cupboard door as if she were concealing a secret. "Yes, of course," she sighs. Interruptions, interruptions. One day I hope to have some peace and quiet so I can follow my thoughts.

She walks down the stairs with Emer trailing behind her. In the kitchen she fills a bottle of water. "Is Zack having fun? Are you hungry for anything?"

Emer gulps down its coldness. "No, we're not hungry, but I think he's wet again."

BELLA

Bella pours water into the bottles. "Here you are. Now send him in. I'll change him."

"Don't you want to come out and run the spaceship for us?"

Bella smiles. "Another time, dear. Another time."

Emer set the bottles in a box. "Aww, you always say that and you never come. Can't you come this once? It's such fun."

Bella simply repeats, "Send him in. I'll change him."

Emer opens the screen door and lets it slam shut behind her, saying, "You're no fun. Why can't you ever have any fun?"

Bella knows that her daughter thinks of her as a stick-in-the-mud, but she doesn't know what to do about it.

Fun?

Fun is for children, she thinks. And in any case, fun—that kind of fun—had died within her and Maman along with her sisters.

She picks up the dust mop behind the stove and walks out to the dining room. The mop drags a dried clump of grass from under the potbellied furnace. She fingers it anxiously.

The day she left for the convent in her pink dress, she finished filling her spring water bottles for Maman and let the fresh smell of the long grass pull her down into it. She lay there gazing up at the sky, watching the clouds dovetailing into each other, contentedly breathing the earth smells. She watched as the clouds formed shapes. Faces. The faces of Aurore, Ophelia, and Thérèse. Tears come to her eyes. And as usual she wonders why they have been taken and not her along with them. She'd slept in the same room, after all. Somehow she always feels she has to compensate for being spared. She feels guilty, for no reason other than she has her life and they didn't get theirs.

"*Je ne comprends pas.*" I didn't understand it then, and I don't understand it now, she says aloud as she shakes the dust into a little mound on the dining room floor. The swarms of dust remind her how huge the August puffballs of dandelion heads had been the summer of her enrolment in the convent. Memories of the stillness as she watched them melt into the blue sky. She was ten years old.

She smiles sadly, remembering that her childhood dialogues with nature began after her sisters left.

Emer's parting shot, "Why can't you ever have any fun, Mom?" clings to her. She knows that it's not the kind of experience she could ever share with just anyone, much less her young daughter.

It had started with terrible sore throats, and then they made loud sounds with their mouths as if they were gasping for air, their small fists grasping above their heads, as if to drag the oxygen into their lungs. Clutching at emptiness.

She remembers the fevers and deliriums in the night.

George, her older brother, sleeps in the far corner. His face to the wall.

From her crib she sees her mother's slippers speeding forward and back with remedies from the kitchen. The pom-poms on her slippers bob and lurch as she marches past. Then there are the leather-beaded moccasins of Grandmère. Hers is a light step that rests at the foot of each of their beds in silence.

Maman rushes about with cold face cloths for their fevered heads and glasses of salt water for their infected throats. To no avail.

Finally, the doctor comes. His black canvas overboots come no closer than the threshold. They don't have the money to pay.

Bella sees the boots turn around and walk away into the snow.

Then a pair of black patent leather shoes comes into the room, lights some candles, burns incense, intones some prayers, splashes some water into her eyes, and leaves a bad-smelling cigar behind it.

The silence after everyone leaves is broken only by Maman's convulsive sobs of *"Mon Dieu, mon Dieu, priez pour nous."* Over and over again.

At times in the night Aurore had cried out, *"J'ai soif. J'ai donc soif."*

The beaded slippers whisper into the room with jugs of water.

One by one, she watches through the bars of her crib as they stopped breathing. All three within one week. No more laughter. Tinkling-bottle-bells gone. Muted.

She was three years old. They had called it a "diphtheria epidemic."

"Where did they go?" she asked.

"Elles sont au ciel avec les anges." With the angels. Her mother rolled her eyes upward.

Memère Tombeau's explanation was, "Everything disappears finally, my child, everything." And she added, "It disappears, only to come back again in a different form. The trees teach us that, the grass, the flowers."

Bella's sisters were viewed in the front parlour. Their blonde heads shrouded in adornments of crinkly white satin with pink rosettes. They held miniature crucifixes in their hands. That very night, she marches down to *la grande source* in her flannelette nightie. She fills a bottle of spring water by moonlight and runs back to pour it in glasses around the three gleaming white caskets. Just in case. You never know, she thinks, they may come back in some form, as Grandmère said, and be thirsty again.

Maman cried for months afterwards. Years, really. The grief never left her.

Sleeping together in bed after that, they cried into each other's arms, and because neither one had words to express their grief, they consoled each other in silence. They'd held each other until dawn, as far back as she could remember.

At three years old, Bella spoke in hushed tones whenever she mentioned her sisters.

Three deaths in a row leave their mark. She knows it, but doesn't know how to stop the pain of the grief. There's no support forthcoming from a God that took the sisters she loved away from her. Her feelings of loss, of utter futile emptiness feel bottomless when they overtake her. The incident doubles in upon itself without wishing it or wanting it, cornering her into the powerlessness of grieving the grief.

"*Elles sont au ciel*," she whispered, looking skyward, imitating her mother, "*avec les anges.*" They're in heaven with the angels.

Several years later her father disappeared and never came back. She hadn't minded that as much as she had minded losing her sisters.

She'd understood even then that he simply walked out because he couldn't handle the grief.

"*En tout cas, il était bon à rien.*" Maman said it that way, that he was good for nothing, because it hurt too much to acknowledge that he wasn't man enough to handle it. She took charge of their livelihood promptly. Marched out the door to scrub her grief on the floors of the Parliament Building.

Bella, however, did not see her father that way. She felt that he genuinely could not cope with the loss. The last she'd heard, he was drowning his grief somewhere in Montreal.

Her older brother George was never around much after that either. Finally, at sixteen, he got a job at the paper mill in Gatineau Mills. He was nine years older than Bella when the job happened. In the years that her mother worked she went to live with her grandmother Tombeau. A small enclave of shacks situated east of her mother's village in Gatineau Pointe on the banks of the Gatineau River.

George lived alone then, some place in the village. He couldn't be counted on to look in on Maman while Bella was with her grandmother. Probably had girlfriends at the time, she thought. But then again, probably not. A woman would be a fool to tie in with him, even though he's my own brother. She looked down on her twisted arm.

"In any case, as I remember it now, Maman had Pierre to look after her at that point," she said to the ferns on the living room wallpaper. Thrusting the mop aside, she examined the walls more closely. The aspidistra Maman gave her camouflaged the ferns and waterfalls somewhat. The leaves were overpowering in their density. A jungle couldn't have been thicker. It reminded her of the swamp at the back of Memère Tombeau's house. The thickness of its waters, of its rich swamp life.

Bella had been born in that house in June, 1909. Born under the sign of Gemini, her element was air, but in reality it was equally water.

From the age of seven she'd been allowed to punt her raft in its comforting jungle silence. Weaving her way in and out of the frondescent lily pads, she listened to the croaking frogs, the whirring sounds of the cicadas rubbing their back legs together, and the birds within touching distance.

Sometimes she lay on her back, allowing her raft to float where it would. She loved to feel the warmth of the sun on her skin while watching the moving treetops.

Suddenly Bella hears the screen door click open. With a start she brushes the last of the dust into the dustpan. Zack waddles toward her. "I, wet."

She picks him up with her good arm. "Yes," she says with a smile, "I can see that. Come, let me change you."

Bella is adept at doing everything with her right arm and has long ceased to think of it as anything special. The left arm usually hangs at her side in a half-bent position. It never looks useless. A long-sleeved smock always makes sure of that.

As she picks him up she squeezes his satin baby-skin to her cheek. She loves the velvety softness of Zack's chubbiness. "Are you hungry?" She glances at the clock on the kitchen wall. "It's almost noon."

Zack nods that he is.

"Here." She had prepared their picnic lunch early in the morning. "Bring these to Emer. They're baloney sandwiches with lettuce and a little bit of mustard."

Zack's short legs teeter out the door.

"Watch your step, mind. And tell Emer to come in and get your milk for lunch."

"It's sour," he pouts, imitating his sister. The screen door slams shut.

"Oh yes, I forgot." She searches for a nickel in the plate-warmer, where she keeps change. Must send Emer to the corner grocer later. Her arm does not fully extend. Bella examines her left elbow for the hundredth time. The doctor had said that in time it would heal. She shivers. He'd mis-set it, so that several bones stuck out at the elbow whenever she bent it. It didn't hurt, but it was not a pleasing sight.

She remembered George's voice echoing to her across the swamp.

"Bella! Bella! Anna-bella! *Viens ici!*" Come here!

They'd had a fight in the early morning over her punt stick. Grandmère Tombeau had made it for her, and Bella had valued it with her life.

BELLA

"Give me my stick!" she wailed.

He came at her as if to ram her through with it. "I'll damn well give you your stick!"

Grandmère intervened, disarmed him, and gave the punt stick back to Bella. Meanwhile, George twisted her arm behind her back so badly that he dislocated it at the elbow. She screamed in pain and fled to her refuge on the raft, alone with her tears, nursing her arm, wondering why her brother hated her so much.

When Maman came home from work she was shocked to see Bella walk in the door at dusk, holding a pillow of fronds and weeds under the weight of her broken arm.

Bella had not wanted her to know. She had wanted to protect Maman from any more pain than she already had.

Uncle Pierre had placed her in the bottom of the rowboat, lying down. They rowed her up Gatineau River to the village hospital, where they set it as best they could.

"That was years ago. The doctor didn't know what he was talking about," she thinks as she stacks clean diapers on the table.

George and she had been such good friends before her sisters died. After that he changed.

Then of course there was the masked Uncle Pierre. On the day of her convent admittance, she was lying in the long grass staring into the empty sky. Pierre appeared.

"*Qu'est-ce que tu fais ici?*" What are you doing here? he had said with a laugh.

His invasion of her world had annoyed her. Besides, she couldn't see what there was to laugh at.

"I'm just looking at the sky," she mumbled, and felt her body tighten.

He picked up the bottles of water. "Come," he said. "Brush

yourself off. Your mother is ready to leave. She wants to catch the three o'clock bus to Buckingham." He scooped her into his arms and carried her back to the house.

"On Sundays I'll come to visit and take you to the moving pictures."

Bella nodded. She always looked forward to their weekly excursions to the Capitol Theatre in Ottawa. Maman didn't care for the moving pictures, so he took her instead. They'd seen all the Rudolph Valentino movies to date, and Pola Negri too.

She warmed up to it a little. "Yes, Laurel and Hardy would be fun!"

He winks. "I'm sure that can be arranged."

The film world became the closest thing to "fun" that Bella would experience. Though walking down Bank Street to the doughnut bakery after the show was a treat too, what with the choice of a hot Mae West doughnut filled with gooey jam or the terrific Chocolate Malteds at Freeman's Department Store on Rideau Street. Pierre had a knack for discovering where the latest piece of decadent epicurean delights were to be found.

She jolted in his arms up the rocky incline.

The bottles of spring water mutely clinked in her lap while he whistled, "You oughta be in pictures. You're beautiful to see."

"Beautiful Bella!" he whispered close to her ear.

Bella walks back into the kitchen humming the song as she pours the rest of the sour milk into the sink.

Emer creeps up to the screen door. "Boo!" she shouts.

Bella jumps, splashing the milk on herself.

"Emer! Don't you ever take me by surprise that way again! I hate it! Look at what you made me do!" She grabs the dishtowel and mops up her flowered smock.

BELLA

Emer presses her nose against the screen. Her arms flail in all directions.

"And just what do you think you're doing?"

"Can't you see? The screen door is a wall." She mimes a set of slow, swim-like gestures. "I'm pretending it's an invisible wall between us."

Bella throws the dishtowel into the washing machine. Her hands shake with fear. "Stop doing that this instant. You'll tear the screen down."

"I want you to come and play with us. I want you to see my spaceship. I've strapped the boards onto my old roller skates now and it really moves! Come and see!"

Bella hides her agitation behind a plate of cookies. "Here, take this. I'll be there in a little while. I've got things to do here and I'm thinking."

"Thinking, thinking, that's all you ever do!"

"Don't you talk back! I'll be there in a little while."

"A little while means never. Meanwhile, Zack and I are waiting for you. Guess we'll just have to wait forever."

Bella watches her daughter as she tramps off.

"I honestly don't know where or how to begin to play with you," she murmurs, hoping that her daughter would hear and understand. Dim feelings of inadequacy glue her to the kitchen floor. The best she can do is keep putting her off. That was her best shot!

Her daughter is growing up. Her spontaneity and directness are alarming. She's no longer the little girl who went into the Sanatorium.

Bella goes back into the front room to lie on the chesterfield, recovering from Emer's surprise attack. To retire within the walls of her convent.

THE WORLD'S FAIR

Mère Marie Thérèse was nice enough. It wasn't that Bella didn't notice the charm of her snugly fitting black voile, her heart-shaped coif, and the subtle scents of lily of the valley emanating from her fingertips.

The nuns simply did not replace her mother. Then, too, she missed the colourful dresses she had worn at home.

The coarse black woollen dress, "below the knees," and the black stockings had itched, and the starched collar and cuffs had chafed at her skin.

She studied the catechism, French Literature, Latin, Arithmetic, and Piano.

The catechism she grew to hate, because there was so much memory work. She found that in order to be successful at remembering it, she had to believe what it said. Bella resented having to take someone else's word as being categorically true. Her own experience was her guideline. She didn't accept the assumption the nuns made, that if she studied it long enough it would become who she was. The dogma appeared to deny her own experience of life, such as it was by the age of ten. She felt trapped by the high stone walls with so very few windows through which to look out upon the world.

In the end, she gave up going to religion class at nine in the morning. She tucked the little brown Baltimore catechism under the foot of her mattress and found herself a hiding place inside the chapel organ. It was bigger than her cell. There she was able to lie down on the thick-carpeted floor and gaze into the silent heights of the disappearing organ pipes while the nuns' beads rattled all about her, asking *"Où est-elle? Où est-elle?"* Where is she? It was no different from home; they too had trouble finding her.

The piano lessons were her favourite. The music teacher, Mère Sainte Anne, said, "*Tu as la sensibilité pour la musique.*" You have a feeling for music.

It amused Bella to think that she possibly had a musical talent. She had been told more than once that she had a light touch. But she hated the monthly presentation in the convent auditorium, where she had to "perform." She played for her own pleasure. It was the private expression of her feelings, not for the general public.

The year at the convent turned into two lonesome years.

Maman and Pierre came to visit every Sunday, and afterwards Pierre had taken her to the movies, as promised.

Toward the end of the second year, just before her mother came to pick her up, she was swimming in the long narrow swimming pool when one of the girls pointed to a stream of blood flowing from her body. Spidery red threads floated into turquoise water.

She ran to Mère Marie Thérèse, who was overseeing the swimmers in the glassed-in booth at the time. "I've been stabbed! I've been stabbed!" Bella shouted.

The nun put her finger to her lips, dried her off, and simply handed her a long white piece of flannelette. She told her to pin it to her underwear.

Bella walked down the long dark corridor to her cell with the piece of flannel in her hand, puzzled at everyone's non-response to the fact that she might be bleeding to death. If she was hemorrhaging, she was even more puzzled to realize that there was no feeling of pain, discomfort, or weakness. She filed the event under secret, along with the death of her sisters and the loss of her father.

Her ability to play the piano, to express herself through music, became her saving grace, to herself, and to herself only. She never consented to play for others after she left the convent. That too became secret.

Bella knew that she held back, but didn't know how to change it. Awareness of it was somehow not enough to correct it. An element was missing. But what? she questioned. The dictums of a convent school training had so raised her ire that it blotted out any consciousness of a spiritual capacity to correct it.

Emer's expressive behaviour unnerved her, because it was a reflection of what was missing in her own makeup. The grey nuns hadn't prepared her for a daughter in whom there were no holds barred.

"I don't really know what would have prepared me." She pursed her lips inward.

Still, she promised herself, "My daughter will not have to go through a convent experience, which would make matters worse."

As for Pierre, that was a total other matter, she thought. Neither did she wish that on her daughter.

Bella came out of St. François de Sales convent exactly two years later, in August, after her twelfth birthday.

She noticed that her mother was paying a lot more attention to Pierre, and did not seem to have too much time left for her. She felt as though the bottom of her world had dropped from view.

Pierre had just found a new job, cooking for the freight workers on the caboose of a train travelling between Ottawa and Sault Ste. Marie. The caboose rattled its way along, snaking in, out, and around the curved tracks through the lush woods of northern Ontario.

Bella helped out in the kitchen, while Maman waited on tables in the adjoining freight car-cum-restaurant as they wove their way north. She found that she had to hang onto the sink or the counter most of the time, because of the unpredictable jolts and bursts of speed.

Pierre put her in charge of climbing up on a stool to close the windows every time the steam engine blew soot through them. One day he threw the tea towel at her. *"Tiens lave la vaisselle!"* Wash the dishes.

As she stooped to pick up the towel, he grabbed her from behind and squeezed.

She screamed, *"Arrête!"*

Through the thunderous noise of steel wheels on steel tracks, Maman shouted, *"Arrête quoi?"* Stop what?

Bella, her head down, said, "I don't like that!"

Pierre shrugged, looked at Maman, and said, "She doesn't want to do the dishes."

Maman, in a rush as always to get back to her tables, said in her sing-song way, *"Bien, Bella, sois bonne fille!"* Well Bella, be a good girl. Do as you are told.

After that, Bella kept pulling away from Pierre whenever he came near. She didn't know whether this was common practice among adults. She wasn't sure that it was right, but she knew she didn't like what was happening to her.

From that point on, Pierre had his hands either down Bella's pants or up her dress. He did it whenever Maman went out to wait on a table. Whenever Bella didn't move fast enough in the kitchen or Maman took longer than usual to return, he forcibly held her in place.

Not having a standard of behaviour to measure it by, she supposed that this was what grown men did to young girls. To compensate for the violation to her body, she would, when she was pinned down, daydream. Bella-daydreams. At other times, when the action got too shocking she vacated her own premises. She never told Maman. She wouldn't know what to do with it, anyway.

And as Maman always said, "We are very lucky to have him. He is a good breadwinner."

Bella didn't want her to lose the one and only good man in her life. So she finally conceded to him. In secret.

⁓

Emer cups her hands around her mouth and shouts, "Mom? Where are you? Where are you, Mom?"

Bella hears her daughter calling. It seemed from a great distance. She locates it as coming from the back of the house ... then closer, almost in her ear.

"Mom? Where are you? Where are you, Mom?"

"I'm in here. In the living room." She feels weak. "What is it now?"

Emer stands in front of the chesterfield. "Is something the matter?" She dreads her mother's answer, because even when it was "no" it meant "yes."

"No. I'm just trying to cool off in this heat," she replies.

"Can I get you a drink of water?"

"Yes, please. That might help."

Bella sits up, wondering where the sour taste in her mouth comes from.

Emer hands her the water and decides not to ask her to come and see her latest creation. Her mother doesn't look good, but she doesn't want to be refused a third time.

Bella sips the water and watches Emer's expressive back. She sees disappointment written all over it, and is about to rush after her when she hears Michael's footsteps on the porch. She pulls herself together and rushes to the front door to greet him. He throws his arms around her warmly.

"Bruneau said 'yes!' I got the job!" he says.

"Wonderful! *Oh, c'est merveilleux!*"

"Won't be starting 'til September, though. We've still got to see ourselves through the summer months."

"We will," she says. "You know we will." They kiss, and the fervour of their old love seems to magically reappear as if it has never left them. Her past dissolves into oblivion.

"It'll be fifty-eight dollars a month," he says as he smothers her in kisses.

"It'll be enough. We'll make it enough."

"But the rent's twenty-four," he says.

"I'll rent the back bedroom. Don't worry."

Somewhere a phone rings.

"It's ours," he says, suddenly looking up.

Bella runs to answer it. As she unhooks the receiver from the wall, raucous laughter greets her from the other end of the line.

"What the hell took you so long to answer?"

Bella eyes Michael, come back from the wars. Her world restored to order.

Cupping the phone she says, "It's your grandmother. It's Alma Longpré."

CHAPTER NINE

Silvy

THE RAIN DRUMS against the cardboard sign "Pups for Sale" in the window frame. Silvy sits on the edge of Alma's feather bed, concentrating on her doll. The light of the brown tasselled lamp falls across the faded rags scattered on the bed and the floor. Deftly she chooses a rag at random. Her fingers close around the limp thing, and in a moment it is transformed into a shapely substantial leg. Decisively, she spears it through with her needle and attaches it to the torso. Spear the leg. Spear the torso. Needle out, pull the thread through.

The scattered rags fill the room, along with her thoughts.

This one looks better than the last one I made. Looks good! The picture of Andrea when she was a baby. She smiles at her accomplishment and stands back for a moment, studying the doll for flaws.

"No, you're perfect. Just as you are." She flicks the flared skirt and pats the blonde curls as she congratulates herself on her artistry.

The phone rings once. She starts. Once, and stops.

Who'd be calling in the middle of the night? Must be a wrong number. Surely not Michael again. She nurses the pain under her right rib cage. God, I wish this would go away.

Every time I think of him the pain comes back. Wonder who that was? Bella? No, not her. She knows I can't stand her. Even so, she did call that once in the middle of the night to tell me Michael and Emer were both in the San. But that was three years ago. She wouldn't do it again! Such a waste of time that was!

Silvy had gone over to console her, but all she found was a dry-eyed Bella.

"Will you be able to manage on your own with Zack?" Of course she would. Her mother and stepfather would help her out.

Bella had smiled. "Yes, I'll be fine."

Silvy hadn't been able to make it out. "Why did you call me then?"

"I thought you should know. You might want to have a few words with Michael in case anything serious happens to him."

"What exactly?"

"The doctor didn't paint a very good picture."

Bella's opaqueness always managed to stymie Silvy. "He'll make it. He comes from strong stock. What exactly do you want me to say to him?"

Bella stared at her.

Her silence unseated her slightly. "That's it? That's what you got me out of bed for? That was a limp excuse for disturbing my rest in the middle of the night."

Silvy knew there'd been something more to the phone call than that. But Bella had hidden behind the pain in her eyes. She wasn't upfront. It irritated her. The hiding made her less than forthright in Silvy's eyes.

I hate people who can't open up, who carry their pain without ever showing it, she thought. I doubt if Bella even shows it to herself. She laughed. She should take lessons from Ma. Now that would do it! How does Michael live with it? He's so outgoing! Silvy sighed. Bella's entirely too secretive. I can never tell what's going on with her; that's what I don't like about her. And then,

Michael: when is he going to let up on the questions? I can't take it anymore.

The pain in her right side wouldn't let up. Liver? Gallbladder?

Have to curb those pork cretons. Silvy shifts the weight of her plump body to ease the discomfort.

Outside, the wind drove the rain against the house. A driving deluge of pellets hit the side of the bedroom wall. She worked, unmoved by the thunder and lightning, her thoughts simmering gently at a sustained pitch. She shook the doll vigorously, and plumped its skirt so that it was a voluminous balloon.

Madame Crevier'd better move out by next weekend. Can't raise pups up on the second floor. I'll find somebody to rent this place to. Must have the downstairs, though. If she can have dogs, so can I. The For Sale sign would get her off to a good running start.

Her tenant was leaving at the end of the month, and as far as she was concerned it wasn't soon enough. Silvy had found an excellent breed of French poodle, and was eager to buy a couple and start breeding as soon as possible. She got the idea the day Alma left. Madame Crevier's barking dogs were partially responsible for her "new idea."

Now that the old lady was gone, along with her income, she and Louie could start living again. His cabby job would tide them over until she could start the dog-breeding business.

She always wanted financial independence, and now this latest idea would provide her with the extra cash she needed, with very little output to get started.

The dogs'll need the yard, though. Pick the pups up on Monday. Make a real business with those dogs, as I did in the old days with Johnnie. Made a lot of money then. People are still nuts on dogs. It's a good business. John always said so, the old bugger.

SILVY

The button-eyed doll sits staring seriously at Silvy. Its skirt dominates the bed from side to side. "There you are, you beautiful creature you." Silvy folds her pudgy hands in her lap complacently.

Outside, the wind hurls the rain against the little frame house.

John Maguire reels crazily up the rickety wooden steps. "Twen'y-one, ... twen'y-two!" He belches, and lurches toward the railing. "Whoops!" And hangs precariously over the railing edge. "Too many bloody stairs. She better be in, after all this," he mutters to himself. His stocky frame heaves with the effort of it as he slowly reaches the top landing. She'll be bloody mad, me comin' at this hour. Ahh, I don't care. He pounds his fist on the wooden door.

Silvy jumps as if she'd been shot in the back.

Christ, now, and who can that be at this hour? She gets up slowly and tiptoes to the sun porch. Her body sways amorphously between the creaky floorboards. She watches through the yellow lace curtains.

He shouts thickly, "C'mon, open up in there. I know you're there."

She smiles when she sees it's John. She quietly draws a wicker chair to the window and gently relaxes her weight into it, watching, and waiting for him to leave.

He bawls through the drizzle, "C'mon, open up. It's not a bill collector, it's only me!"

She whispers to herself, "Go away. Go away."

"Open up. I'm getting pissed on out here."

She takes a deep, nervous breath. "Go away. Should have fallen over the edge of the banister an' broken your skull, silly bastard." The strap of her nightdress falls over her tremoring arm, revealing a portion of white breast. "Put some sense into you."

"Open up." He pounds. "Open up, or I'll break in."

THE WORLD'S FAIR

Her body tenses. He'll break the door down sure.

"Open up!" John hammers on the door with his thick fists until the lock begins to rattle under the strain.

She sits nervously on the edge of the wicker chair, watching. Stupid bugger'll wake up all the neighbours.

He pounds on the door and makes as if he's going to break through with his shoulder. "I'll burst the goddamned door down if you don't answer me, Silvy. I know you're in there."

Exasperated at last, Silvy runs down the hall. "Stop it! You'll wake the neighbours."

She unlocks the door, but firmly holds onto the handle.

"Ahaa, my little chickadee, tryin' to hold out on me, eh?" he says with a charming grin. "I tried phoning, but then I decided to come"—he opens his arms grandly— "in person! Ta-de-la-dum!"

"Go home, John. It's late. You woke me up."

He tries to edge past her. "Well, go back to bed. Who's stoppin' you?"

She blocks him off. "Oh no, you don't. Not tonight. I'm in no mood."

He beams, happy to be out of the rain. "So who said you had to be in a mood?"

"Go home, it's late."

He starts to go. "Well, I just thought I'd come over for a talk, that's all."

"Goodnight," she says from the doorway.

In an instant, he turns and leaps past her into the hallway.

"You conniving bastard!"

"C'mon now," he says as he closes the door, "make me a drink. I've got things to tell you."

"You've no right bustin' in on me, John."

"I know, I know. But I wouldn'a come if I didn't have somethin' important to tell you."

Her voice is flat. "It could have waited." She shuffles toward the kitchen with an air of resignation, grabbing a robe from a hook on her way. *Just when I was beginning to enjoy being alone, too.*

"It couldn't have." He surrenders himself to a long loud belch and looks in Alma's room as he goes past. "Where's the old lady?"

Silvy fills the kettle full of water. "Sent her to Andrea's."

He eases himself into the snug. "Was she kickin' up that bad?"

"The kickin' up wasn't half bad. It's just that I've had her ever since Poppa died, with one break when she went to Andrea's, in between. Sure, she started livin' with us when we was just breakin' up."

Although she's French, Silvy speaks with all of John's inflections and expressions. He'd been a visitor to the house since she was twelve. She learned to speak English from him. A French accent, laced with an Irish brogue.

"Yep, yep, that's right, too. How the years go by! Seems t'were only yesterday we decided to call it quits."

The gas stove made a loud pouf sound as she lights it. "Yeah, don't it though! Anyways, it's high time Andrea started pullin' her end of it. God knows, she owes it to Ma."

"That she does. That she does."

Andrea was a year old when Silvy left her off at Alma's. She wasn't John's child, and he insisted that he and Silvy start together on a "clean slate." Silvy hadn't objected. At thirteen years old she didn't know how to handle a baby in any case. Alma was twenty-eight at the time and John felt that she was more capable of looking after a baby.

He watches her round, soft body move around the kitchen. "She told me you were there last Saturday. I figgered you were makin' arrangements."

She stops and stares at the spout of the kettle. "Oh? Last Saturday was it? Did Ma tell you I was over there?"

He nods, "Yeah. She did."

Her eyes narrow on the kettle until all she sees is the spout. "What time were you here at?"

"Dunno. Late afternoon, I guess it was. 'Bout four-thirty maybe."

Silvy purses her lips, trying to suffocate her laughter.

John frowns through his thick red eyebrows. "What's funny?"

Her shoulders shake with restrained laughter. "Oh, nothin'."

"Well you can't be laughin' at nothin'!"

"It's nothin', I tell you." She wipes a tear of laughter from the corner of her eye. Old Ma, she thought, bless the cockles of her heart. Still the good liar she's always been.

"Well, there's a place for people who laugh at nothin', you know."

Silvy swallows hard, trying to choke the rising bubble in her throat, not wanting to arouse any suspicions in John.

Although they'd been separated for more than twenty years, they still lived by a fidelity code all their own. And that was, in Silvy's own words, "Never let your right hand know what your left hand is doing." They both tried to play the rules of this game.

She says, "It's just that I never told her I was going to Andrea's place, and it's funny she guessed it … that's all."

She swills the hot water around in the kettle. My God, wait 'til I tell Louie this one. She watches John's face to see if he buys it.

"You shouldn't leave her alone, though. In case of fire or somethin'. She wouldn't have a chance." He looks around the kitchen. "A real matchbox this."

Silvy takes a deep breath, anxious to be onto another topic.

"Ah, she was safe enough. Safe enough." Hands on hips. "Besides, I've said it before an' I'll say it again, my life and the way I run it is no business of yours, John Maguire."

"Ah, Sarah Bernhardt now…." He enjoys her theatrics.

She takes the kettle off the stove and pours hot water into two tall glasses.

"Well then, drink this an' then you can leave. I'm not entertaining you all night."

He loves it when she gets belligerent.

He pulls on his red nose and speaks through it. "Christ, you call this entertainment? Got any brandy?"

"I had a quarter of a bottle left, but I gave it to Ma. She drinks it in the morning with her eggnog."

"Now, I ask you, how can the old lady break the habit when you encourage her?"

Silvy shrugs. She stirs some gin and sugar into the hot drinks.

"Ah, you make me sick. You talk as though you're concerned over Ma's health and all along you're mad because I gave her the brandy. You two used to fight like cats over the bloody brandy."

He smiles and imitates her French patterns of speech: "You gotta good memory, you." And then back to his own: "What's that you're after makin'?"

"Sloe gin with nutmeg an' sugar, an' if you don't want it I'll drink 'em both."

He hastily covers his glass. "No, no, I'll drink it. Jus' want to know what I'm getting, that's all."

"Since when are you so worried about your drinks?"

"Yeah, but I've changed, my chickadee."

"Well so have I," she almost shrieks. "And stop calling me

your chickadee!" He probably got it out of some movie, that and the patronizing tone that went with it, she thought.

He tears the cellophane off a package of Craven A. "Well now, don't get your dander up. I was just remarking. So you got rid of Alma, eh?"

Silvy smooths the flowered tablecloth. "I decided I had to. I'm goin' into business raisin' dogs again, John. I'll be having my hands full, and I can't have her round here, trippin' over them."

"Yeah, yeah, I guess you're right."

She glares at him with embers of old anger. "You're damn right I'm right. I can't live on what you send me every month, so I'm going into business."

He offers her a cigarette. "Sorry I can't give you more money, Silvy, but hell, things are tough everywhere. I'm damn lucky to have a job at all." He was happy that she was going back into the breeding business. It made him feel good that he'd left her with some kind of skill so she could look after herself. He still had protective feelings about her, but couldn't understand why, for the life of him. Maybe it was because she had been so vulnerable when he first met her.

She had run straight into his arms, pregnant and all, from the episode in the derelict house across the street from Alma's and Choe's. Been raped, she said. He'd had a terrible time calming her down. Felt sorry for her. It took months of consoling, just holding her in his arms.

"Sorry I can't give you more money, Silvy," he says.

"Something the matter with you? You're beginning to repeat yourself." She watches him out of the corner of her eye as he blows smoke rings over his head.

He was giving her his standard line. A tightwad of the first order, she thought.

SILVY

But she looks at him and smiles. "Oh, don't worry about me, John. I'm sure what you say is true."

He throws his hands behind his head, mellowing a little.

"How're they doing over at Andrea's?"

He had pleasant memories of the three of them out in his old Ford coupe, driving down the bumpy dirt roads to Papineauville, north of Ottawa, to visit Silvy's grandfather Longpré, and all her distinguished French uncles from law school.

Andrea singing, screeching, and laughing, with her long, fair hair flying over the rumble seat of the old Ford.

"Andrea's running a beauty parlour on Elgin Street. Works her fingers to the bone, poor girl. Do you think you could try to find something for Gerry?"

"Look Silvy, every time I see you it's the same thing. I tell you there's nothing doing. People are being laid off in the boiler rooms; that's how bad it is. I'm just lucky I'm not one of them."

"There must be something you can do for them."

"Not a thing. I'm having a tough enough time holding down me own job without tryin' to find someone else one."

She could hear herself shouting, "Selfish bastard. Only thinkin' of your own skin. After me, I come first! That's you!"

Quietly, he says, "I know you so well. You're only concerned about getting Gerry a job because the old lady is there now and you know that if Andrea and he are away at work, then Alma can stay there indefinitely. Isn't that so?"

"That ain't true!" Silvy loves to express herself in colloquialisms. It was a form of inverted snobbery.

"Isn't it, though? You're concerned because you don't want the old lady back here again. So I'm not the only one concerned about me own skin." He downs his drink. "Yyyup! You're only fooling yourself, that's who. You're a good actress, though," he concedes.

"Ahhh, you're so smart...." She slams her drink hard on the table.

What he was saying was only partly true. Like her mother she wanted her son-in-law to take his hands out of Andrea's handbag. Her earnings had developed into his stash of racetrack betting money. If Gerry had a job it might give him more respect for hard-earned cash. Still, she didn't have the words to defend against John's one-sided logic. If he couldn't help, he couldn't. And she was learning to let it go. Why did he persist in taunting her with his anger? The old pain under her right rib cage comes up to plague her again.

"No, I'm not the only one that's selfish around here...."

He looks around the kitchen and the idea strikes him. "Matter of fact, there's a difference between being selfish and filthy selfish. And you're fi...."

Silvy stiffens. "What are you saying?"

He controls a mounting fury and says, his head close to hers, "I don't forget how you hogged this whole house to yourself, Bernhardt!"

He always calls her that when he remembers the scene of her in bed with Gustave Renault. She'd played it well. A good actress. There was no doubt about it.

She clutches at the heaviness in her right side. "Ahh, are we going to go into that old song and dance again? Every time you come you bring it up."

"Not true!"

"Oh? Twenty years off and on, and you've never missed a chance to remind me. Don't you think I'm not sick of it? You were as involved as I was."

He pokes his chest with his thumb. "An' me, how sick do you think I feel when I know this house was mine from the very beginning?"

The weight of her heavy breasts across the table pushed the fat up under her chin. "In the beginning, dear boy," she glowers at him, "if you really want to go back that far, I did the work. The house by all rights is mine."

"The old man signed it over in my name. Legally, it was mine." John toys with his empty glass.

The experience was etched in their memories. They exchange long, hard looks, and in the silence decide not to pursue it. Silvy settles back in the kitchen snug, trying to distract herself out of time remembered. Finally she has to concede that it had been her idea and it had served her well.

"Poor old Renault," she says, shaking her head sadly. "Couldn't take the scandal. Ah well, that's life. Some are strong and others aren't." And then as if to forgive herself, "I was just a kid. Didn't know any better anyway. You were the adult!"

He suddenly explodes. "Christ! How can I forget about it when you screwed me out of my legal rights?"

Silvy rises from the bench. "Now calm yourself, John. You'll upset your blood pressure, burst a gasket, and you don't want that!"

"I'll have another drink."

"There ain't no more."

"I'll have another drink." He hated her when she became stubborn.

"Here. Here's the bottle. It's empty."

He rises from the bench and noisily opens all her cupboards.

She watches him as he moves. "There ain't no bottles there." Perfectly coordinated. Pissed to the gills and he can still hold himself sober. She watches his back muscles tense as he searches the topmost shelf. Hasn't put on an ounce of fat either, she thought as she finished her warm drink. His muscles still look as hard as the first day she knew him.

Discouraged, he sits down in the snug and stares at her.

She closes the cupboard doors and puts things back in their place. "I told you there was nothing there for you."

He nods and belches. "Yeah, s'cuse me."

"Should think so."

John feels the weight of the alcohol in his system now and is tired. "Well, I guess I better be goin'. I'm sure you've got some hid somewhere." His tone was wheedling. "But I didn't come up here to fight tonight." He walks out to the hallway.

"Christ, that's rich!" She laughs more with herself than with him. "You didn't come here to fight, an' that's all you been doing since you got here."

He pauses at Silvy's bedroom door. The floor was littered with her rag dolls. "I see you're still playin' house," he sniffs.

Empty-eyed rag dolls. They remind him of the day he found her lying on the summer kitchen floor, clutching a doll to her chest.

He remembers how he'd sat on the end of the bed upstairs, putting on his pants and shoes. Alma had asked him to look in on the children on his way out, as she usually did.

"They're in the summer kitchen. Right underneath us. Make sure they're behaving," she'd said.

Opening the door a crack, he saw Silvy's rag dolls scattered all over the floor.

He heard the back door click itself shut.

Silvy lay in the middle of the room clutching a doll to her heart, rocking herself. "Where's your brother?" John had asked.

"Out," she'd lisped, in her childish drawl.

He thought her colouring a mite red but was never sure afterwards.

His questioning look had pierced itself into the present moment. Silvy blushed. Not so much at the mess of dolls on the floor as at John's intense look. Searching her out.

They both looked at each other wrapped in their personal confusions. She breaks it.

"Look," she stammers, rubbing her right side, barely conscious of withheld feelings of turmoil. "I thought you told me you'd come up here to tell me something important."

John throws up his arms in astonishment. "Ah yes, so I did."

Relieved to be released from the unfamiliar feelings vibrating between them, he goes back to the kitchen. "Nearly forgot." He sits down heavily in the breakfast nook and rubs his forehead. "Now where to begin? Let's see...."

"C'mon now, I haven't got all night."

John clears his throat. He's finally faced with the distasteful reason for his visit and can prolong it no more.

He begins, "Well, I was over to Maura's and Meg's an' they're after tellin' me that they're going to lose the house, if they don't raise the money by the end o' the month."

"What for?"

"For the mortgage, in part. They fell behind a little. And then the new rates came in and they can't charge old man Latouche any extra. He doesn't have it."

"How much are they looking at?"

"Five hundred and thirty dollars." He says it quickly in the hope that it would sound less.

"What's so important about that?"

He crosses one leg over the other and nervously squeezes them together. "Well, they asked me if I could find someone would lend them the money...."

"Yes?" Silvy's blue eyes narrow imperceptibly on John's face.

"Well, the fact of the matter is...." He wrings his legs, one against the other, until the pain is almost intolerable. "I thought of you."

Silvy shows no surprise. "Oh, did you?" Her sense of irony at his gall overpowers in her any sense of surprise she might have. He sounds almost contrite.

"Yes, I did."

"You know full well I don't have that kind of money."

He leans forward, knowing how good her business sense is. "You'd have ways and means of raising it, though."

Silvy is flattered at his compliment, but she backs off.

"They're your sisters, not mine. If they're in a pickle let them work their way out. What have they ever done for me? In forty years, they've not said a word to me." She throws her hands up in disgust. "Nah, I'm not stickin' my neck out for anybody."

Visions of her and her mother sitting in a pew, dressed to the nines, being ignored by parishioners. Parishioners who had judged them as being red-letter women without knowing the actual facts. The burning humiliation of no one to speak to, with perhaps the notable exception of a nod or smile from Maura when Meg wasn't looking.

There follows the longest silence. John painfully uncrosses his cramped legs.

The rain pelts hard against the kitchen wall.

The house on Beechwood would be lost and there was nothing he could do about it. The house that had been in the Maguire family for years, ever since they'd come over from the old country, that they'd worked so hard to buy and never fully possessed. It would slip through their fingers. Meg had never approved of the Longprés. Maybe it was too much to ask in the light of the long-time feud.

He had loved both women, something Meg could never forgive. "Do you think Andrea would loan me the money?" he asks.

"Why should she? What have you ever done for her?"

"Just wondering...."

"Well, you can stop. Every penny she earns goes on food and payments on her house. She's got nothin' left over for investments."

He drums his fingers on the table, exasperated with himself for having mentioned it to her at all. What a fool to think that she'd loan the money, even if she had it. Still, he shouldn't blame himself. Silvy was only running true to form. Stubborn....

Maybe.... if she thought there was something in it for her....

"Well, if that's all you have to say, I'll be saying goodnight to you, John Maguire." She stifles a yawn with the back of her hand.

He bites his lower lip in desperation. "What about Michael?"

Silvy stops dead in her tracks and looks at him.

"Christ, now I've heard everything!"

"When does he get out?"

"He is out. Go on over and pay him a visit, why don't you? He should be pleased to see you, all things considered. Taking an insurance policy out on him indeed!"

John was thinking fast. The money he'd invested in an insurance policy on Michael's life before he went into the San was now money down the drain. He was confused. "Ah, you make me sick." He stalled for time staring at the cracks in the ceiling. God help me to think of a bait that she'll bite on. She's my last chance. There was no one else that was more ingenious at raising money. She had a real knack of it.

"You and the old lady, two of a kind."

Silvy hates the comparison. "Now you leave Ma out of this." In no way did she feel that she and her mother were the same.

Alma's house had become a brothel. Lots of young girls running in and out of the house while she'd been in the States. Toussaint was driving a cab at the time. He'd picked up the girls in the Byward Market. He took "Baby-face" home that first time and Alma gave her a room upstairs. Louie'd said she did it out of "compassion." What did that mean?

The next night the doorbell rang. It was a "John," but Alma thought it was the girl's boyfriend. From there, more homeless girls arrived on the doorstep. Her mother was entirely too naïve.

She never closed her doors to anyone. Hot soup was always on the back of the stove for whoever dropped by. It was something she had slipped into without giving it any forethought. That was the main issue Silvy had with her mother. She hadn't any forethought. So she and her mother were decidedly not the same. Not at all the same.

Seeing the look on Silvy's face and not wanting to stir up trouble, John says, "Always looking for an argument, the both of you."

He stirs her anger, instead.

"You never cared two cents for Michael or what happened to him. Your own son."

He counters with a wink, "Now, how can I be sure about that?"

Silvy is inured to his time-worn remark. "Ah, you know damn well he's yours. Got your ways and mannerisms all over him."

"Has no resemblance to my side of the family." What John really wanted to say was that Michael looked French, he didn't look Irish. But he held his tongue. Don't give cause for provocation. Instead he said, "Jesus Murphy, you ran around so much you couldn't remember who you'd slept with." He laughs bitterly, remembering.

The floorboards creak as Silvy shifts her weight. Feeling weak, she leans against the sink, folding her arms tightly across her chest, nursing her side. "I don't want to talk with you any more John, you can go. The door is there." She indicates with her head.

Her personal secrets would die with her.

He stands, drawing himself up to his full stubby height. "Goodoh, I'll go," he says, faking an English accent. The clock on the icebox ticks thunderously in his ears. He lurches and the table breaks his descent. He straightens himself with dignity. "Sorry."

She glares at him.

The window rattles miserably under the weight of the rain.

She is speechless. He has no sense of fatherhood, regardless of whether the boy was his or not. She suddenly finds him distasteful. Go, go, go; she seethes with the pounding in her gut. He couldn't claim him as a son, but could go after him for money? Silvy tries to remember what it was Bella had said of him. She and Michael had laughed at the cleverness of it. She hadn't much use for Bella's long silences, but every now and then she came out with a natural-born witty remark. "Long pockets, short arms," she'd said of John. She was dead right, too.

John sighs inwardly. "All I can do, when it comes right down to it, is go with the flow." He breathes in deeply and says as a last resort, "If you loan them the money, they'd make you a good deal."

"You're still on that, are you? All right, what's the deal?" she asks out of habit, wishing she hadn't.

"Well, you see, it's this way...." John plods around for an idea.

Not just any idea; one that would appeal specifically to Silvy's sense of adventure.

She glances at the clock impatiently. "Christ, we'll be here 'til the cows come home! C'mon now, what's the ticket?" she asks flatly.

He clears his throat and plunges in with purpose. "Well, ... if you loan them the money over a period of six years, they'll sign over half the deed of the house to you." He rubs his hands together. There now, that's done. He watches her carefully. Does she bite or not?

She thinks for a moment. "The other half of the house?" Her mouth curves upward slowly in a smile. Yes, the idea pleased her. "Is that so?" she muses. "Sit down, sit down." She waves him back to his seat. Their personal clashes are fading into the distance.

She walks slowly back to the snug and sits.

The other half of the house for a loan of five hundred and thirty dollars. She couldn't read or count, but she knew a bargain when she saw one.

John sits down.

She laughs. "Why didn't you tell me this at the start? Ah, you're a cagey one, you are."

"I didn't think you'd be interested."

"Well," she cajoles, "this is a horse of a different colour."

"Yes, I guess it is." How was he going to explain this to his sisters?

"That means I'd be part owner, right?" She's speeding in leaps and bounds. Her eyes sparkle and she beams a long, toothy smile on her ex-husband.

"That's right."

She could see the little brown, wooden house on Beechwood as clear as day. Clearer. She could even see the knots in the wood, the porch with the partition dividing one half of the house from the other, and the little shiny parlour windows with the lead piping. "*Comme une boîte à bonbons.*" She laughs out loud at the thought. As cosy as a box of chocolates, with some land at the back, too. My, what a bargain. Bargain basement! She can't believe it.

Silvy's eyes become pinpoints.

"You're sure you're not making all this up? Your sisters never did take me in. Why should they offer me this bargain?"

"They're desperate for the money."

"As long as there's no hanky-panky an' you're being honest with me." She searches his face, trying to detect traces of dishonesty. She knows the signs so well.

"Of course I'm being honest." His voice rings out with firmness. "Why should I go to the trouble of thinking up a story?" God forgive me, for I know not what I do, he thinks. Both his legs are numb with the tension in them.

Silvy is well satisfied with his tone. "Well, then, does that mean I could live on the other side of the duplex?"

"Well, I don't see why not, if you can raise the money."

God help me, I hope she can't now. Let them lose the old house. They'll lose it in the long run if it's in her hands, any way I slice it.

Out loud he says, "Course Mr. Latouche has been livin' there for years. You'd have to get him out, get it written in the agreement and all that."

She turns this over in her mind. "Hmm." The thought of becoming part owner in another piece of property excites her. An opportunity not to be missed, really. Five hundred and thirty dollars to be paid up front. She'd rent the house here, top and bottom, pull in maybe fifty a month. It'll cover the interest too. She'd keep Madame Crevier. Yep, she'd go to the bank tomorrow and offer the house up as collateral on the loan and pay it all back in less than a year.

Breeding was a good idea after all. The sale of the dogs would bring in the ready cash for groceries and living expenses. Her computing abacus was in full swing. Yes, sir, this is going to be easy. She slaps her hands together. She's good at rapid calculation. Plus, he'd presented her with a good script.

"Well, I'll do it." It appeals to her sense of family drama as well.

"What's that?" John is dazed. Things are moving too fast for him.

"I'll try an' raise the money." Then she adds, "Providin' one thing."

"Yes?" he says dully.

"The whole thing will have to be drawn up legal-like with proper lawyers witnessin' signatures an' all."

"Oh sure, sure. You know Maura. She'd never go into a thing blind."

"All the same, I'll not have any monkey business. I'll not invest my money and then discover I've been squeezed out of my share of the house."

He took his shoes off to rub the numbness out of his feet. "Of course not. You can rest assured, they'll do the whole thing up proper."

"We'll see." She rises from the table.

John watches her in a stupor.

She lifts the lid of the washing machine. Half her body disappears. Her voice resounds from the depths of the unwashed linen. "How about a snort of cognac, John?"

"Well I'll be damned," he says with a laugh. The night was saved. "I might of known you had some hid in that contraption. Haven't changed a bit, have you?"

She laughs good-naturedly. "Guess I haven't, have I? My fault, I didn't remember. I was savin' it. But this is a very special occasion, isn't it?"

"It is at that." He sighs.

She pours them each a drink in her best snifters and stares at the three stars on the bottle. "Have you far to go home, John?"

"You know full well it's an hour's walk from here when the buses aren't runnin'."

There's a long silence. Then, in a moment he reads her meaning.

"Why?" he almost whispers.

"Oh, I was just thinkin'." She fingers the label on the bottle.

"What were you thinkin'?"

"Maybe you could spare yourself the walk." She holds both drinks and smiles at a spot over his head. "An' spend the night." Her sense of timing and the rhythm of her words excite him.

He blinks at her. The witch! Bewitching witch!

They clink their glasses and burst out laughing. Each for a different reason. She gathers up the cognac. He switches out the light.

CHAPTER TEN

Next Door

AFTER EMER AND MICHAEL got out of the Sanatorium, their first family address was an apartment at 272 PROSPECT STREET. When the two-storey duplex next door came up for rent they moved in. After that, 272 changed hands, with many families coming and going.

Bella is on the second floor in the front bedroom doing her morning exercises. Legs up slowly, and down slowly. She watches glittering particles of dust floating in the sun's rays as they beam through the bay window, like her thoughts.

The rented room barely covers their food. Baloney and hamburger constitute the main fare, at five cents a pound. Stable enough for a while, but boring.

September is still a long way off, and Michael won't be paid until the end of that month. She suddenly remembers that Maman and Pierre are coming to visit, and they'll be bringing their usual supply of weekend groceries. It means fresh Byward Market food on the table. We're very lucky at a time like this, when there are no jobs. This was followed by the stunning thought that she could make a special dessert for the occasion. Baking is always a wonderfully distracting escape from the depressing facts of life. Right? And escape was what was called for. She's not a good cook but that does not deter her enthusiasm. The energy transmutes itself into flavour. She loves to sit and watch the children munching, round-eyed, as Maman had done with her.

Her mother gave her a jar of maraschino cherries from the Tecumseh kitchen. They'd go well with the stored coconut, raisins, and nuts. She considers herself lucky to get supplies from her mother's kitchen. Well, not exactly from her mother's kitchen, but the Golf Club's kitchen. She worked hard enough for it God knows! And for so little money too!

"Good enough!" she says aloud. "I'll do it now! While Michael and the children are out and before the heat of the day starts. Surprise Pierre and Maman! Everybody!"

She gets out of her shorts and puts on a flowered cotton dress with her long-sleeved green smock on top. The new house is beginning to feel good to her. She can breathe more easily now that she's alone.

At least Bruneau has assured Michael of the autumn semester. And Granny Alma is coming to live with them. They need the money God knows! All's right with the world! If not, she's going to make it as right as she possibly can.

Bella hums as she walks down the stairs. "The mixing bowl and cake pans will be in that large box by the dining-room window." She finds what she's looking for, and fires up the wood stove while the house is still cool. Michael taught her how. It's easier than she thought. She switches on the little Marconi. At first there's static, and then the voice of Pius XII winding down with "These are uncertain times."

Bella thrusts her hands up to her wrists in flour, butter, and eggs. Pierre had taught her. "You have to use your hands," he'd said, "to get that light cake texture." Her fingers work diligently, squishing all the lumps out into a smooth paste.

"And now for Paul Robeson … 'The Bluebird of Happiness.'"

She sighs with contentment as she listens to his mellow

voice. She never tires of hearing it. Robeson stops singing and starts to speak:

> The poet with his pen,
> The peasant with his plough,
> It makes no difference who you are,
> It's all the same somehow.

And on it went. Corny but cathartic. The song worked on her every time. It is *not* the sombre voice of Lorne Greene droning the events in Europe. Or Pope Pius for that matter. "T'anks Got!" as Maman would say.

In the process, she finds that she has smeared her cheek with pastry flour, getting some of it in her eyes. She starts to laugh at herself. Her laughter mounts until tears roll down her cheeks at how ridiculous she can be at times.

"So be like I," Robeson sings, "Hold your head up high, Till you see the Bluebird of Happiness!"

"That's the most beautiful piece I have ever heard." She laughs and cries by turns. Tears cascade down her cheeks as she pours the pastry into the cake tins. With one sweep, she pops it into the oven. Tapping the wooden spoon on the edge of the bowl, she marvels at how much better she feels after a good cry. "Tears are always such a great relief. Good for the Dream Bars too!"

She licks her finger and glances out the back door at the oncoming day.

A tall, dignified-looking woman stands in the middle of the yard with an empty cup. Her black crêpe sheath, heels, and upswept grey hair were incongruous against the sheds and shacks in the yard.

Bella calls through the screen door, "Yes?"

The woman jumps. "Oh, I'm sorry to bother you, but can you spare some molasses?"

Bella hesitates. She could never bring herself to borrow, even when it meant not eating.

In Sudbury, working on the train, there wasn't always enough to go around. Maman and Pierre just spread it thinner then. They never asked to borrow what they didn't have.

But the next-door neighbour strikes a chord in Bella. "Come straight in," she calls.

The woman thanks her, and Bella notices that she walks with a slight limp.

She pours molasses from a glass quart bottle.

The woman holds the cup in both hands. "That's far too much. Thanks ever so much. It's for a cake. You're very kind." She glances around the small kitchen. "Well I guess I'd better be toddling." She walks toward the back door, hesitating, not knowing what else to say. "Mmm, what's that wonderful smell?"

Eyeing her crêpe dress, Bella explains, "They're squares. I'm baking Dream Bars."

Suddenly the woman sits down opposite Bella. "Tell me, are you French by any chance? Excuse me for asking, but it's the accent."

Bella is surprised. "Yes, I am." Not many people pick up on it. Her English is flawless.

The woman puts her cup down on the table. "Say, I've got a lot of French Canadian friends. You been here long?"

Bella bites the insides of her cheeks to keep from exploding with laughter. She could hear the deep-throated tones of her grandmother Tombeau—"Since before the *Mayflower*!"—and wonders if the woman read thoughts too.

Out loud she says, "About three weeks." People who ask too many questions put her on the defensive.

"Is that so? Well I guess we're both new to the street. I'll have been here a week tomorrow. We're from Detroit," she volunteers. "We ran a horse farm; went bankrupt."

Bella listens while she chats about her week spent unpacking. About her twelve-year-old daughter, June, who was tall for her age, and her husband, who was never home to give her a hand. "Of course I can't complain, really. At least he's got a job now. He came here ahead of me and took out citizenship papers." She shakes her head. "That was hard going for a while. Thank God he's got a good job now. We're just starting to get on our feet after the big crash and all."

"Really?" "Crash" was not an event in Bella's lexicon. It translated as ceaseless disaster. The mere thought of the word silenced her.

"Well, I guess I must be going if I'm going to do any baking today." She shrugs. "June adores cake, so I bake cake. Takes a child to hammer you into shape, I always say. You do things you'd never do normally."

She waves the cup. "Well, thanks a lot for this. If ever you run out of anything don't hesitate."

The limp gives her a dignified air. Bella calls through the screened window, "You didn't tell me your name!"

"Jean. Jean Drake. Just call me Jeannie." She laughs and, as an afterthought, adds "with the light brown hair."

In the quick opening and closing of Jean's back door, Bella catches a glimpse of white frilly curtains and a shiny checkered linoleum. 272 Prospect had vastly improved.

Blinking into a snapshot of spanking newness, Bella quickly glides into the front room with a hand whisk to get her mind off it. She brushes the dust from the chesterfield; it rises to the ceiling and settles down again. By the end of September we should be able to afford something nice, she thinks, looking at the bare wood floors. She pulls on a piece of toffee stuck to the arm of the sofa. "Damn those kids anyway. Teeth marks and all in it. Right into the rep."

"Anti-ma-cassars." She bites into the five syllables. Hard to get your tongue around that one! "Maura said we'd need them for the children. She was right. Strange English word. Best of all, though, is 'ga-zee-bo.' Now that has a musical ring to it." To distract herself she chants it as she works.

⁂

The word was out: "Mr. Freeman's building a gazebo up on the rooftop!" That's where Bella eats her lunch, on top of Freeman's Department Store on Rideau Street.

"Ga-zee-bo." It has a bittersweet taste to it.

She dyes her hair bubbly blonde and gets a job selling men's shirts, to get away from Pierre. And runs into Peter Rodney; she'd sold him a shirt over the counter. They had lunch in the gazebo on the roof that whole summer. She got pregnant. He married her in the Church in her second month and left her immediately after signing the registry. On the proverbial church steps.

Bella miscarries from shock and Maman says, "What could you expect from *un Orangier*? Might as well have married an orang-utan as an *Orangier*. He was not only English-speaking, he was from Toronto! He was not only from Toronto, he was Protestant! He was not only Protestant, but Orange!"

All in all, Maman never had much hope that the relationship would have amounted to anything anyway.

As for Rodney, his father was a man of the cloth. The girl was obviously not socially acceptable. She was from the Gatineau, in Quebec! Other side of the river and French to boot! The Battle of the Boyne relived in rural Quebec. Old world conflicts re-emerging in new world relationships. Consequently they were divorced, post-haste, in 1929.

Bella was seventeen.

Maman grieves and moans, "*Ma pauvre fille*. Who will want her now?"

When she returns home, Pierre simply continues where he'd left off. Choice doesn't enter into it.

Maman looks the other way. It's either Pierre or the poorhouse.

Another form of orangutanism.

Freeman's, Bella discovered, was not a livelihood. Then, too, the packages were sometimes awkward to parcel. Her left arm was no longer flexible enough to handle them, and the long-sleeved blouses got kind of hot in the heat of summer.

After the divorce, Bella cut off her bubbly curls. She took to wearing hats with wide, low brims: Greta Garbo hats that slouched low over the brow. Hats that protected her against the world's prying eyes. Not to mention that the world was also protected against her invitingly flirtatious green eyes. Under the brim of her disguises she could be anybody she chose to be.

That summer Maman paraded her through Par-en-Bas every Sunday after Mass on their way to visit Memère Tombeau.

Downriver from Gatineau Pointe village.

Bella waits for her outside on the church steps overlooking the river.

Maman said that Monsieur le Curé ranted in the pulpit about divorce and that it was a mortal sin. She thought she might stop going to the Sunday morning service altogether, but then the evening benedictions were such a comfort.

Bella herself had long since stopped going to Mass. It was

merely a display of hypnotic sorcery as far as she was concerned. In her world a wooden cross conveyed the concept of conflict. Either that or life was something to be endured in pain. Neither of these images work for her.

Either way the sacred isn't there as she feels it to be in nature.

Despite the divorce, and now M. Le Cure's comments in the pulpit, Maman parades her daughter as they walk down the river road.

The village runs along the coast of the Gatineau River and is divided in two, Par-en-Bas downriver and Par-en-Haut upriver, with the village between them, where Maman and Pierre lived, on rue Principale. The houses there huddled in a low-lying cluster at the foot of the steeple.

In the hope of finding a local suitor, Bella went along with the parading and smiled bravely through the charade. To please Maman.

As they walk down the dusty river road, friends and relatives run down to their white picket fences to get a closer look at notoriety. Her divorce appeared on the front page of the *Ottawa Citizen*.

Wreathed in unabashed leers they lean against their picket fences, curious to see what sin looks like up close.

"*C'est la belle Bella, la fille d'Anna.*"

Bella sees their thoughts. A divorcee at seventeen. And hears their whispers. "*Dans un ménage à trois avec Pierre!*" Hands up to their cheeks in horror. "*Le savez-vous?*" A threesome, don't you know?

Inscrutable only to themselves, but not to Bella. In her heart wishing they could recognize what it was she had *done* for her mother, she holds her head high and walks down the road, smiling graciously at everyone in spite of Maman's ulterior motives to marry her off to a local boy. Natural grace was Bella's way of defending her right to be alive.

Nevertheless she still felt the electricity of their dark questioning looks all the way down the river road. It was closely related to being famous—or infamous for that matter. In later years, when she mentioned her divorce to her grown children she said, "But you know, the people in the court were so nice to me. The lawyers all laughed and joked with me all through it."

She had allowed herself to be cheered by litigationists who didn't want trouble, while her young heart broke at the prospect of having to return home to Pierre. So she had never had a life of her own. On her own.

The small taste that she did get of it, away from Pierre, had been fully enough.

With a sigh, Bella hangs up the whisk in the kitchen. Smells of Dream Bars everywhere. She pulls them out of the oven and puts them on the windowsill to cool.

Jean shouts across the way, "That smells pretty good. Would you care to come over for an apéritif before lunch?"

Bella was glad to have an excuse to escape her thoughts.

A bluebottle fly buzzes around her head and lands on the butter dish. She searches frantically through the as yet unpacked kitchen boxes for the fly swatter.

"I'll be over in a minute," she shouts into the box.

"Bloody bluebottles! If there's anything I hate it's a fly in the food."

She searches through the drawers and cupboards. Finally she settles on a rolled piece of newspaper, lunges at the fly, swats, and misses. "Geez!" she yelps. Too late! The butter smears Chamberlain's face.

"Hey there! A little appetizer before lunch? A little sherry, maybe?"

"Yes. I said yes. I'll be right over."

As Bella steps into the bright, shiny, new-smelling kitchen, Jean pulls a bottle of sherry from under the sink.

She flashes Bella a conspiratorial smile. "Have to hide it. Les and June pour it down the sink when they lay hold of it. Fifty cents down the drain, too, damn them."

Bella grimaces. Jean has magically erased any image of sophistication that Bella had held of her. I never was a good judge of character anyhow, she thinks.

"You've got a real nice kitchen here," she says, to cover.

Jean pours them each a tumbler full of the sweet, sticky liquid. "Yes, well, it's not bad looking—for the area, I mean." She shrugs. "Rats in the back shed, though."

"Really?" Bella shudders. "Gosh, I hope they don't come over to our place."

Bella was familiar with rats. They'd come out of the swamp at the back of Memère Tombeau's house. Sometimes right into the outhouse. It wasn't that she was afraid of them. She simply didn't care for their darting movements.

She glances around the kitchen for a second time, on the alert. Just in case.

"Never fear. We feed them too well here." She clinks her glass against Bella's. "Here's looking up your kilt."

Bella watches as she swills the syrupy amber liquid down her long throat.

"Look, if you're too hot in here we can sit on the back steps.

I've got the wood stove going for the spice cake. First time I succeeded in getting it started, too." She wipes her mouth with the back of her blue-veined hand.

"No, I'm just right, really." Bella stares at her, fascinated by the dress and elegant costume jewellery that did not relate to her words or mannerisms. Maybe she was on her way to a party? In any case she reminds her of a jigsaw puzzle with a missing piece. Better: an unfinished symphony. Bella isn't sure how she feels about her. She lets the sweetness roam around in her mouth. Her eyes settle on a strange, wonderful-looking hat sitting on the sideboard. Actually there are two hats, now that she looks more closely. One on top of the other. The one underneath is a khaki-coloured wide-brimmed felt hat.

Jean follows her glance. "I'm a milliner. The bottom one is Les's hat. He's a Mountie. Wears a red uniform and all the paraphernalia and crap that goes with it."

Bella's eyes widen in childish wonder. She sits up straighter and is relieved. Well, yes, of course she's a milliner. That's why she's all dressed up. In case a client comes to the door for a hat.

"He covers Rockcliffe on a horse and is in charge of the stables."

"Really? Does he? I'm terrified of horses but I respect them a lot."

Jean grabs the top hat and says, "But this one I made."

She plops it on her head. It sits askew, like a distinguished piece of impromptu art.

Bella falls in love with the spontaneous gesture immediately. "It's a total happening!" she says with delight.

"Here, hang on, I'll go unpack my collection in the bedroom."

Glancing at the Mountie hat, Bella remembers when she was eleven years old. Pierre got them part-time jobs with a travelling fair while they were in Sudbury. He'd rented some Shetland ponies, and she rode up and down the paddock, displaying her non-existent riding skills to the young giggling children, while Maman sold tickets in the little box-office cage.

She was petrified of horses, never having been on one before, but she managed to look good in the saddle and the Mountie hat.

Pierre had said, "Look at her, she's a natural," as she sat quivering on top of the quivering animal.

Maman said that she took after her blood father in that. According to her, "Maurice had been a showman with natural composure."

Bella reckoned that it was the Mountie hat first and foremost that had given her the courage to sit in the saddle without falling off.

With several hats on her head and one on each hand, Jean appears out of the bedroom, the essence of a walking hat rack. "The circus is where he belongs when he's all dressed up. Up there on his horse ... his high horse," she sniffs derisively, struggling with the hats.

Bella holds her breath to keep from bursting into laughter at Jean's disarming ingenuousness.

Jean continues, "On his high horse...." She laughs from the pit of her throat. "He says that Americans eat it up madly, though." She throws them on the table.

Bella saves the glasses just in time, as the hats tumble and roll all over the table and floor.

"And he should know, being one. Apparently they click their cameras all over the fool place. And what's more, they keep asking where the Indians are. Isn't that rich? Les says the government is seriously thinking of hiring a couple of hundred of the unemployed and dressing them up as Indians to attract more tourists." She takes her glass from Bella and savours another sip. "I think it's a pretty good idea myself."

Bella looks at Jean across the mound of hats in disbelief. She doesn't know whether to laugh at the joke or run. She mutely swallows the sudden lump of shock instead. Memère Tombeau is Algonquin. Being native to the country isn't considered the social register in the white man's world, but it is to Bella. "I guess the capital city should be noted for something besides Parliament Hill," she says limply, but silently feels insulted. The woman doesn't care which way she swings the bat when she swings it.

Bella decides not to say anything about her people. Memère Tombeau's philosophical tone rings in her ears. "There's no point defending yourself against the indefensible." In the convent, Bella had seen how the nuns treated the native children. It was not a pretty sight. She changes the subject. "If tourist money is coming in our direction we've nothing to complain about, though." *Des Platitudes*. Platitudes. They always work well in English as fillers. It was called having social skills.

Silence drifts into the room. Bella rotates the glass in her hand and watches Jean attentively behind her long eyelashes. She notices that she has a cast in one eye. It makes her look cross-eyed. She'd had a Siamese cat similar to that once. Bella decides that she likes the look; it reminds her of her own vulnerability. Jean may have a sharp tongue but she has a warm look.

She sorts her hats on the table according to style and colour. Out of nowhere she says, "Your English is good. Do you translate everything you say into English, or do you think in English?"

Bella tries a hat on, looking at herself in the mirror above the sideboard. "It doesn't matter, one way or another. The images are the same in both languages." She pulls the brim down on one side, affecting a French persona. "But when I feel strongly about something, it comes out in French … it all depends on how the hat makes me feel."

Jean limps over to the sideboard for a cigarette, eyeing Bella in the hat.

"My grandparents were French. Beaumarchais. That's my name. Can't speak a word of it now, though." She snaps her Ronson lighter. "You look good in that. Softens your features. You have real style. Always remember I said that."

Bella tries another hat on. "That's why you have such good taste," she says, as she flips the brim up, along with her chin.

Jean smiles at her, "Because I have some French in me? Really?" She offers Bella a Sweet Caporal cigarette. "That your husband, the urbane, dark chap I see around?"

Michael? Urbane? Now there was an English word she didn't know. Bella exhaled the smoke through her long thin nose. Urbain? "Citified?"

Jean offered, "Cultured, wears his hat well."

"What makes you say that?"

She adjusts Bella's hat just a touch. "I *know* people. It comes from working in a hat shop, I guess."

"Yes, that's my husband."

The minister's voice echoed through the empty hall, "I now pronounce you man and wife." The X-ray results had come back positive. Michael had been forced to marry her. Not exactly what you see in those Hollywood movies. She herself was happy enough with it, except that it would have been better if he hadn't felt so desperately pressured. On top of which, it had to be so very secret.

Michael hadn't wanted the university to find out. The Jesuits wouldn't buy it and the Bishop would definitely be on their doorstep.

A marriage in the United Church was not part of their script. Then too, there was always those bothersome villagers.

Maman said it was just as well that it was secret. A Protestant marriage was not something, as the old English expression went, "to write home about."

"Yes, that's him."

"Nice-looking man. What does he do?"

"Teaches at the university," she says, proud that she, with her elementary school education, had married into the right side of the tracks. Basically, she felt her spirit strong enough to be able to take him on.

"Handsome."

"Yes, women are attracted to him." The late nights. Never knowing where he'd been. Bert always supplying the alibi. Straight face. She ended up calling Bert Mr. Straightface, to his face.

"Pardon my grammar, but ain't life grand?" Bella sighs.

"Are those your feelings or are you just quoting the song?"

"Both."

Jean looks at her derisively as she hobbles over to the stove, not knowing what to make of Bella. She peeks in the oven. "Damn, it's not even rising yet!" She fusses around the stove with toothpicks and pot holders.

Bella had got her own back though. Those pre-Sanatorium days had been difficult. Pierre welcomed her back. It was better than nothing from Michael. Besides, she'd grown used to Pierre now. She'd never had an orgasm with anyone anyway, so what was all the fuss about?

She reasoned that changing partners was not so serious, because if she wasn't having an orgasm then she wasn't in love. That was back in the days before the San. Now she changed her views on the subject. She merely dropped the whole idea of ever having an orgasm and that it possibly was not related to loving anyway. She did not connect the dysfunction with the sexual abnormalities in her childhood.

Jean finally settles for closing the air vent and pulls on a couple of keys. "There now. That ought to do it. Now where were we... ?" She lurches into her chair and proceeds to tell Bella that being a Mountie doesn't require much in the way of brains. "In my experience, Les wasn't there when God was handing them out."

Bella wonders why she is negative about her own husband. You could think those thoughts but you didn't speak them. Those kinds of things are best kept to yourself, she thinks.

She struggles with a bit of thread from a hat. "Oh, well, the honeymoon doesn't last very long, does it?"

Bella nods in agreement, although she'd never had one herself.

"'Kiss the joy as it flies.' Now who said that?"

Bella fingers more hats. "What are they made of?"

"Crepe paper. I call them straw hats because you can't find straw anywhere these days. Lots of fine fabrics for dressmaking, but straw is unavailable for milliners. Shortages going on, you might say. Dunno why." Jean circles the rim of her wine glass with her fingers. "Do you think we're headed for war?" she asks darkly.

The question startles Bella for an instant. "Well, Chamberlain doesn't seem to know what he's doing, does he?" is the best she can come up with, seeing that he'd just had his face smeared in the butter. She feels insecure about world events. She doesn't feel like she has a solid grip on political issues. Nor does she feel she is educated enough to venture an opinion, for fear of being laughed at, particularly by Michael.

Bella feels instead the texture of the black and white hat. "How do you make... ?" A hacking cough burbles up. She doubles over in her chair. The stove imperceptibly emits smoke from the cracks in the lids.

"I braid the different coloured strips together. That one you have there I call tweed."

Bella tries it on. "How does it look?"

"Great! But on you, smashing! It gives you another dimension."

"I love it!" she says, choking. "Jean, you're sure that everything's okay with that stove?"

"Sure, kid. Don't worry. Got the damn thing working after one solid week of trying. Not going to stop now."

Tears start to roll down Bella's cheeks. "Yes, but maybe you should leave the vents open?"

"No, the cake won't bake then." Jean's tone changes to mildly reassuring. "It'll straighten itself out, don't worry."

"Fine, but let's go sit on the steps outside."

"A'rightio."

Bella staggers outside with Jean behind her, clutching the sherry bottle.

"Here. We'll sit here." She puts the bottle down on the top step between them. "Now then, where were we?"

Bella drinks some sherry to stop the coughing. "Can't remember." The fact is that she doesn't want to remember. The topic of war is not in her repertoire of facile conversation.

Jean slaps her on the back. "Any case, it doesn't matter."

The bottle tips over. "Oops! The bottle!" She grabs it and holds it to the sunlight. "Well, there's another thirty-eight cents plus tax left, I'd say. Have another?"

Bella giggles at the distortions through the green glass.

Jean's back door suddenly swings open. A gust of grey smoke

explodes from it. Eyeglasses tower above their heads, shimmering in the sunlight.

"Mother, what in hell is wrong with this stove?"

Jean stands up, trying to focus on her daughter through the clouds of smoke.

"Oh dear. Goodness me. I forgot all about the cake. I'll fix it right away."

The twelve-year-old bars her way into the kitchen. "June dear, this is Mrs... Mrs...."

"Maguire." The cold reflection of the glasses is suspended above her.

June stares at her mother. "Another one of your pals? Didn't take you long to find someone, did it?"

"Now, now, June, don't be bold." She jockeys for the door. The girl won't let her in.

"The place smells like a brewery on fire." She indicates the darkened step with her foot. "You spilled it, didn't you?"

Bella backs away from the steps.

Jean laughs. "Well, I must get inside. See you again soon.... Mrs... Uhhh...." She picks up the sticky bottle and disappears behind the door.

The girl sneers, "Mrs Uhh. That's not her name."

Bella hurries to her back door. In the coolness of her kitchen she hears June shrieking, "I'll tell Daddy on you. I'll tell him!"

Bella looks out the window. Tears are streaming down the child's face. "You're not going to get us thrown out of this place too! I'll tell Daddy." Her voice bounces off Jean's wall onto theirs, echoing through the narrow laneway into the street.

Thrown out of this place too? My God, was the woman an alcoholic? You don't have to go far to bump into the world, she thinks anxiously. It's right on your doorstep. Bella plugs her ears. The screaming is frightening. A streak of summer lightning lights up the kitchen. The screaming stops.

In the silence she hears the children's footsteps on the front porch.

Bella throws open the front door. "Is it true, Michael? Is it true that we may be going to war?"

"What brings this on?" he asks.

"The woman next door seemed...."

"Whoah, wait a minute."

"Well, what do you think?"

"It's true that the news from Europe doesn't present a good picture. There appears to be a depression there, too, and that can presage war. But we have business people here on this side of the water who have just opened the World's Fair in New York; that doesn't augur war to me." He pauses for a moment, taking her in, this old lover but now anxious wife of his. He decides to reassure her. "On the contrary, that indicates confidence in our economy. I was in fact just reading at the library that the Czechoslovakian Government in exile have opened their own pavilion in New York. That's the action taken by business in face of the fact that the Germans are at this very moment occupying their country. It's a clear demonstration against the German occupation, and for the liberation of the Czech Sovereign State. There are still good signs of life emerging on the business horizon."

Although she doesn't understand all of it, Bella is satisfied with his response. It's what she likes about him best: his clarity ... when it comes.

CHAPTER ELEVEN

Emerald

THE SCORCHING HEAT of June 1939 finds Prospect Street full of people sitting on their porches day and night. They never seem to move from there. They're there at night before she goes to bed and they're still there in the morning when she gets up. They rock back and forth, watching the traffic, languidly fanning themselves with the latest news of the day. They're there when the milkman arrives with his horse and cart at seven and when the iceman arrives right after him. They're there when the breadman's buggy turns the corner in the middle of the afternoon and when the vegetable vendor arrives, hollering his wares, just before supper time.

"*Des tomates, des cornichons, des navets, des patates, des oignons. Cinq cents la livre.*" Five cents ... five pennies nobody has.

People watch and rock.

By seven o'clock on Friday evening the fresh smells of the vegetable wagon are gone. And the street reeks of horse piss and manure. That's when the street flushers flush up the week's debris; the water rushes up to the curb and, with tidal strength, into the swirling sewers.

Emer watches Monsieur Larocque, who quietly sits with his chair tilted against the porch, chewing on a matchstick. She notices that he never gets it wet. He slouches back against the brickwork. His red-rimmed eyes half-closed, he scans the people on the other side of the street. She peers over the partition of their duplex to observe him. Roy Rogers without Trigger, she thinks. There was a resemblance. His eyes are very small, but well delineated, sharp, and darting, just like those of the movie-star cowboy.

Madame Larocque is perched beside him in a straight-backed rocker that never rocks, her knees jammed together tightly, her eyes wide open, unblinking. Seemingly unseeing.

Her father calls it "catatonic." Something to do with cats, Emer supposes. The way they stare at nothing for such a long time. What the "tonic" part of it was, she didn't know. Emer could only guess that staring at one spot for a long time might feel like a tonic to some people. Madame Larocque appeared to be one of them.

Across the street, on his front stoop, Monsieur Chapelle is eating from a bowl. He dips his crust into his "ragout," a combination of hamburger and pig's feet. She stands on tiptoe on the balcony banister, clutching the pillar, and catches sight of a pig's hoof hanging over the edge of his bowl. As he eats it, she wonders how it goes down and stays down.

Emer hears her father say that he'd never seen the likes of it, and that things seem worse than before he went into the San. She wonders what he means, because everyone seems quite happy to be sitting around doing nothing. The summer heat of course is a factor. Still, the street is a big change from the desolation of the rooming house on Waller Street.

When she got out of the San her mother had found a room for all three of them. The one window looked out on a convent on one side and the bars of the prison house next door on the other.

This is different. Here there is life. Lots of people.

To Emer the display of smiles does not hide their sad eyes. Although she is too young to be aware of need, she still senses the forced optimism.

It's July first, Dominion Day.

The street is alive with the excitement of celebration—anything to break the boredom of the heat and the unemployment.

Two policemen saunter by on their usual five-thirty beat. Small billy-sticks by their sides. No guns. Chatting amiably. The supper hour, on a weeknight. Quiet. No full moon in sight ... yet!

Suddenly, young voices fill the street from end to end. "The flushers are coming! Flushers are coming!"

Emer rushes down to the curb to join Zack, who's already waiting for the Friday night water tank to arrive, with its cooling sprays. As the truck starts down the street, she sees the steam rise from the wet pavement in an undulating haze.

Two men sweep horse manure to the curb ahead of the splashing truck. The water comes rolling in toward them in clumps.

Children suddenly appear out of their torrid houses, bumping into each other to sop up the cooling sprays. As the flushers hit the pavement in full force, Emer feels the delicious showering on her face and bare legs, along with the primal smell of earthiness that only water can dredge up from its crevices.

Pirouetting in the gutter, she breathes deeply into the ecstasy of the experience.

Bella calls from the window. "Emer, will you and your brother get up from that dirty gutter!"

Her mother's voice startles her.

"The wringer on the Beatty is broken and you know I can't wring things out by hand. You hear me? Get out of the gutter! I'm the one does the washing around here! Mucking about in the muck!" she grumbles.

Emer hops up on the sidewalk, barefoot.

Her mother screams, "And put on your shoes!"

Zack remains in the gutter, hiding his feet behind the curb.

"You too, Zack. Up here on the sidewalk." Her mother's voice always sounds a lot mellower when she talks to her brother. Almost kindly. She never speaks to her in that tone of voice. Never that she could remember, anyway.

"Sit on the porch, not on the curb. Not when the water's going by."

The boy looks at her stubbornly, but doesn't budge.

"Do I have to go out there with a stick?"

Emer hates her when she loses her temper. The idea of her mother with a stick in her hand is silly. "She can't hit a baseball with a two-by-four, never mind the two of us," she mutters.

Zack hesitantly puts one bare foot up on the sidewalk, then the other, tensing his shoulders about his ears, waiting.

And it comes. "Where in heaven's name are your boots?"

He stiffly points to the little pile on the street.

"*Mon Jupiter! Mets tes bottes toutes suite, ou j'te tu.*" By Jupiter, put those boots on right away or you're dead!

Emer helps him get back into his boots as he gulps back his tears in great musical notes.

"You! What's wrong with you? *Dans la lune tout le temps!* Always in the moon. Can't you watch him?"

Emer blushes. The neighbours all heard it, no doubt. She feels humiliated.

The fact that her mother speaks French and English interchangeably is, in Emer's view, her only saving grace. She bends over her brother's laces, waiting for her to leave the window. Swamped in her anger.

"Mommy mad," he pants, trying to help his sister tie the laces into a bow.

EMERALD

Emer, burning to her roots, fervently wishes that her mother bore a stronger resemblance to radio's *Ma Perkins* than to the Bad Queen in *Snow White*.

"She's so mean to me," she says to Zack, play-acting the role of Snow White speaking to the dwarves.

They sit solemnly on the top porch step, watching the other children squealing with delight as the city flusher splatters them with cool water.

Emer watches June Drake wade in up to her ankles. She's lucky. Her mother lets her do what she wants. Probably isn't even home. She's real lucky.

A fat woman with a turban that looks like an inverted pot appears on the upstairs porch of the duplex over June's, shouting, "Joce-lyn Gosse-lin! *Débarque de d'la!*" Get out of there!

The woman is perched on the edge of her jutting Juliette balcony. Emer marvels that it doesn't collapse. "Wow! A Visigoth! The only thing that's missing is the shield!" Madame Gosselin creates the exact image of the pictures in Emer's encyclopedias. "No horns in the pot, that's all!"

A brown head of sausage ringlets emerges out of the crowd onto the curb. She's a small dainty child in a homemade frilled-up pinafore that looks out of place on Prospect Street.

Emer watches as Jocelyn's mother walks back indoors on the balls of her feet. "My, my, an accomplished ballet dancer, fluttering wrists and all! A bobbing balloon, pretending she's a feather." Emer's anger takes itself out on Mme Gosselin.

Suddenly, across the street, a man with a long beard comes into her sightline. He's wearing a black beanie and chanting in front of a bookstand.

She stands on the railing of the porch to get a better view.

She knows his boys by sight. The eldest one, Arnold, is splashing about on her side of the street with his younger brother, Percy.

As she stands on the railing the skullcap turns around and faces her, still singing.

At the same moment, Percy whispers through clenched teeth, "Arnie wants to kiss you." She loses her balance and spins out of control onto the small patch of front lawn. On her back, looking up at the sky through the oak leaves, she wonders what Percy meant. What did he say?

Zack's voice fades in on her. "Le's play nurse and Doctor, Emer."

She investigates her scraped knees, keeping a sharp eye on Arnie and Percy in the water, though why she's doing that she doesn't know.

"Oh, you always want to play that silly game."

"C'mon," he pleads.

"Naw. I'm sick of operating on you. Same ol' thing."

"Aww, c'mon."

"Nope. Don't want to. Too hot."

Kiss me? Why? Images of pictures from her mother's movie magazines. People kissing. Wow!

As she squints at Arnie splashing about with his head down, his ears appear to be red. He pretends not to have heard his brother.

"Well, le's play house then," Zack continues, undaunted.

"No. Too hot."

"You be the baby." He pulls at her dress. "I'll be the mother."

"No, I told you."

The red ears are fascinating.

Her mother's voice rises behind the lace curtains. "Emer, Granny Longpré is coming. Go play at the back and don't move from there. I'll call you in when she arrives."

"Oh? No one ever tells me anything around here." She is fond of Granny Longpré. She has a rough, sandpapery, low voice, with hands to match.

The first time Emer met her, the old lady had grabbed her to her beaded bosom. She felt her up and down. Checked her out everywhere. Even her crotch. She remembered squirming uncomfortably. Her head, entangled in masses of ebony black beads, bounced off Gran's bony breastbone. In self-defence, she was about to say to her mother, "I'm for out!" But eagle-eyed mother caught her eye, fixing her until Emer thought better of it. Instead, she allowed Gran to "see her." The truth of the matter was that her mother didn't want to be left alone with Great-Grandmother. Emer knew that much. Her truculence frightened Bella. When the old lady was in her cups, she was prone to talking about things in the past that made Bella feel uneasy. Emer had actually seen her mother tremble from head to toe when Gran started in on past events. The last time she paid them a visit was before her father had left for the San, and he had disappeared for two days. He was no better at handling the old lady than her mother was, that much was clear.

Bella peers through the heavy curtains.

The children haven't budged.

"I'm telling you again, git! Don't let me say it three times!"

Emer bounces back onto the porch and glances at Monsieur Larocque through the slats in the partition to see if he'd heard the humiliating witch. But his magic wet-proof matchstick never stops moving from side to side as he watches his wife stare vacantly at some point in the distance.

Apparently one is deaf and the other is blind, Emer surmises.

The two policemen now wend their way back on Monsieur Chapelle's side of the street. The old man smiles and waves at them.

He knows them well. They're like old friends. They'd taken him to jail last Saturday night. In a sidecar.

Poupoune and Emer find front seats, on the curb.

Sitting low down in the sidecar, only his head visible, he waves at the gathering crowd like the Queen Mother from her carriage, waving and smiling with his handkerchief.

Such grace!

No one ever sees his wife. She's presumably sitting inside beside the phone, ready to dial when things get rough.

The police nod and smile back. Monsieur Chapelle waggles his finger at them as if they've been two naughty boys for carting him off to jail.

Emer wipes her wet bangs. They're standing straight up in the air. "It's too hot in that back shed to play," she says to her mother, eyeing the cooling swirls of water rolling into the curb.

"Well, play in the yard then. Please understand that I want you off the front steps so that Gran' can make her way to the front door without tripping over you."

"Do I have to?" Emer longs to be playing in the midst of the wild screams of laughter.

Michael stands in the screened doorway. "What's going on?"

"Oh, they don't know what to do with themselves," Bella replies from the bay window. "And they make me nervous hanging around the front of the house when your grandmother's moving in with us, with her suitcase and all."

"What's the matter, Emer?" he asks.

"Nothing." Her heels turn inwards. "It's just too hot to do anything."

Michael looks at their streaked faces. "Your Great-Grandmother is coming here to live for a while. Your mother and I want to have the front steps clear for her when she arrives. Try to be accommodating and play at the back."

Across the street the chanting begins in earnest.

"There goes the rabbi." Michael looks up toward the figure in the open window. Emer watches as the two men nod at each other across the splashing pandemonium in the street.

On the window seat, Bella leans into the path of a breeze. "Look at that," she sighs. Everyone's windows are wide open. "God, what a street for noise! Houses are too close. Just listen to the volume on that radio next door!"

Mexicali Rose, I love yooo,
Dry those big brown eyes
And please don't cryyy.

"Where's it coming from?" Answering her own question, Bella says, "The Truro Apartments across the street, where else? Between the pop song on the radio, the chanting rabbi, and those excited children, it makes it difficult to think," she says to no one in particular.

Michael clears his throat nervously. He doesn't like to hear Bella complain in front of the children. "That's a rabbi, Emer. A Jewish clergyman," he says almost reverently. "He's a chess master. Played him at the chess club. Came over from Poland three years ago with Boyateerchuk, another master. Mr. Boyateerchuk will be teaching in my department come September."

Emer looks in awe at the singer. "Oh, a master huh? I wonder if Arnold plays chess."

"Ask him and see."

Emer casts the boy a long look, trying to assess his chess abilities. "Oh, well. C'mon Zack, let's go to the backyard." Emer trudges toward the laneway.

As she pushes the heavy wooden gate into their laneway, she catches sight of Poupoune turning the corner at Routhier's.

She's carrying a heavy basket covered with a white cloth.

"Find a place in the shade to play in," Bella shouts from the window.

"Say," says Michael, "how about a nice tall, cool glass of lemonade?"

Two beaming faces look up at him.

"There aren't any oranges and we don't have a lemon," the witch says. Emer was capable of holding a grudge for a while.

Michael puts his book down on the verandah. "C'mon, let's go buy some at Routhier's."

They walk down to the corner store hand in hand.

"We'll make some for tonight, too," Michael says, swinging their arms. "When we fire off those firecrackers I bought this afternoon we can drink some lemonade."

On their way, they meet Poupoune.

"What's in the basket?" Emer asks.

Poupoune pulls away from her. "No look, no look." Her face is red.

"I missed you. Where were you?"

"*Le marché.*"

"The market?" This puzzles her. "*Pourquoi?*" Emer lifts the white linen and peeks under it. It's a chicken.

The front door to Poupoune's house suddenly swings open against the wall, rattling on its hinges.

"*Ma 'tite chienne!*" The hurled words force both girls to duck. "What took you so long?"

"I couldn't sell the last chicken," Poupoune says as she scuttles past her mother.

"*Quoi?*" She cuffs her on the side of the head as she runs past.

This time Emer doesn't wait to have the door slam in her face. She runs to join her father and brother up ahead.

Selling chickens at the market alongside real shopkeepers was something to be admired, she thinks. I couldn't do that. It takes courage to do that. She wonders why Poupoune's mother doesn't appreciate her courage.

"You kids choose," says Michael, lifting Zack up to the counter.

M. Routhier smiles encouragingly as he slides the back of the candy display case open.

They feasted their eyes on B-B Bats, great big chunks of caramel on a stick, Honeymoons, molasses-flavoured taffy covered in chocolate, and then black and red candy balls, and cinnamon fish as burning hot as horseradish. There were hundreds of enormous purple balls of peppermint bubble gum, and chocolate-covered marshmallows in the shape of miniature brooms on a stick, alongside the mouth-watering homemade butterscotch, and scads of long, braided licorice whips.

Emer swoons, finally murmuring, "Caramel B-B Bats, Dad."

"Settled," he says. "Two B-B Bats for a penny, please."

A very special and rare treat.

Arnie and Percy are sitting on the curb on her side of the street. She musters up her best piercing look at Arnie, trying to assess his chessmanship.

Michael takes the front steps three at a time. "I'll bring the lemonade out back."

Percy hisses as she disappears down the laneway, "Arnie wants to kiss you."

Emer pretends to glower at both of them, B-B Bat in one hand, brother in the other. She'd been told never to speak to a stranger, much less kiss one, and as far as she was concerned they were both strangers.

Michael brings out the pitcher of lemonade. He sets it down on the sloping floor of the back shed and sits on the threshold.

Although he's curious to see his grandmother again after so many years, he notes that he's no longer anxious. He trusts that he'll ask the right questions at the right time. He feels that's a plus in his favour.

Every now and again Bella leaves her magazine by the window seat to listen to Emer and Michael chatting.

༄

Poupoune escapes to the backyard from under her mother's thumb. She gives up feeding the baby in the high chair. He doesn't want any more of the mashed carrots anyway. She wipes the orange splatter from her face and saunters over to her father's red truck. There it sits up on blocks, handsomely gleaming, beckoning. Temptation itself.

Teddy, the long-haired chow chow, limps behind her.

Although irresistibly drawn to sitting in her father's truck, she hesitates.

His voice rings out clearly in her head. "*C'est défendu d'embarquer dans mon truck.*" It's forbidden to get in my truck.

Not that he would deter her. She loves the excitement of getting him riled. He would beat her, but she no longer cares. He does it anyway, on the slightest provocation. Maman and Papa both beat her. But her spirit is unbeaten. The excitement of "driving" the truck is worth the risk.

Hearing voices on the other side of the fence, she peers through a loose slat.

Emer looks up to see Poupoune beckoning her.

Squinting through the slat, she sees Poupoune's yellow-haired dog behind her. Both ears point straight up to the sky.

"You wanna drive in my car?" Poupoune nods toward the red truck.

"Is your dog mean?"

"Mean?"

"Bite. Does he bite?" Growling, she bites her arm.

The girl smiles. "*Non*," she says, "*il est trop vieux.*" He's too old.

"Yeah, he must be thirty if he's a day. His white hair's gone yellow."

Suddenly some leftovers are pitched out Poupoune's kitchen window; the dog scurried away.

Emer hears her gate squeak open. The two of them. There they were. Behind her. Percy and Arnie.

Percy shouts, "Arnie wants to kiss you."

She scrambles over the fence into Poupoune's yard.

"Catch me if you can," she shouts.

Giggling, the two girls bounce into her father's truck, slamming the doors shut. Poupoune's dress smells of rough brown bar soap that Emer's mother washes floors with. Barsalou soap. Or maybe she washes her skin with it. It isn't nasty, it's just rough-smelling floor soap.

Emer turns the windshield wipers on while Poupoune puts the car in gear and honks the horn.

"*Watchez-vous les gars on s'en viens!*" she shouts. Watch out, boys, here we come!

Percy screams, "Yeah! C'mon, let's get into the thing!"

They pull the doors open and sit themselves on either side of the girls, with Arnie in the driver's seat. The dog growls on the roof of the cabin. In the next yard a buzz saw starts to hum and whine.

The children become one mass, tugging and screaming for the driver's seat. "I'll be the driver!"

"Naw, you're not good enough to be the driver."

Fat Percy screams, "I'm a good driver. I'll be the driver and the rest of you passengers." He turns on the ignition.

"Vrroom! Vrroom! Watch out now, we're going ninety!"

"Wheeee....!"

"We're going ninety!"

"What a tub!"

"We're turning a corner. Hold on!"

They giggle and squirm climbing around each other, in and out of both doors trying to push each other out of the driver's seat.

Finally, the girls find themselves sitting up on top of the cabin with the dog. Their bare feet dangle in front of the windshield.

Percy peers up at them from behind the wheel, "How can I see the road? You be the passengers. Sit in the back of the truck!" he commands.

Poupoune retorts, *"Nous prends tu pour des vaches?"* Do you take us for cows? Emer laughs at the smart reply.

"We aren't taking a back seat," she shouts, "so there! You take the back seat. You be passengers. Any case, we have the better view up here."

The boys howl with laughter.

Emer clambers over the cabin on her stomach and tries to pull on Arnie's pant leg, while Poupoune, whose arm is longer, succeeds somewhat on the other side with Percy.

He tries to hold onto his pants and struggles for control of the steering wheel at the same time.

"Débarque, bon! C'est le char de mon père, pis moi, j'veux le runner," she says. Get out! It's my father's car, I have a right to run it.

At just that moment Poupoune's father comes tearing out the back door.

Screaming at the children, he splutters unintelligibly. With shaving cream halfway down his face, he holds his trousers up with one hand, a straight razor in the other. As if that isn't horrifying enough, his glass eye reflects the rays of the setting sun like streaks of lightning.

They all bolt over the fence, minus Poupoune, through a flurry of white chicken feathers and barking Teddy.

They run to the other side of Emer's house, out of earshot of the "licking" that Poupoune was probably getting.

Emer feels her body pounding in her ears with fear and excitement. "I'm all puffed out!"

They stand around for a moment, not knowing what to do next. Hearing Poupoune's stifled cries, they toe the hardened earth into mounds, quivering.

Percy starts swinging on the creaky wooden gate.

"You've got a baboon face," he says.

"She does not," says Arnie.

"See? He wants to kiss you."

All three children start swinging on the solid wooden gate.

It slams shut a couple of times.

Emer can see her house shudder with the bang.

Bella calls from the kitchen window, "Get off that gate! It's old, you'll break it!" They jump off, all three at once.

Percy's sing-song begins. "Baboon, Baboon, Arnie wants to kiss you." Emer looks straight at Arnie. All she sees are his red ears again. Judging from his ears it must be true, then. She had never seen anyone wanting to play chess with red ears.

She bolts down the alleyway in confusion, then through Madame Gosselin's back garden. She runs over the cucumbers, radishes, and squishy tomatoes, then squeezes herself between the back of the corrugated garage and a fence, ten inches from it. Leaning against the hot tin wall, she feels the sweat pouring down her face.

The chase is alarming and exciting at the same time. The feeling is new to her. The rat-a-tat-tat of her body gives her away when she finds the opening in the fence into the next yard and through it into the street to the north.

She turns the corner in great glee, mopping her forehead with a maple leaf. She has escaped!

Walking along King Edward Boulevard she regains her breath.

The breadman's buggy is delivering his day's supply of "Miracle" bread to Monsieur Routhier. What makes that cotton mush miraculous? Maybe because it's pure white and wheat is naturally brown, she thinks, answering her own question. I prefer the Jewish bread Dad buys at the Bakery Oven while it's still hot. Yum! Rye with caraway seeds and a hard crust to chew on. She pats the horse on his velvety brown nose, thinking how much more she likes saying *mon-see-oor* Routhier than just plain old "mister." It wasn't as musical, and after her escape she was in a musical mode.

The two boys sneak around the buggy.

She catches them creeping up behind her. They immediately adopt a *"laissez faire"* attitude.

Percy whines, "Aw c'mon, Emer, he just wants to talk to you. We're tired of running after you."

"Well, let him talk then."

The three of them walk down Prospect Street toward her house in silence.

Emer ambles along on the inside, as far away from them as she can without walking on people's crummy lawns.

The grocer's house has a small patch of yellow grass that is surrounded by a fence of green bars.

Holding her balance on the bars she repeats, "Well, go on. If you want to talk to me, say something!"

"Cause you're always running, that's why." Arnie is walking backwards, ready to catch her if she falls. Emer imagines collapsing into his arms. Right into his arms.

Two nuns in black were walking toward them.

"Look," he whispers, "two scarecrows."

"So? Who cares?" Head down, concentrating on the bars, she knows the nuns are watching them. She hears their beads rattling past. She also notices Percy has disappeared from her range of vision.

"Where's Percy?" She jumps off the bars and discovers him creeping up behind her on all fours. As she backs away she bumps into Arnie, who makes a grab for her. For a chess player he's pretty swift. She rams into him with all her might in the hope of knocking him down. They struggle with each other until they get to her front door.

Emer notices that no one on the front porches seems to be the least bit interested, least of all her neighbour, Monsieur Larocque, with his old toothpick.

Noticing the belt on her dress, Arnie grabs it and drags her behind the wooden gate in the laneway. The world spins in enormous circles.

"It's dark back here, behind the gate," she whispers.

Her father's voice emerges in the darkness. Something from the Bible, no doubt. Not that he was a Bible thumper. He was just an avid reader who always had a *bon mot* for every event in life.

The voice cleared its throat.

"The sins of the father are visited unto the seventh generation."

What does that mean? What are sins?

She senses that kissing is wrong in his view. Is doing something wrong, sin?

Mother, father, family, crowd around, pointing fingers. "She's too young to kiss. You're too young to kiss. Don't let him put his tongue in your mouth, you'll catch his disease."

The voice intones again. "The sins of the father are visited unto the seventh generation."

What did that mean?

The voices are so deafening that she no longer hears her own voice.

Feeling the tendril of the boy's excitement against her thigh, she whispers, "No, no, no." Suddenly, out of nowhere, she decides yes, and kisses him. Kisses him on the cheek.

The world comes to a full stop as she hears the front screen slam shut on its spring.

"*Bienvenue,* Alma," she hears her mother say.

Oh gawd, Great-Granny must have driven up. She wonders why she hadn't heard the car. Granny. Emer smells the ice-cold snow of winter, Florida Water, and a black seal coat.

Both children stand awkwardly in the stifling heat.

Her lips feel dry, seared even.

What did the seared feeling in her lips mean? The street lights came on. Sparrows rustle in the trees readying to settle down for the night. Crickets begin their chirping. Across the street, the rabbi calls Arnie and Percy. Arnie's stance stiffens at his father's voice. Percy peers up the black alleyway, softly calling.

"Arnie, are you there? We have to go in now."

Emer and Arnie stand with their backs glued to the brick wall. Minutes pass and still they stand there waiting.

She hears her father ushering Granny into the front parlour.

A lot of laughter and babbling sounds. She strains to hear what the voices are saying through the open kitchen window above her head. The sound of Granny's voice excites her curiosity. She loves the old lady. She gives no indication of being sightless. Her sentences are short, clean, and to the point. No repetitions. No loops. "Don't miss a trick there, me." That's Gran.

Arnie, thinking that her excitement is a reaction to the kiss, promptly plants another one on her mouth.

"I'll call her in," she hears her father say. "She'll be happy to see you."

For a moment they stand staring at each other in the dark, not moving, not knowing, not hearing. Not hearing Percy telling her father where they are. Not hearing her father's angry voice calling her indoors. The words and tone of his voice slowly turn up to full, like the volume on a radio.

The effort to make sense out of what Percy was saying and then her father's angry response roots her in fear.

"Big, ugly Percy," Arnie mutters. "I'll get him."

"Never mind," Emer says. "It doesn't really matter."

She runs up the dark laneway, into the shed, and in through the back door. In the kitchen she hears the front door slam and her father tell her mother and Gran how out of hand she is and that he would settle this once and for all. Settle what? His footsteps walk toward the kitchen. As he turns the electric light switch, Gran shouts from the parlour.

"Take it easy now! Don't be too hard!"

Emer looks up at him from the rocking chair. Her eyes squinch up from the glare of the bare bulb. She bends down to scratch her shin as casually as she can make it.

Wordlessly he unbuckles his brown leather belt, swiftly grabs her from the rocker, sits in it himself, and throws her over his lap to give her a thrashing. She's stunned.

It comes without warning.

Before the second lash on her numb bottom, Emer looks up to see a small woman under the light bulb with her little black glasses glowering down on her father's head, saying, "*C'est assez!*" That's enough!

"But she's too young for that sort of thing."

"Yes, but it's enough! We all get the point." She reaches for Emer.

"Look at you, you're shaking," Gran says.

Hard to tell who she's talking to.

As he buckles his belt back on, he notices his rage. It's out of proportion to the event. He was emotionally charged, almost out of control with anger and not knowing why.

Through the blur of Emer's tears she remembers the smell of Florida Water and a woman in a black seal coat. She picked her up off the day-bed in the sun porch. The room was cold but comfortable. She was dressed warmly and was wearing a white angora bonnet with white satin rosettes over the ears. It felt and smelled delicious on her head. The windows surrounding her were little squares with globs of snow. The walls were green. She lay in pale green satin and wine velvet. The woman inspected her closely. Emer watched her as she examined every feature in detail. She wriggled a little. The scrutiny made her nervous, but Emer looked her straight in the eye and saw round black eyes and a pug nose. She put her back down safely between the flouncy skirts of button-eyed dolls. Through her numbness she saw the same woman. It was Granny Longpré.

"Don't miss a trick there, me."

Neither one of them missed a trick.

Catherine wheels, rockets, and firecrackers fill the night skies as Emer watches from her bedroom window.

Out of nowhere, Poupoune silently sails into view on the shed roof in the shimmering light just below her window. She squats down on the warm tin of the roof. Emer finds the rough old Barsalou smell comforting. Her cheeks feel stiff with dried salt tears.

"We're seventy-one years old today," she says, standing on a chair, making conversation, pretending sociability.

"Seventy-one?"

"Yep!"

The French girl shrugs. "What means?"

"Dunno … I guess we're just a little older than Teddy." She rubs her numb bottom.

"Who, seventy-one?"

"Canada."

"Teddy is good dog."

"Yeah, except when he's mad."

Affronted by her father's thrashing, she adds, "Daddy sometimes has the anger of a mad dog. Dunno why. Makes no sense."

She watches the display, her head silhouetted against the dark sky.

Mme Gosselin appears on her second-floor back porch, still teetering on the balls of her feet in her sleeveless sundress, with Monsieur Routhier-the-grocer and Jocelyn-with-the-long-ringlets. "OOO! Awwww!" She raises her arms in wonderment, revealing masses of rolling flesh hanging down from under her arms.

"Look at that!" Emer marvels bitterly. "She has four tits. Two at the front and two under her arms. Quadruplets! Wow!"

"What means...?"

"Never mind."

She sees Zack parading around waving the Union Jack under Granny Longpré's nose. Granny sits in the rocker, balancing a teacup very daintily on her lap. She is socializing as if she's attending an animated tea party. From the window she can't see her mother, but knows that the movie queen Lana Turner with the glamorous puss is down there somewhere. She can smell her Tweed perfume. She never comes to her rescue. Granny does. Her father is conducting the fireworks with great aplomb. Never a dull moment, she thinks jeeringly. Always something going off, or moving in all directions. She never knows what he's going to fire off next! She's angry not so much for the numb bottom as the suddenness of his temper.

Mixed in with the sulphuric smell of the firecrackers in her nostrils was the smell of his cigarette smoke. "Lucky Strike Means Fine Tobacco, L.S.M.F.T. So round, so firm, so fully packed, so free and easy on the draw. LSMFT, LSMFT."

Emer mimics the radio announcer on the Jack Benny program. She pinches her nose and does an imitation of the auctioneer selling off a swatch of tobacco leaves. Rapid fire bursts of farting firecrackers.

Poupoune tries to imitate the auctioneering nasal quality but breaks out into laughter instead. Emer sighs as she watches the "show" from the perch of disenchantment with her father. The spanking was humiliating, mortifying. She's unsure whether to run away or stay under the same roof with him.

A huge blast of light fills the sky, lighting up her brother's pumpkin face and all the neighbours.

Mme Gosselin in her awe topples down the stairs, two-at-a-time. Bump-a-dee, bump-bump. Down she goes! Tits over heels. Literally.

Mr. Drake and Michael rush forward, too eagerly. Emer notices with derision how their willing hands settle into three inches of soft warm flesh.

Mr. Drake, back from the wars, dressed in his black boots and jodhpurs, just off from work. "Never fear, the RCMP is here."

She swallows back her loss of pride. Not even the policeman came to her defence. But Gran did!

Downstairs, June is watching from her verandah.

Watching from upstairs, Monsieur Routhier and Jocelyn hypnotize themselves with their loud "Awws."

Emer watches the spectacle of the men groping to get Mae West's corpulence to a standing position. Poupoune snickers. "Now there's the spectacle!" Emer says.

Difficult to see in the strobe-effect lighting of the whirling Catherine wheels whether they're "Awwing" over the fireworks or over the men struggling to straighten her out. Emer leans so far out the window that she hangs there by her knees, raging over the shed roof. Don't give a damn there me. From this position the whole scene is a silent flick.

STARRING.... "Emer as Buster Keaton," she mouths into her rolled fist.

FANFARE: TAH, TAA....

Buster Keaton with a megaphone silently shouts, "Ladies and Gents, step right up and see ..." Monsieur and Madame Larocque sit bolt upright in pressed back pine chairs. A sprinkling of mica dust scatters over the heads of all and company. Bindu lights glitter directly in front of their unseeing eyes. Look at them! Look! Seeing is believing! For they truly see not!

Granny Longpré looks directly up at her in the wake of a shower of swirling Catherine wheels, reflecting in her little black glasses.

"Get yourself down here, girl! You're missing all the fun!" the low gravel voice shouts. Emer jumps out of the window onto the roof. She's been waiting for this kind of a break.

Holding Poupoune's hand, they alight into the flickering world of reality. Or was it unreality?

No matter, into the main feature. Now showing! Her father's creation. Her mother's too. The old lady grabs her to the rocker. Emer's head clunks against her rattling beads and washboard chest. Gran's backbone is straight and strong. Nothing soft about her. Her bony hands pull Emer toward her.

"You come from good stock, girl!" It was a conspiratorial whisper. "Never forget it. Great-Grandfather Choe came here on a boat. Straight from France! The King gave his father a seigneury, Papineauville, on the St. Lawrence River. Choe was a fine gentleman. No matter what, never forget it! You have hard lessons ahead of you, but you'll learn." Her tone was comforting. "So has your father," she adds as an afterthought.

Gran's words puzzle her. Emer feels her shame and wonders what happened to her father's closeness. To live with it in later years she learns to translate the experience into his expression of "tough love." French love handled in clear English.

But on that day, all she experiences is her father's spanking. She understands him only in hindsight. Which, she figures, is where the word got its meaning.

CHAPTER TWELVE

The Theatre

MICHAEL SPENDS MOST OF HIS TIME preparing for the autumn semester. There are good reference books on Fermat's work at the Ottawa Library, but it's the University Library that has the definitive information. He looks forward to delving into its comprehensive math stacks when he starts teaching in September. Might still be able to pick up his Master's in his spare time if he could manage it. The mere thought of it excites him, not just because it's an essential step to the doctorate, but because winning the prize money will enable him to keep his promise to Emer to move the family to a warmer climate. He looks at the clock. It's noon already. He wonders where the time goes. In the excitement his mind scatters. There are so many things he wants to do and not enough time to do them. Playing chess with Bert is no great shakes anymore. Michael needs tougher challenges. Bert's son Mo won a bicycle in a yo-yo contest. The kid has eyeglasses like bottle bottoms. Quite a feat in itself. However, Bert behaves as if Mo just got his degree in massive intelligence. Maybe he has. Go figure.

Michael's mother phones mainly to find out if he knows where Gran is. They finally make an arrangement to meet up. Maybe today he'll get some of the truth out of her. He picks up his strewn papers and stuffs them into his briefcase. I'll get her a bottle of sloe gin on the way. Her favourite drink, hot with nutmeg and sugar. That should help things along some.

He takes the bus to the end of the route, which is a semicircle lined with tall maple and pine trees. The white frame house appears suddenly in the middle of an open field, its red-peaked roof outlined against the blue sky. The driver winds the grinding steering-wheel around the semicircle. Michael sees her standing in the upper sun porch waiting for him. The heat and the uneven ground enervate him on the long walk to the house.

A virtual stampede of French poodles and Pekingese rush at him as she opens the door. Small distracting pups tear about with full command of the upper duplex. He shouts his greetings to make himself heard over the barking.

Thinking himself well-armed, he puts the bottle of gin down on the kitchen table and slings his jacket on the back of the pressed wood chair. When she sees the bottle, she bustles most of the dogs into the basement and puts the kettle on to boil. She ensconces herself carefully in the captain's chair at the head of the table.

Michael observes that she's wearing a black velvet dress with one string of pearls and that her hair is freshly hennaed. Full regalia battle dress. She has a sense of occasion. Enjoyment sparkles in her eyes at having an audience. She has a taste for showmanship, he thinks disdainfully. The gin warms her up. She starts to talk. "You were taken from me as a baby. Your father hired a sleigh in below-zero weather with snow piled up on either side of the road. Some of it piled up to second storeys on each side."

She sips her hot drink. "He'd wrapped you in your flannelette blanket and kidnapped you to Maura's house."

Michael watches her eyes intently as he palms the top of his glass. He'd heard the story before.

"I ran alongside the sleigh, screaming." Silvy gets up and looks outside the window. "No, I'll never forgive John Maguire for that!"

THE THEATRE

The story is straight out of *The Perils of Pauline*, though Michael knows she can't read. As usual, she turns in quite a performance. Melodrama, he thinks. Then again, maybe it is the real thing. He couldn't be sure before and can't now; she's that good at it. Maybe *she* can't be sure any longer either.

She wipes a tear from the corner of her eye. Michael slides into home plate. "He *was* my father then?"

She caps the bottle of sloe gin, returns it to Michael, and begins her delivery in a reproachful whisper. "Who do you think I am?" Silence. Followed by the shrieking vocal dynamic she was so good at. "I'm your mother. How can you doubt my word?"

She could have been an opera singer given half a chance. Incarcerate her in a vault and she'd still be singing her arias to the last breath, he thought.

"What difference does it make, anyhow? You are *who* you are!"

This truth appalls him. He starts to leave, knowing that her next line will be, "Get out. My knees are swelling again." The only difference this time is that her rage is total. For the sake of the neighbours and propriety, she grabs the fly swatter and swiftly whisks the barking pups out the back door, pretending to direct her coloratura screams at them. "I can't handle it anymore. Out!"

So, as always, he leaves. He knows her scenarios well. Michael remembers the sense of defeat he'd had over this precise issue when he entered the San precisely. He would die and she would let him die, never knowing who his father was.

Trying to pick up the pieces, now that he's out, is not as simple as it first looked. Walking back to the bus stop he remarks that perhaps Bella was right: "Let's just get on with our lives and leave the past behind us." Maybe so, he broods, not sure. The troubling question of his paternity is still there. He needs a change of emotional venue, he thinks. Away, far away, from the centre of the painful question that Silvy would not or cannot answer.

At the bus stop, Michael slumps under a maple tree. He dialogues his way out of her negative potholes, as is his usual way after these dead-end visits.

It's good to have Alma living with us now. Straighter than an arrow. She's a tartar. With his illness had come the longed-for time to heal old wounds; to heal unworkable family judgments, his own, theirs. Out of respect for her age he'd always held back from asking her the question.

But now that she's living with them, it seems the obvious thing to do.

The bus driver swings around the circle. Michael hops in. He sits in the back seat and realizes that he forgot to pick up his books. His emotional state got in the way of walking out of the house with books that were key to the solving of Fermat's theorem. In shock, he wonders how he could have allowed such a thing. For an instant he kicks himself, which only worsened the feeling. You'll pick them up another time, another time, he whispers in consoling tones. That over, he swiftly turns his thoughts to his grandmother.

Life has a way of walking into the front parlour, he muses, looking forward to a chat with Alma. She is grieving Horace in her room. He's ill and can't come to see her. Michael postpones talking with her until things get better. With any luck, some place nice and quiet, out in the country. She's in the middle bedroom, where she can reach out the window and feel the sunflowers with her hands. That and feeding the birds keep her occupied. It doesn't take much. She's a lot easier to please than his mother makes out. As long as she stays out of the kitchen, Bella's happy.

THE THEATRE

Together they have their five o'clock apéritif. He plays Beethoven's "Moonlight Sonata," Chopin "Études," and some snappy jazz pieces.

"On your visit to your mother's you didn't tell her I was here, did you, Michael?" Alma asks anxiously.

"No, of course not."

"Play 'Sophisticated Lady'"

The choice pleases him.

"Everything in moderation, I always say." Alma is in her "middle-of-the-road mode." They are all enjoying it, for as long as it will last.

***

That evening he takes Emer to see a stage version of L.M. Montgomery's novel *Anne of Green Gables* at the Capitol Theatre on Bank Street. They have complimentary tickets in the front row. It's a cinema house that occasionally rents out to local theatre groups, in this case The Glebe Players.

The Capitol's lobby boasts a gleaming Carrara marble staircase with an upstairs gallery that sweeps around it. A magnificent crystal chandelier dominates the lobby, giving it an added air of European elegance. The regal wine carpeting is slung across the centre of the stairs, with casually placed armchairs and sofas in the gallery completing the picture. While they are waiting to be ushered to their seats, Emer suddenly stands stock still at the back of the house. She gapes down the raked aisle at the proscenium arch draped with blue velvet curtains that reflect the coloured footlights.

He whispers, "The proscenium is the open fourth wall."

She whispers in reply, "The silence! Feels like I'm in a church."

He smiles at his daughter's choice of words.

As they follow the usher down to their seats, Michael observes that she's mesmerized. Parents and children dressed in formal clothes. Scented silk dresses rustle up and down the aisles, finding their seats, waiting in hushed silence for the curtain to go up on the first act.

Michael inhales the steamy air of expectation that fills the house. The four gem-encrusted boxes hover over the stage apron on either side, with every seat within them filled. The anticipation is palpable. He breathes the excitement into his pores.

Michael had met the director Kurt Hellman a few nights previously. He had been performing some of his more polished tricks for a small audience at the Magicians' Club on Sparks Street when Hellman came in and sat down. He was displaying his sleight-of-hand tricks with coloured ping-pong balls and silk handkerchiefs. Michael's style was crisp, deft, and precise that night, and he knew it. He owed his talent to the time spent in the Sanatorium. The tricks he practised for the patients depended upon misdirecting their attention. These tricks also distracted himself and them from the all-pervasive grief in the ward. "See?" he'd say, pointing his right hand to his left. The left opened, revealing emptiness. Back and front. Then a right-handed pass. In the flicker of an eyelash the left hand held a red ping-pong ball.

Pure magic! Guffaws of laughter and applause. His audience welcomed it. He loved it. Afterwards, he swiftly improvised a soft-shoe and sang, "There's No Business Like Show Business."

Hellman was impressed and gave him tickets to his production of *Anne*.

Bella thought the theatre was a ridiculous place. "You're filling Emer's head with a lot of unreal ideas! I remember having to perform at the convent. I was so nervous! And all that phony applause afterwards."

THE THEATRE

"It's a children's play. It's good family fare!"

"Theatre people are not film people."

Point-blank! He looked at her in astonishment.

She went on. "They're a phony bunch. Larger than life, off-stage and on. They have a need for recognition."

"A bit strong, don't you think? In what sense do you mean that?"

"I mean that film people have to be 'real,' because the camera never lies. The theatre is exaggeration. Actors sell themselves short by doing that. That's how I mean it. They're lying to get an effect."

"If the camera is on you or not, there's an audience to play to," he reasons. "An effect has to be achieved. Do you call that lying?"

"Yes. More of that goes on in the theatre than in film."

"That's a generalization. In any case, I think it's relative."

"Maybe, but I'd prefer to see Emer go into film."

Michael walks away humming "Oh, don't put your daughter on the stage, Mrs. Worthington," ignoring her displeasure.

When Emer asks him what she meant, he simply shrugs and says ask your mother. When Emer asks her, she says, "*Modère tes transports!*" Moderate your transports. Which was what the nuns told Bella when she got over-excited. When Michael hears of it, he objects. He reads her tone as meaning, "Don't get too carried away with yourself. Don't let it make you big-headed."

"And why ever shouldn't she?" he says behind closed doors. The pounding in his chest has to be expressed, shouted from the rooftops. What the pounding is, he isn't sure; he only knows that the energy is large and has to be expressed largely. How could it be any different for his children? "Moderate your transports, indeed!" What is youth all about, if not that?

Bella murmurs, "You're filling her head full of dreams!"
She aroused his anger.
"You can have dreams but your daughter can't?"
"No," she counters, "that's not how I mean it."

He feels his temper rising. "Either that or you don't approve of your own dreams." Michael thought it was the latter but stops short, knowing he's walking on the edge. He steps out into the back yard to cool out and think about it.

When they first started going out together he took photographs of Bella in different costumes. They were good. She had a good profile. Right or left. She not only knew how to pose, she had a translucent aura that instinctively knew how to project itself into the camera, producing close-ups that were, in his view, a knockout. Plus she had a large repertoire of personas. Japanese geisha girl, 'twenties flapper, Sonja Henie on skates. Pola Negri slung back invitingly in a wicker chair. The epitome of a sultry, smouldering, sexual spitfire. And for the folks next door, the June Allison pose. A red-cheeked girl biting into an apple.

Michael smiles, remembering her ambitions of being discovered by a talent scout. The miraculous era when you could be discovered on a drugstore barstool sipping a milkshake in a tight sweater.

Dreams all come to naught. Had he stood in her way? Maybe. But he didn't think so. She was good at posing in front of the camera. Perfectly natural. She had a talent for tapping in on her inner emotional energy so that it manifested in the photograph. It was a private affair, between her and the camera. He'd seen her do it. Emer's energy is outer. Even if it displeases Bella, Emer has to gain the experience and try it out for herself.

If she feels larger than life, why not let her be larger than life? "It's perfectly acceptable to live out all your dreams," he tells Emer. "Don't ever let anyone tell you any different."

Bella sighs into her resignation.

On the other hand, he also knows that Bella wants what she perceives as safety for her daughter. And the film world is safer to her than the theatre world, because the work is inner. So it appears to her. Then.

They both have idealistic ideas about their respective worlds.

As he sits in the Capitol Theatre Michael thrills at the sound of the "live" orchestra tuning up in the pit. He wonders if they need a violinist. Not a bad thing to do over what was left of the summer months. He did it for the silent movies at the *Français* on Dalhousie Sreet when he was a student. It had been a good chance to study the actors, and the money was good. As he listens to the orchestra tuning up, he supposes that his penchant for drama comes to him via his mother. His gut tightens at the very thought, but can't avoid it. He casts a glance at Emer. She stands in the front row leaning on the edge of the stage.

"I'm standing here for the whole performance," she says, peering over the footlights.

He smiles.

"I want to get as close as I can." Her head revolves from stage right to left and then up into the flies.

He calls to her, "There's a 'catwalk' up there; that's where the stagehands hook up the flats and fly them onstage. Saves a lot of carting around."

She nods as she watches the men walk on the narrow plank.

Bert is in the audience too, with Mo, his teenaged son. They nod briefly at each other across the rows.

Before the curtain goes up Kurt Hellman drops by to say hello. "That was quite a show you gave the other night. I'd heard you were back in the circuit again. Glad I caught it." Kurt grins and asks him if he'd like to direct anything with the Glebe Players. Michael is taken by surprise but says he'd give it some thought. *Harvey*? Maybe. *Playboy of the Western World*?

"Think about it," Kurt says.

Though he'd directed at the university before he went into the San, he swore he'd never do it again.

Father Bruneau had asked him to direct a production for the Christmas program. "You've been raving about your trip to New York and seeing Molière's *Les Fourberies de Scapin* with Jacques Copeau. Why not try your hand at that?"

Naively thinking it would be fun to direct *Scapin the Schemer*, Michael consents. He chooses Molière's play and bites off a larger slice of hilarity than he and the cast of male students can handle. This result, combined with one of his last encounters with his mother, took him to Oka Monastery, outside Montreal.

He and Bert (his then lighting technician) spent three weeks in sepulchral retreat. They'd eaten steamed vegetables, and Oka cheese that the monks made themselves. Bert was assigned work in the garden. Michael learned how to make cheese. Back to basics! They sat up all hours discussing the works of Thomas Merton. Theatre of a different order.

He smiles and settles in as the house lights dim and the orchestra fades. Silence for ten whole seconds. Good, he thinks. He loves the repose that silence brings. The Gothic-shaped windows cast shadows on the opposite wall. They activate images of the apse in the monastery, and how they'd chanted Latin matins at three in the morning, clad in brown robes and hoods.

THE THEATRE

He'd seen *Anne of Green Gables* several times in his youth. This production is mainly for Emer's benefit. He lets his mind ramble in order to experience the triggers that live drama inspires in him. The catharsis of theatre in free-ranging thought-association is his form of healthy therapy.

He sinks down comfortably into the aisle seat, preparing himself for this contemplation as he usually does at live performances. The world of the stage and the world of real life. So-called real life. What's the difference? he asks himself. Where's the line? Is there a line? Where does the illusion end and reality begin? Or is it all illusion? He rolls his body from side to side, trying to centre his weight. Michael smiles at the magician in him that responds, "The theatre is an illusion inside an illusion." The pristine child within him is happy with his response.

Michael watches the curtain undulating into the flies as the overture from the orchestra pit starts again. Happy sunshine music. The pacifying music and the shadowy set in half-light bring back the few moments of peace experienced in the monastery.

The three-in-the-morning chanting and the long silent meditations in the Cistercian medieval monastery with its turrets and cupolas readjusts his sights. Life in the limelight is not what he wants, he decides. He has to live it out, to find out. The university production was a disaster! His encounters with his mother even more so. His earlier university production efforts had been far better than the Molière fiasco. However, now with this invitation from Hellman, maybe he could retrieve himself by directing a production for The Glebe Players? Maybe.

Mrs. Rachel Lynde suddenly sweeps into the room. Her makeup is overdone. So is the acting, he thinks. A smidge over-theatrical. She reminds him of his mother. Noting his rising anger he shifts his attention to the serious look on Emer's face, drinking in the make-believe. She examines every last detail as if it is sacred. The costumes, the makeup, and the props.

He glances back to gauge the interest of the young audience and sees Bert studying the program.

He remembers that he and Bert stayed up long hours studying Thomas Merton and *The Confessions of St. Augustine*. Together they'd decided to apply for entry into the Cistercian Order.

The chest X-rays were positive. If he was going to drop the body, he wanted to be in the right place when it happened. He told Bella as much.

At that time, the Oka Monastery seemed to be the best choice. Time ... he'd needed time to heal. No matter that he'd tried it once before at nineteen and been refused. He hoped the rules had changed. This was going to be a second time around. A conscious re-alignment of where to place his disappearing energy, where it would reap the most benefit for himself and in consequence for his family. Not practical, but worthwhile in itself. He wouldn't leave them a chest full of gold, but treasure of a different order.

On fire with this new idea, they both turned in their applications at the same time. Bert was accepted and Michael was rejected. So Bert never went "in" and Michael never recovered from it. They wanted his birth certificate again. Of course there was none to be found. Mother was mute. The gulf between them left him full of unanswered questions. He was confident that he had a "vocation." A "calling."

Mrs. Rachel Lynde distracts him from his ruminations. She too is full of unanswered questions about dispossessed children. Children from orphanage homes. Or "home children" as Montgomery puts it. He's hearing the words as if for the first time. Had

THE THEATRE

he been a "home child"? How ridiculous. Of course not! He knows who his mother is. It's just the other half of the puzzle that's missing. So in that sense he's just "half-a-home" child. Pierre, on the other hand was a "home child." So Bella kept saying.

Returning to proof of birth, the abbot said, "We need a birth certificate as proof of who you are."

As if he doesn't exist without the piece of paper.

"Are you the legitimate son of John Maguire?"

Good question. "'Tis a wise man that knows his own father," is on the tip of Michael's tongue. Like the Host wavering on the edge of its communicant, he thinks ironically.

"You understand of course that legitimacy is of the utmost importance in the Cistercian Order. You must have it to take holy orders. Sit outside and wait for our decision."

As he sits in the dark lobby, visions of the bleeding Christ return to haunt him. Feeling that he has been thrust into the emotional breach, he writhes with a sense of shame as he swears that he will never again put himself in such a position.

Brown robes fluttered in and out of cavernous passageways like the wings of a dying bird. Not undone by the abbot's refusal, he went, on Bert's advice, to see Father Brennan, an old colleague of Bert's who had taken holy orders. His parish was in Darling, hours from Ottawa, out in the country. He lived there with his housekeeper.

Michael asks him for a birth certificate. The priest rises from his swivel chair, pushes a blank certificate and rubber stamp in his direction, and says, "I didn't see you." And vacates the premises. Under those circumstances, Michael can't bring himself to do it. He looks at it for a long time. He flails his fists as his anger flames skyward. The monastic dream slips away.

THE WORLD'S FAIR

In his turmoil he bounces from one bed to the next. Ruth, the lady with the beautiful legs and big heart. Never knowing why he did that. But driven to anyway. A grey bleakness overcomes him. Now he's drinking, playing chess, and never making it home to Bella before four in the morning. She was not fooled. "You're just trying to recapture the rapture, Michael!"

When Anne finally makes her entrance, Emer looks back at him and smiles in sheer delight, pointing at the garish vividness of her red hair. He smiles back, enjoying her enthrallment, and murmurs a quiet prayer. Thank God we both made it to here!

The curtain comes down on the first act: thunderous applause! From backstage he hears someone hiss, "House lights!" He watches Emer rub her eyes. She's speechless, but nevertheless she directs her attention in a fixed gaze over the footlights, intent on not missing a single thing.

Michael sees the stagehand preparing to turn the lever on the curtain pulley. It hums up swiftly again on the second act.

Marilla and Matthew Cuthbert are having a steaming argument over Anne now. Matthew and Marilla are brother and sister, he remembers with a start. What an unlikely plot! He fidgets in his seat. But then it's for children. What the hell! The inner roller coaster of his feelings moves faster than he can see it.

In consequence of his poor health he and Bella both fell between the cracks of non-communication. Never-ending green, thick, slimy phlegm. The chest. Grief. He knew that much. The bloody Bishop's Palace. Not enough money to buy her an annulment.

Bella permeates the walls of their small apartment with a minor-key dirge of information from the newspapers. "Tyrone Power and Annabella got an annulment. Why can't we?"

"Money, m'dear, pure and simple," he says. "Cross my palm

with silver." Doing an oily imitation of John Maguire doing an imitation of W.C. Fields.

He keeps going back to Oka. On retreats anyway. Just in case. They might change their minds.

"What are you retreating from?" Bella asks.

He has to concede a smile. "I don't have an answer for that." She is catholic but with a lower-case c, which provides her with a viewpoint that is freshness itself. However, it still disturbs him that she will only attend Sunday Mass on condition that he take her to the cinema afterwards. Bella has long ago turned her back on religious rituals of any kind.

"They're only meant for people who need trainer wheels on their bicycles."

He laughs at her wit. "I don't have an answer for that."

No answer. No matter.

On a totally different topic, his mother's answer when she hears they're getting married: "But she has no education to speak of." This from his mother. She, who could not read her own name if it were in boxcar letters in front of her! Go figure! Nevertheless, she did acknowledge Bella's genius for repartee. That was a big plus in Bella's favour he felt too. So they got married. Never knowing why he did that. Well, yes, he did know. The grief in his lungs manifesting as TB pushed him into it. That was how he understood it. There's a breathless silence in the house.

On a dare, Anne stands precariously on the ridgepole of the house. He sees Emer holding her breath.

With a start he realizes that he's holding his breath too. Over the success of his marriage. He hopes that he's done the right thing in marrying Bella. In itself it had been a good thing. At the time. But now?

The Relief money had kept her off her mother's doorstep. Pierre's too, for that matter.

The icebox became well-stocked with Oka cheese, between X-rays and visits to the monastery. A stinking reminder of what might have been.

Bert had asked him if he loved her. How could he know?

"What's past is past," Bella said after they were married.

"Yippee!" They both shout and congratulate each other on the church steps. Bella wears her splashy-in-good-taste flowered dress with her white sailor-boy straw hat with the navy-blue trim. She holds onto it as they rush out the tall open doors. They stop on the first landing, spontaneously pretending to be the invited guests as well. They shake hands, hug, and kiss between giggling gasps of incredulity. "Congratulations! A great production! May you have a long and happy union!"

He buries his nose in her delightful nosegay of wild flowers. They laugh and applaud while out-throwing each other with great clouds of confetti all the way back to the car and the waiting children.

The final curtain comes down. There's a thunderous round of applause.

"Bravo! Bravo!" The audience dries its eyes between curtain calls. The actors take their bows.

As the curtain sweeps up and down several times, the heavy smell of Leichner's theatrical makeup sticks wafts over the footlights in waves. He loves the smell. The successful illusion. That's entertainment!

The orchestra picks up its lively overture. He takes Emer backstage afterwards. She shakes hands with the director and the actors. As they walk up the darkened aisle to the front of house, she says, "I know what I want to be for the rest of my life, Dad. I want to work in the theatre."

"In what capacity?"

"As an actor or a director," she says with firmness. That's final. He knows it.

Bert approaches him in the lobby. "What did you think of the production?"

"Not bad. The live orchestra was a great touch! It covered what the actors couldn't reach for."

"What did you think of the lighting?" Bert-the-lighting-technician asks.

"The pink and amber gels worked well together for the outdoor backdrop. But they need a dimmer for changes of moods."

"Yeah, that was noticeable, wasn't it? Did they ask you to do anything?"

"Yes. I'm thinking about it. Time is money and they don't have any, of course. Money, I mean."

"Would you do it, if they did?"

"Decidedly." And then, fixing Bert with a long look, "Seriously, where are the professional theatre companies in this country? And I'm not talking about the imports."

"There aren't many choices, are there?" says Bert with a groan.

"Many? You mean any," says Michael.

Bert cups a match to his cigarette. "Anyway, there aren't any self-supporting companies in this country."

"True," says Michael.

"Born ahead of our time," Bert says ruefully.

The choices for the exploration of Michael's talents were few. There are no whetstones to sharpen his creative talent on. He can't find an outlet for their expression other than venues. Life had looked promising at eighteen.

At thirty he is discovering reality.

Bella had called his talents "distractions."

He corrected her. "They aren't distractions. They're my interests. I love theatre, among other things. But there are no outlets in this country for its development...." Then he added, "Yet!"

That he never developed it was, he rationalized, because he was "in" the world and not "of" it.

"And I'm not about to run off to Europe on a hunch, when I have a family to support." Nevertheless, European culture, especially that of France, captures his interest. In his first year at Ottawa University he hears that Copeau is coming over to New York from Le Vieux Colombier in November of 1917. He saves his violin-playing money and hops a bus in January of 1918. Copeau was playing Scapin in *Les Fourberies de Scapin*, by Molière. Michael is blown away not only by the *commedia dell'arte* style of acting but by the team spirit among the actors. Their give and take in delivery is clearly visible. No stars! A total group in the best sense of the word.

Ireland? The Abbey? Maybe. But he'd never been there. Only hearsay. Their cultures were older.

Emer looks up at her father. "Why can't we do something in the back shed?"

Both men are stunned. There's an embarrassed pause.

Bert finally clears his throat. "Because it's inappropriate."

Michael takes Emer's hand. "Out of the mouths of babes," he says, and then, with enthusiasm, "Maybe we could rent a good garage!"

Bert stomps on his cigarette. "No. You wouldn't rent an office for my teaching idea, Michael. I'm certainly not going to do

THE THEATRE

lights in a garage. Ceilings aren't high enough. A barn maybe, but not a shed."

"A barn? I know of a barn!" Emer shouts.

"Where?" they shout back.

"Behind Aunt Maura's garage!"

"Good girl! We'll pay her a visit!"

The three of them walk out on a hum. Pinned like specimens to the wall they fly in their dreams. Ahead; there is no other way to go!

CHAPTER THIRTEEN

The Businesswoman

SILVY LEASHES SEVERAL PUPS; she's in a hurry. She wants to get to Clarkstown ahead of the movers. But she also wants to tell Ma about it first. With any luck the old lady will have forgotten about their little fracas. Silvy thinks of it as little because she herself has seen worse fallings-out with her mother. She flags a cab over to the dusty curb.

As soon as the cab driver sees the dogs, he's none too happy. But damn him anyway! Dogs will be dogs! Especially excited pups.

"You could've phoned first," Andrea says. "She's not here."

"You can't see who you're talking to on that thing," she says defensively. "What's the use of that?" Dialing numbers was not her forte in any case, so she hasn't got a telephone. So what? She raged silently at her daughter's impudence. Numbers, yes. She loved numbers. Especially adding. But dialing them, no. "Where did Ma go?" she snaps.

"She's staying with Michael and Bella." Andrea eyes her.

Silvy allows the dogs to tug at her arm while she attempts to restore her inner equilibrium. "Ma is at Michael's?" she whispers incredulously.

Andrea looks the pups over and wonders what her mother is cooking up now! "Always something on the back burner, right?"

"Right," she says astutely. Then, ducking any further unwanted remarks from her daughter, she adds, "Well, you're looking good." She eyes her blue-eyed daughter with satisfaction, and passes her free hand down the side of her shoulder and thigh. They resemble each other in many ways, except that Andrea is slimmer. Her long blonde hair drapes her shoulders gracefully.

She smiles. "Gerry got a job with Canadian National Railways, in the office."

"Good girl! The two of you must be doin' something right."

"Thanks, Ma."

"The old lady been acting right?"

"She's been good. When she's sober, she's wonderful."

Silvy stares vacantly down at the dogs, never having had the "wonderful" experience herself. "Hard to believe." She scans her daughter's face openly and risks it. Once over lightly. "You love her, don't you?"

Andrea giggles. "Yes. She's fun to be with. Always was. Michael will be getting all of the fun with her now, though."

It hurt to hear it. "Well, best be moving on." She'd brought that one on herself good and proper! It was best now not to tell Andrea her good news. The visit had been an all 'round bad idea.

"Nice bunch of pups," says Andrea mechanically. Dogs were not her favourite animal. They were always Silvy's excuse for not taking her and Michael back as a child.

Silvy fakes a jovial wink. "Yeah, well, they're a beginning. A new beginning."

There's an uncomfortable silence. There were parts of her mother that Andrea dared not query. There'd been too many "new beginnings" to name. None of which she had ever figured into. Changing the subject, Andrea says, "Horace died."

Silvy stops in her tracks. "Really? How?" She remembers the piggyback rides she and Toussaint had with him in the back fields whenever John Maguire came visiting her mother.

"In his sleep. Had no relatives. Left everything to Granny."

"What do you mean, everything?"

"She was the sole beneficiary of his insurance policy. He had no living relatives. That, and his cottage in the Gatineau."

The other side of the tracks, for God's sakes. "The Gatineau?" Bella country. "How much did he leave her?"

"Somewhere in the order of three hundred and fifty dollars. She gave him a good funeral out of it though.... I'm surprised you didn't hear about it." And before Andrea can stop herself, she blurts, "It was in all the newspapers." If you could read you would have known. The thought communicates itself in an accusing look.

Silvy feels slighted, but shrugs, "So what?"

They stand looking at each other in the silence again, not knowing what else to say.

"Well, I'm happy for Ma's sake." Silvy flounders for words. "But it's a bit of a mixed blessing. I hope she doesn't drink the money away, that's all."

Andrea nods. "I don't think Michael will let her do that."

The dogs chase each other around Silvy's ankles. Glad of an excuse to do something, anything, she bends down to unravel their leashes. In the confusion she asks, "Who was there?"

"Everyone. Molly Gleason, Baby-face, Michael, Bella, Louie...."

"Louie?"

"Yes, I'm surprised he didn't tell you."

How could he? She hadn't seen him in a month, because John was on her doorstep. Lots of ground to catch up on. Must attend to that.

Silvy suddenly becomes businesslike. "What streetcar do I take to get to Clarkstown from here?"

"Take the Lindenlea down at the corner. It'll get you right there."

THE BUSINESSWOMAN

Silvy hoped her daughter would ask why she was going to Clarkstown, but she didn't. So she didn't offer to tell her.

Andrea left her in an empty vortex of confusion. Getting on the Lindenlea she feels the old familiar "hanging" feeling. It was always that way. Always. Whenever she walked away from her. It was not anything Andrea said. It was what she didn't say.

It's nothing new. Best to forget about it. She hadn't raised her. Had no claims on her. Ma was right. Not that her being right changes things any.

Silvy's acknowledgement to herself doesn't lessen the pain of her daughter's coolness. It should have, but it didn't. She'd become too attached to it. Who would she be without her pain? God knows. Frightening thought.

She sits in the back seat with the dogs, alone on the streetcar. As the tracks narrow, branches of trees scrape the tram, popping in through the windows.

Languidly she feels the leaves floating past her in the breeze. Toussaint, Pa, and now Horace. Sometimes she feels she'll explode with grief. What's it all about anyway? To add to it, Andrea's detachment hurts. Silvy massages the pain on her right side. And then there's Michael. Oh God, Michael. As a young mother there hadn't been too many choices. Running away with old man Tremblay to the United States after Michael was born, with Andrea a year old, was her best shot at the time. Her marriage to John ended three months later.

She moved back into her father's house with the two children in tow. It was hardly the place to raise children, with Toussaint bringing starving young girls home from Byward Market. By the time she was fifteen, life wasn't worth a plug nickel. Sitting at home with two babies under her father's roof was not her idea of a good time. She hid her feelings as best she could until opportunity presents itself in the form of George Tremblay. He feels sorry for her. "C'mon, let's get out of here!"

So she runs away with him.

"It's better for the children too," he reasons. "Your brother and his family can raise them."

The circus and Tremblay took her mind off whatever compunctions she may have had. For a time.

But now the children are a grown son and daughter. Andrea has no room for her in her heart, and Michael's problems are magnified ten times over. Silvy wonders how much longer he will persist in his questioning before he drops it. She'd hoped that his Sanatorium experience would heal his pain, and now if anything it had only made it worse. Sometimes she feels as though she's in one of those speeded-up silent movies that Tremblay took her to in New York. She shrieks her anguish into the passing bushes with all her might. "There is no such thing as hell! I'm in it, right now! This is it!" She hurls her secrets into the seclusion of the passing trees, then sits back in silence. The tramway rattles on, carrying her muted truth. That gave her some relief. Not much, but some. She's being hard on herself, she knows, but she doesn't know how to stop. She had written her own script, and no longer knew the road back. For as long as she could remember she'd always loved drama. It came to her from her mother. Whenever she thinks of it, it makes her angry. Not so much with her mother as with herself. Instinctively she knows that her actions are inherently predicated on the historical past. Silvy would not have expressed it that way in so many words. It was more of a gut feeling. "Life is just a fluke!" Silvy bites into the words. "Why was I born into this family and not another?" She ponders the question. Forgiveness was not anything she had ever personally experienced. It wasn't in her lexicon of feelings. Oblivious to that part of herself, she functions as best she can, lugging the past along with her into the present. "Best to forgive and forget." She mouths the words, unable to experience her own forgiveness. The words vaporize before they reach heaven.

The acrid smell of hawthorn berries wafts past her. She links it to life, and making love in the open fields behind the house. Bittersweet! And there it was. That loneliness again.

Ma had a fit when she found out about them. Didn't want to see them anymore. Though she'd never admit to it now. She forgot it. Totally.

Silvy looks up at the moving sky. The sun burns a hole straight through the clouds, shining down on her face. Pa had said, *"Honi soit qui mal y pense."* Years later Baby-face had translated it as, "Honey your pants are down!" She laughed at the time. But it wasn't right. It was funny, but not right. Pa had said that the translation was "Evil to him who evil thinks." The Order of the Garter. She smiles, remembering his bookishness and how he'd always added in the next breath that it had been the motto for the English Order of Knighthood in 1346.

Pa was a philosopher. She loved him for that. He didn't judge. He minded his own business. But take Ma now: judgments were her private bailiwick. Ma said that it was because she could feel her answers in her bones and that thinking per se had nothing to do with it. That gave her the right, Silvy supposed bitterly.

The streetcar swerves on its narrow track. She holds onto the dogs until the car straightens out.

The conductor shouts, "Lindenlea! End of the line!"

Through the trees she can see the brown clapboard house with its two front porches. The jabbing pain on her right side starts up again. The truck is in the driveway already and John is directing traffic. Damn. They got here ahead of me.

She straightens the seams of her nylons, adjusts the circular garters above her knees, and checks her hemline for a slipping slip. No corset as of yet, thank God! She can't stand the pain of the digging stays. She pulls herself together and disembarks.

Maura stands on the porch waving and smiling at her. Meg sits in the wicker rocker, scowling. Silvy holds the dogs firmly on their leash while she brushes the dust off her best silk dress. Ready for battle. If, that is, there is going to be one.

"Welcome!" Maura shouts across the road.

Silvy doesn't have to look at Meg to see her response. She feels the disapproval clear across the road. The dogs start to growl.

"Dogs, indeed!" Meg hisses under her breath.

Silvy gives a sharp tug on the leash. They all walk across the dirt road with dignity. She's in full command. John watches from behind the truck. God, what a figure! What style! She's still got it, bejaisus! She smiles and watches the movers push her ornate woodstove around to the summer kitchen on a dolly.

"Watch the door on the plate warmer!" she shouts. "It's a little loose."

"I'll fix it when we get it in!" John shouts back.

Standing on the curb as she smiles at Maura, her mind races at his response. Did he think that because she'd been successful in this mortgage transaction with his sisters, that made them a couple? She shudders at the thought. His eagerness under the words suggests it. Have to straighten that out with him.

She was good at organizing money, but had not seen its implications ahead of time. It came to her, standing there greet-

THE BUSINESSWOMAN

ing John's sisters, that her life, such as it was, would no longer be protected from prying eyes. Or maybe even from John himself, for that matter.

Still, she isn't too worried. Silvy knows how to keep her life secret. She'd started the process early.

Sort it out later. In the moment, she decides to brazen it out, as she usually does when in a tight spot.

"Welcome!" says Maura, extending her hand.

In her confusion, Silvy extends her free hand, looking toward John for reassurance. He ducks into the truck.

She hears Maura saying, "Looks as though the stove will take some time to get set up, with the stovepipes and all. You are very welcome to come over here and have lunch with us."

Glancing at Meg, she sees the impossibility of it. "Thank you, but I prepared some cretons and baked beans in advance."

Meg visibly winces, muttering behind Maura, "Pork, in the middle of summer! My word! Probably eats brains too!"

Gratefully, she let the pups pull her out of earshot, toward her new house. "Thanks anyway," she calls back.

"Well, I'm right here if you need me."

"Thanks again." Silvy doesn't know what to make of gentle kindness. She understands it as Maura's way of showing appreciation for the five hundred and thirty dollars that she'd laid down, cash-on-the-line.

Gentle kindness in itself doesn't exist. It has to have a reason.

※

John set up her four-poster in the front bedroom. The clanging of the tramway could be heard from time to time, but other than that it was country living. The same as Eastview.

THE WORLD'S FAIR

They sit up in bed, in the glow of the pink lampshade, feasting on pig's knuckles and beer. John's favourite. They share the *Ottawa Citizen*. She takes the front half, he the back.

She loves to pretend to herself that she can read. It gives her a feeling of importance. She looks at the picture on the front page. "My gawd! What are all those people doing?"

John glances over and reads the caption. "It's a bread line. They're all out of work."

"Where? Here?"

"No. In Europe."

"Looks bad."

He growls. "Yeah. It's bad all over."

She watches him lick the grease off his fingers. "Guess we're lucky, huh?"

He goes back to his comics. "Guess so." No comment. Full stop.

She turns to the second page, scanning it for pictures. She points to some people standing behind a model of a dome and a tower. "What's this?"

He sighs. He can't get to the end of *Alley Oop* with all her questions. "It's the model for The World's Fair next year. An' don't always be interruptin' me."

"The World's Fair." She lets the words roll around in her mouth. "What's that?"

He puts his paper down in exasperation. "It's where everybody in the whole world comes together in New York to celebrate all our inventions to date." He rattles the newspaper.

Silvy thinks about this for a while. "Oh. A fair, huh?"

New York. The name. Simply the name of the place gives her the shivers. Shivers of excitement. That's where, in her opinion, the hub of the universe is.

THE BUSINESSWOMAN

Sarah Bernhardt played there once. Silvy had seen her with George Tremblay when they were on tour with the circus. George had even taken her to Harlem to hear Charlie Parker, the jazz saxophonist, as well as some of what was playing on Broadway.

But Bernhardt. Now there was a woman! She only had one leg then, but she crashed around that stage as if she owned it. Silvy beams with the wonder of the French actress's talent.

Suddenly she says, "I'm taking Emer there next year."

John ignores her, intent on trying to understand the funnies. Silvy lies back on the bolstered cushions, hands behind her head, staring at the ceiling, picturing the trip in living colour. Emer in one hand, suitcase in the other, looking up at the huge dome and tower. Experiencing Emer's delight. The delight she had missed having with her own children.

Silvy was aglow with the memory. She'd take Emer to the Cotton Club and see Duke Ellington again. Billy Holiday, for God's sake. She shivered, recollecting the goose bumps when she heard "Strange Fruit." Maybe even see a play. The Lunts. Light fare, but entertaining. That's it!

"Well, I'm doing it!" she shouts.

John picks his teeth as he looks up from the paper. "Doing what?" He'd come to the cigar part of his meal and lit up a White Owl.

"Never mind. You wouldn't get it."

He shrugs indifferently and returns to Daisy Mae's curves in *Li'l Abner*.

Looking at him, she decides this will not do. It won't be easy telling him, but as she breathes into her new plan she knows that, finally, he has to go.

Silvy is up at dawn. She nails a Pups For Sale sign on the front porch. John hears the banging from his bedroom upstairs. Bleary-eyed, he comes down in his blue-striped pyjamas, scratching his belly and waggling his dry mouth. "Bejeesus! an' she's wakin' up the dead now!" he moans.

Ignoring Monsieur Latouche's vegetable garden, she sets the kennels up as close to the back as she's able to heave them. She disturbs the crab apple tree in the process and some of the riper tomatoes.

She's had a bad night with her side again so she takes it gently.

The drapery of the lace curtains on the other side of the house flutters more than once.

Silvy hears the back door open on Maura's porch. They nod and smile at each other across the fence. She likes her manner; there's something familiar about her that she can't put her finger on.

Meg suddenly appears and fumes loud enough for her to hear. "What does she think she's doing?" Her white face blends into her nightgown, making her image all of a piece, with the exception of her long white hair, which flies in all directions.

Maura remains Maura. Centred.

"What does she think she's doing?" Meg repeats as she tries to tie her hair back into a bun.

"What are you doing?" John shouts from the bathroom window. "Starting a business?"

"You're damn right." Her head appears above a tomato plant; both are red with the glow of exhilaration.

"You can't do that here. It's residential!"

"You don't say!"

The dogs start barking.

Whatever else they say to each other gets lost in the barking.

THE BUSINESSWOMAN

John sees Meg on the other side of the fence waving her fist at him.

"Can't wait to get out of here fast enough," he mutters. "Shit! Silvy's always stirring it up. No matter what you do for her," he groans as he pees into the toilet bowl. "Gads, Meg is in an uproar," he mutters. As he struggles with his pants he knows he'll never hear the end of it. " Oops! Both legs in the same pant hole. Shit!" The soured beer churns around his insides. Swinging his braces over his shoulders he grabs his windbreaker and flees, forgetting to pull the chain.

Silvy never saw him again. She'd not planned it. Like everything else in her life, it happened. She'd never had to say a word.

That summer, Silvy's pedigreed poodles became a big item in Ottawa, thanks to Louie. Every morning he'd take two of the pups with him in his cab. He sold them to the civil servants and MPs on the Hill. Though she could only count to ten, she knew the value of a dollar, and re-invested her sales back into the dogs. In tens. There was cash flow.

With the money, she bought four more bitches, and before the summer was out she had a going concern. The kennels in the back garden were full. The dogs were prizewinners in all the contests. There was no profit yet, but business was building. It would come.

She tells Louie, "I intend to take Emer to The World's Fair with the money."

"What a great idea!" he says. "You know they have a great new invention they're called a TV set."

"It's a set?" she asks. "Meaning two of them?"

"Well, no, not exactly. It's a box with some electronic components that allow you to see movies in your own home."

"Really?" Silvy swallows in astonishment. "Movies in your own home? Is that really going to be happening?"

"Not just that. They've come up with computerized machines that enable you to to play games … among several other things."

Silvy sits in her chair, mouth agape in total wonderment. "Well my, my, my!"

"There's so much being invented right now," he continues, "that I just can't seem to get my mind around it."

Her mind runs ahead of her, trying to work out how that might possibly improve the business of raising thoroughbreds.

" So yes, I think we'd better pay it a visit."

"Most certainly so."

It becomes a project between them that they share and work on. They would go to the fair, all three together.

On the other side of the house Meg both grieves and is angry at her brother John for leaving, and now for her son Louie for taking his place.

Maura busies herself with her everyday chores. She takes it moment-by-moment. Because, as she often says, "That's all there is, dear."

So while Meg walks up and down the hallway wringing her hands, periodically putting her ear to the wall and crying her eyes out, trying to comprehend the incomprehensible, Maura weeds her garden and feeds Silvy's dogs over the back fence.

She smiles at Meg through the kitchen windows on one side of the house and suggests to Silvy on the other that she take some olive oil and lemon juice to flush the stones in her gallbladder.

THE BUSINESSWOMAN

By the middle of August Silvy starts to feel much better, and is grateful for Maura's advice.

She turns John's old cigar box into her safety deposit, and stashes the profits under the bed. Things are going so well that she decides to invest the money in a few more kennels, and bring them and the surplus of pups over to the old house on Dagmar, where she has more land.

"Think I'll build a fence for them out there," says Louie, "so they can roam around more freely."

Things are decidedly moving fast now that John is clearly out of her life. "I'll take Emer and Louie to The World's Fair. Michael will be proud of me. Maybe even Ma will be too."

She knows that she can no longer risk Meg's ire.

"It's just not good business," she says to Louie. "Being half-owner of the house alongside Maura has its responsibilities."

Her new business partner takes front row centre.

CHAPTER FOURTEEN

Other Dimensions

AFTER SUPPER MICHAEL PLAYS a fast-moving game of chess with Emer. They use the double clocks. A minute a move. She wins. Time, weather, seasons disappear under the spell of combative intellectual wizardry. He smiles, thinking it time to teach her more openings. She could be a master.

That night he plays Boyateerchuk at the club. He's going to win, by God! That's his intention. He'd first heard of the chess master while he was in the San. Michael played him from his bed by post. Special chess postcards with men printed on them. He lost every time.

But tonight his footsteps along Rideau Street are energized with determination. They are well into the second game when Michael finally sees an opening. His heart is pounding with the excitement of his "find."

He makes his move. "Check." He knows that the next move is "Mate."

Boyateerchuk looks up solemnly from the game and, in his deep Polish accent, says, "It's good." Then, after a long pause "… but it's not beautiful."

It's not what Michael expected. Something in the old man's tone makes him see it as an epitaph on his tombstone. Michael has been defeated by a judgment. The old man has sidestepped his win.

Michael is disappointed. A win, but not beautiful!

Which was less beautiful, his game or Boyateerchuk's response? He can't make up his mind. Was he mirroring back at Michael the ungracious thrust of intellectual battle?

Nevertheless, on his way home he whistles happily. Love of the game is more important than the game itself, he thinks. Like his grandmother, he always wins; he never loses. Even when he does lose, he wins. It's three in the morning. Bella will be up, twisting with worry. He hates that about her—her fear-ridden anxieties.

"I hope you aren't starting this pattern again," she says quietly.

"No," he says. "It's the last time. I won the game!" He crashes into bed without another word.

The next morning he wakes up from a heavy sleep. A deep, disorienting, drug-like sleep. For no reason. For several moments he has no idea where he is. Slowly he focuses on the green wallpaper. Small white snowflakes fluttering on ladies in long, full skirts getting into carriages, assisted by gentlemen in top hats and tails. A blizzard.

A blizzard of ladies with muffs. And mufflers. Muffled. Aware of a hard lump in the back of his throat, he swallows into the silence of the falling snow. Where in hell am I? The question looms larger than his ability to respond. Too large to have a response. No response. The women all have their feet on the bottom rung of the carriage with the men bending over them, holding their top hats to their chests. Helping them up in deep ... reverence? Lust? Difficult to discern the difference.

Where are they going? On a journey. But where? Don't have to know where. The destination will bring you there. In the silence of the snowstorm.

Michael looks at the clock on the night table. Time doesn't register. Forgot to take my temperature. He reaches for his thermometer glass. Not there. Nurse'll be in to do it when she takes pulse.

Wonder who died today. Sinking heaviness. Beads of perspiration. A cold sweat. Fear? Or the body shutting down? Apparently not my turn yet! Must breathe some fresh air. Sticky hot here.

Image. Him in a top hat and a black silk cape lined in red satin. Powdered white hands flicking cards.

"Watch this! King of Hearts! Whammo! Changeover! Queen of Spades!" Faster than the twinkling of an eye. And it's over!

Through semi-slit eyes back to the muffled ladies. Opening his eyes more fully, he sees that the ladies are all muffled. He feels as if there's an old sock in the back of his throat. It's choking him. Image. He's making love to his mother. Their bodies snake around each other. He can't breathe.

"Air. I need air!" he shouts. "Must break free!" He feels vomit coming up the back of his throat. "Tom," he croaks. "Can't breathe."

Tom leans out of his bed and whispers, "Pranayama, Michael. Pranayama. Breathe in and out. In and out."

He focuses on breathing in and out.

"Good. Now you're doing it."

He breathes more easily. "Yeah. I'm doing it now." The nausea subsides.

Repetitive dreams.

Dreams within dreams. Maybe he'd been too active the day before? Done too much? The Boyateerchuk win?

As he lies there, once again trying to figure out his dreams and why he's still having them, half awake, he hears a loud gasp.

The silence is broken. Someone in the next room? He smiles. Home. I'm home. It's Alma. Her snuff, no doubt. And then a loud "Ahhhh!" followed by a loud raucous sneeze.

He sinks back into the pillows with the green satin comforter tucked under his chin. He shivers in distaste. His farcical jingle,

OTHER DIMENSIONS

"Oedipus, Shmoedipus, as long as you love your mother," had sickeningly come home to roost. He tries to swallow the sourness, but the sock hasn't gone away. It smothers his words, his inner dialogue. He knows it, but has grown not to mind. Ignore its presence. He's lived with it too long, and so returns into a light sleep with its familiar fuzziness lodged in his throat.

When Michael finally wakes up it's to the sound of voices downstairs. They travel up the hole in the floor where a stovepipe used to be. He leans over the edge of the bed and sees the top of Pierre's thinning hair. Memère Duval is unpacking vegetables and red meat on the kitchen table. Must've just got back from the Market, he thinks. Eager to forget his dreams, he allows himself the distraction of the kitchen activities.

He looks at the eight-day clock. Eleven-thirty. Market day, Saturday. Bella's family. Madame Duval, punctual as usual. The table is laden with food. Disjointed sounds of words below. The primal sound of French words wafts upwards, along with delicious smells of an early lunch. For some reason the language gives him a feeling of sitting low in the saddle. It speaks truth to him. Michael's mother is French, but he was not raised in the world of French words. Aunt Maura couldn't speak a word of it. He feels securely grounded in its music. Bella's French lineage is what attracts him to her, he feels. Even now. More than that, he cannot explain. Simply put, she is a pragmatic woman who balances the scales with *joie de vivre*. That was how he saw her in their best moments.

Leaning out of bed a little further, he sees Zack in his high chair piling into a bowl of fruit. Emer is standing largely in the middle of moving traffic, joining in the conversation. She jumps nervously from one to the other in the manner of a Mexican jumping bean.

Bella shouts, a little too loudly, "You're getting in the way, Emer!" as she hands Pierre the vegetables at arm's length.

Michael notices that Bella neatly avoids splashing her stepfather's corpulent body as he hurriedly rinses the warm earth from the vegetables under the cold-water tap. Michael watches as they circle each other and the food on the table.

Pierre walks from the table to the kitchen sink as if he owns the place. Michael tries to calm his fears. He reassures himself. The kitchen is his domain; after all, he's a professional cook.

Memère is cooking home fries on the wood stove in the noon-time heat. Her back to everyone. Bella is shucking early corn on the cob. At first glance, a convivial family scene. Suddenly it's All Partners Change! Wordlessly, Pierre continues with the frying while Memère takes his place at the sink and Bella switches to chopping potatoes.

The shifting patterns of their movement seem balletic. Swift. Sure. Direct. Bella stands beside Pierre and drops another tablespoon of butter into the frying pan. She doesn't miss a beat. No collisions. Pierre melts it briskly into the hot skillet. They dovetail in and out of each other's paths. Silently.

Pierre brushes past her on his way for more chopped potatoes, his easygoing hands waving in the breeze, loosely brushing Bella's thigh. Accidentally on purpose? Michael freezes in disbelief.

He watches Emer watching them. Bella's face impassive. Emer's face impassive.

"Whaat?" he whispers in disbelief. "They aren't reacting?"

He vaguely remembers Bella saying, "He doesn't do it anymore."

Michael had thought that "it" had been nothing more serious than bottom-pinching. Now he isn't so sure. His anger flares. Getting out of bed, he determines to settle this thing. He'd been justified in the first place! Michael looks again, but can't see. Memère sees, but doesn't look.

As for Alma, she allows her eyesight to go to black, because in her life she looks, sees, and doesn't want to see any more.

When he's dressed and shaved he goes downstairs, nodding in on her as he passes her door.

"I heard you shouting in your dream," she says.

"Bella's people are here," he says tersely, not wanting to get into it just yet.

"I know," she says. "I want to be alone."

"À la Greta Garbo?"

"Yeah," she says with a smile, "à la Garbo," and waves him on down, empress-style.

There are hugs and kisses and pats on the back. A warm welcome from Pierre and Memère. Celebration is in the air. He smiles through his discomfort and marvels at the provisions they've brought.

"*Ben, c'est une fête!*" says Memère. "We celebrate your getting out of 'ospital."

Celebrating life. His life!

The conversation centres mainly on the welcome food, and where to store it. Some he puts into the icebox. The vegetables go into the cold pantry in the cellar. Hopefully they'll keep until his first paycheque arrives at the end of September.

Noon finds them sitting around with quart bottles of beer, pepper steak, mushrooms, with tea sauce, home fries, peas, and fresh corn. The food tastes good but settles like a lump in his stomach.

"Like old times at the Tecumseh," Pierre says.

He's been manager and cook at the golf club ever since he closed his café opposite the paper mill about two years ago.

"Just Bella and Zack. And of course Anna." Pierre hangs his arm around her neck. In ownership. Bella, head down, slices the French stick with vigour. Memère looks toward the back door and smiles as if someone has just come in.

Michael compliments him on his cooking. Pierre expounds on his latest discovery: black tea poured into the frying pan over the butter sauce after the steaks have been pulled out of the pan.

"Ingenious," says Michael, thinking that he might well have said "insidious." That's what he basically feels about him. As Pierre talks on, his open hands are disconcerting. Are they too open? At any rate, they're too casual. Almost careless in the way they touch things. Was Bella soiled? Or is he soiled for thinking it?

He can still taste the sourness of his revolting dream. Was what he'd seen from upstairs true, or a projection of his own dream-state? Where's the line? Plato had something to say on the subject—the outward being a manifestation of an inward state. His inward state? Must read that again!

Bella had left home at sixteen. He had sympathized with her, though he'd not fully questioned the whys of it. It was all in the realm of surmise on his part and innuendo on Bella's. The innuendo was the mystery that held him in place. Her mystery. The eternal femme fatale mystique that reminded him of the house where his sister Andrea had grown up.

Alma's house, where the rising-beautiful-sun girls mysteriously beckoned his puberty out of the cradle. His young, naive heart had gone out to them.

Meg's finger waved in his face. "Don't you ever go there again!"

Ahhh. Forbidden fruit. How delicious! Bella held that same air of mystery for him. His desire for her had veiled his ability to see her. He knew that. She had kept him occupied helping her with the children, the financial running of the household, the domesticity; and there was always her arm to consider. His desire for her was a driving force, but the fact that she needed him was perhaps the compelling issue.

And now Pierre appears on the horizon and Bella's various and sundry problems once again pull him away from his own truth. In the process, Pierre escapes him, along with Zack in the high chair. His own unanswered questions loom larger than his ability to formulate questions about Bella's family life. And so, no questions asked. No answers given.

In this mode, Michael sits at the dining room table, holding forth on the latest topical subject. The teacher in him wants to initiate a rapport with Pierre, not only to establish an acceptable standard of behaviour within the family unit, but to sort out his own thoughts on the subject as well. "What does moral re-armament mean to us?" he asks.

"Moral re-armament?" Bella smells fire. "Sounds like war."

Michael smiles at her response. There are things about her that endear him. "No, it means to re-evaluate our thoughts on what we think morality is."

They all bow their heads in solemn agreement, including Memère, though she doesn't understand a word of it.

Pierre clears his throat and jumps in. "I know what you mean. My mother and father died on the boat coming over from Belgium. I was raised in an orphanage home as soon as I arrived in Canada. Morality was a big issue there." He didn't say how, or elaborate, more than "There was a lot of coming and going there. I mean the staff changed about every three to six months. I had many different people looking after me when I was young."

The gleam of his wall-to-wall smile disturbs Michael. A little too ... what? Open? Knowing? So Pierre had been a home child. "What was that experience like for you?" And he added, "What did that question I just asked mean to you? I mean in the sense of re-arming?"

He catches Emer rolling her eyes. Unusual for Emer. It jolts him into deeper reflection. The man hadn't had much in the way of an education, after all. One couldn't put him on the spot by asking him to elaborate on something he probably can't remember. Even if he does remember, Michael doubts Pierre would have the language to express it. He shrugs off his feelings of patronage. Patronage reveals itself in Michael when his emotions stand between him and sound judgment.

Bella's head moves mechanically from right to left as if she's watching a tennis championship match. He concludes that she doesn't know what they're talking about, that she's pretending interest.

Memère has her head down, sopping up "butter-tea" gravy with her French crusty bread. Four corns heaped up on the side.

The green-eyed Bella-sharpness assesses the outcome of the match nervously.

Emer concludes, "Love all." Barely breathing.

Michael decides to drop the issue. Just as well. It is too hot to handle. The moment of Pierre's version of "morality in the orphanage" forever lost to whatever questions he could have asked. Michael notes, however, that the tension in the dining room spoke for itself. The electricity that hung over the dinner table gave him a dark picture of Pierre's "home" life. For some odd reason Michael notes that the episode opens his heart to the man.

Hastily Pierre picks the baby up and sets him on his feet. He starts to sing an old song he'd learned from his carny days in Sault Ste. Marie.

Oh the merry-go-round
Broke down and it went
Round-and-round.
The people fell off
And they got cross
And the merry-go-round
Broke down
Pah, pah.
Umpah, Umpah, Umpapah

On the Umpapah bits Zack moves his bottom up and down as Pierre had taught him, while the adults comment on his dancing abilities.

Michael bites his lips. "Where'd he learn that one?"

"He'll be another Fred Astaire. Just you watch. Look at him. The kid's musical. He's got rhythm." And on and on.

"While we were away," Emer whispers.

The distractions from the truth were endless. He holds Bella's hand across the table. He isn't able to settle the issue with words, and trusts that the situation between her and Pierre has never grown any worse than what he had seen that morning.

"When do we go to Peru, Dad?" Emer asks from nowhere.

Or so it seemed, because he did get the point.

CHAPTER FIFTEEN

The Pointe

BELLA CAN'T WAIT to get to the Rockcliffe Lookout. Its green tiled roof stands out handsomely, perched as it is on the edge of a cliff overlooking the Gatineau River. She loves to look at her village from across the water. From the Ottawa side. Her head feels clearer for it afterwards.

Zack holds her hand as they get off the streetcar. She sees Michael manoeuvring Alma across the tracks. Emer is standing stock still, gazing upward. At what? The pine trees?

Hurrying along with Zack, Bella says, "What's up there, Emer?"

"It's the smell. It's positively dee-vine!" she says, imitating Katherine Hepburn.

Bella smiles as she sits Zack on the balustrade. Memère Tombeau's unpainted little shack stands out against all the other houses with its rustic weather-worn pine boards. Bella can't see the hand-painted flowers on the doorknob but she knows they'll still be there.

The freshwater smell of fish in the air makes her skin tingle with memories from her childhood. The air is keen and somewhat cooler by the river. She shivers slightly, not from the coolness, but from the memories. It had been a favourite place in their courting days. They kissed there, she and Michael, in the shelter of the shadows, before Monsieur Séguin's little yacht putted over to bring her home. Those were the days when Michael was playing at the Standish. After her divorce.

When they got off the streetcar, he offered his arm and held her tightly to him on the way to the Lookout. He made her feel precious. The violin case was under his other arm.

She watches him now, ambling along with Alma, still with his violin case.

They smile at each other. He laughs. "Never thought I'd make it back to here. It feels good, though."

She smiles and nods. "Our very own gazebo!"

Some gazebos had good memories.

He shows Alma to a bench. "Here, Gran. Rest your feet, because after this it's all downhill to the ferry."

The old lady chuckles.

Michael takes out his binoculars and scans the little houses on the Gatineau side of the river. He studies them for a long time, and then focuses on Gatineau Pointe.

"What are you looking at, Dad?" Emer asks.

"*Par-en-bas*. Down below, where your mother was born." Then, turning, he scans the more distant view. "And Gatineau Mills, where you went on a visit once."

She doesn't need binoculars. Memory has its own reality. She'd been there before. Her mother had sent her there for the country air.

Bella tightens her lower regions. Her bottom is rigid as she waits for Emer to say something smart, like "I went for fresh air and got fresh Pierre instead." She's on the alert to step in, if need be, to divert attention—one of her major talents.

But Emer doesn't say anything. She only casts Bella a long look. Bella knows it well. But she doesn't know if she can trust her daughter to keep the secret. Only time will tell. And so she has to be on the *qui vive* … every moment. There's no telling how Michael would take such a piece of information. She hasn't as yet experienced any serious anger from him, but she isn't about to push her luck.

Bella looks across the river at Gatineau Mills, northeast of Ottawa, where Pierre tried to get funny with her daughter. Finger to mouth, she'd said to her daughter, "Shh, be quiet, muffle up." History repeating itself.

"He was raised in an orphanage, you know. His parents both died on the boat coming over from Belgium. He was a 'home child.'" As if that explained it. Mainly because Pierre had often said it himself. Apparently he thought it was self-explanatory. Though of course it wasn't. Who could have known what his experience was?

Anyway, it's finished between him and me. It lasted while it lasted. He had been a gentle man, a big-hearted man, as Maman had said. But I have drawn my line, and my line is my daughter. Something of the sort must have happened to him in the "home."

Bella wonders if there were any other women who were as trapped as she had been. No choices. Was she the only one?

It's Alma's idea that they all come here for the final two weeks in August, before Labour Day, when Michael goes back to teaching. "Get out from under this insufferable heat," she says. Bella agrees, and knows that it will be a good place for Michael and Alma to talk. The sooner Michael knows the truth, the sooner they can get on with their lives.

Not her truth. His truth. God forbid he should know hers.

She watches the crystal-clear waves lapping up to the beach below and knows that it will be a cleansing place.

THE POINTE

Michael adjusts the binoculars, fixing his sights on the Pointe, on the village where she grew up. Since his mother has not been forthcoming, his frustration focuses on Bella's lineage. He puts the glasses down with a sense of futility. "Who are those people? I'm curious to know where they came from and why they chose to live with the river in front of them and the swamp behind. I didn't know who you were when I went out with you and I'm no further ahead now."

"It was pretty exciting though, wasn't it?" She says with a smile. There's no sense in articulating what to her is plainly obvious. She doesn't understand that he has to worry it, that lineage has become his preoccupation. Life does not have those complexities for her. It is what it is. It's all so simple.

He repeats, "Where did they come from? Why did they settle here?"

Ten small houses on the edge of a swamp, facing the Gatineau River. The church steeple comes into view. It dominates Up-Above and Down-Below. "Here." He hands Bella the glasses. "I can't make out why your people would move to such a location. It must be hellishly cold in winter with water all around like that. Here, you try."

"Try what? What am I looking for?"

"Focus. Just focus."

When she sees the familiar steeple of the village church up close, she involuntarily jumps. The cross, like an X on its side, signifies conflict to her. There is no escaping its gleaming, man-made rays. Twisting everything it touches.

Re-focusing quickly, she sees the ferryman's big white house on the opposite bank. It's the biggest of the ten houses. Monsieur Séguin and his gentle blonde wife live there with their eight children. Bella looks for him in the ferry, skimming the clear water. His face is permanently tanned from the sun. Leatherish. Deeply etched in lines. Warm face, laughing eyes. Always a kind word for everybody. Good man. Happy man. A little bit of a leer. Somewhat of a masher. He'd take it from you if you weren't alert. But if not, that's fine too.

"*Un matou!*" her mother once said in disgust. A rover.

On the river there are men with long poles organizing logs. Lashing them together, forming booms. Tugs chug, their motors laboriously lugging the booms past the Ottawa River, going northeast to the Gatineau, to the paper mills.

Bella sees the Queen's Hotel overlooking the river at the end of the village road, high up on the embankment. Her relatives own the hotel. They take turns working there during off-season from the booms, in the dead cold of winter. *We Sell Beer and Wine.* The red and yellow neon sign flashes off and on across the river. At night it's reflected in the water. Underneath it, *Patates Frites.*

Cousin Anna painted that sign herself. Bella's entrepreneurial cousin has six children and a go-getter husband. They run the place.

On weekend nights in the dead of winter, Ottawans mush it on foot across the frozen Gatineau for a drink. No prohibition in this province. They hope that the temperature will have dropped by the time they return. "Paqueté," as Anna remarks anxiously, an anglicized French word meaning pissed to the gills. Her husband belongs to Alcoholics Anonymous himself. Hence she's protected from such worries. Even so, Anna and her husband watch their customers through the picture windows of the hotel as they weave their way across ice that crackles underfoot.

Bella focuses on the front steps of the hotel. Groups of people darting in and out of the saloon doors. Waving at each other. "Come this way." "No, go that way!" Waving hellos, waving goodbyes. It looks farcical to her, like a cartoon. It's so familiar that she feels she can actually hear their dialogues. "Don't pee in the road, too many cars—pee up against the side of the building." "Watch that mongrel! Looks vicious!" A dog with his tail between his legs. "Watch him! Could bite. Drank too much beer." Zip! Zip!

The Queen's conjures recollections of the smell of hops, malt, whisky, fresh sawdust on wood floors, and a ceiling fan that whizzes stale cigarette smoke out the swinging doors. Forced laughter. "We're all having such a good time!" "Everyone in the village is here!" All crammed into the saloon. Yachtsmen, and the men who work on the booms behind them, with nails in their boots that bite into the slippery logs.

The louvered swinging doors waft forward and back with breezes from the river. The familiar smells of freshwater fish, wet logs, and fumes from overloaded tugboats assail her nostrils. Their chugs echo up and down the river as they pull booms of wood heavier than they can handle.

"That your youngster, Pierre? Cute kid. Here's a nickel, Bella. Sit on my lap."

Oh no, you don't. Hold my own here. I'm nobody's "cute kid!"

"*Calice. Tabernacle. Sainte ciboire. Hostie. Jésus Christ. Vierge. Putain. Plotte. Fourre-moi donc là!*" The sacrosanct, laced with the smell of sexual profanities, burns the incense called anger. Then acrid smoke floats upwards, stinging the nostrils. The chains rattle against the incense-burner. Its sulphuric contents permeate the surrounding air, making the heart turn over as it gushes itself out onto a pile of cold grey rocks.

Fear and fury turned in on itself to the tune of "Beer Barrel Polka" coming from the flashing red, pink, and green jukebox … together with the seven o'clock Family Radio Rosary. "*Tous le monde a genoux!*" Everyone on your knees! shouts Anna to her six children in the back kitchen of the hotel as they pull out their little rosary beads.

> *Pater Noster*
> *Qui es in Coelis*
> *Sanctificetur*
> *Nomen Tuum*

Prayers overriding the statically charged hourly news from England. Disturbingly dark.

"But William Lyon Mackenzie King will look after every last man jack of us. Just you watch and see!" Voices echoing across the river. Bella sighs heavily as she moves away from the Hotel.

Michael is impatient. "Well, what do you see?"

"Everything. I see the whole village." She scans the houses west of the Hotel in an attempt to control her sadness "I see Grand-mère Tombeau's house, where I was born."

Michael looks across the river. "How do you know?"

Bella adjusts her sights. "It's got a white porcelain doorknob with painted flowers. Grandmère painted them herself. She brought it with her from Maniwake, eighty-five miles northwest of the Gatineau."

"She walked?" he asks incredulously.

"Some did. But she came by canoe with her father. He was the Chief."

"When was that?" Michael asks.

"Well," she says, "it was about 1895. She's old, you know. She's older than Alma."

"Maniwake?"

THE POINTE

"You remember her, don't you? Catherine Tombeau, my grandmother. She raised me as a child. I introduced her to you three years ago. Maybe you didn't register, because it was just before you went into the hospital."

"Guess I was distracted at the time."

"It will be good to see her again, don't you think?"

He isn't sure. "What else do you see?" he urges.

Bella looks up at him, holding the binoculars to her chest. "Maman, les ma tantes Rosa, Manna, and Nina were all born there too, along with mon oncle Emil." She raises the glasses and continues, "in that order."

"How do you know?"

"Grandmère Tombeau told me. '*Dans cet ordre*'."

"Catherine Tombeau. Yes, I remember her now. Quiet, soft-spoken lady. Powerful in some way," he says pensively.

"That's right."

"Anything else?"

"Ma tante Rosa's big house with white wooden pillars. They always looked so out of place there. They're similar to Greek pillars you see in books," she giggles.

"Ionic columns." He smiles at her family's exceptional talent for duplication.

Bella scans Rosa's house more closely. She was Maman's second sister, Maman being the eldest. Rosa with the long black hair. Every room in the house was empty except for the kitchen and the bedroom. By choice. She loved the open space of empty rooms.

The bedroom curtains are pinned together. She's sitting on the edge of the bed, no doubt braiding her hair, a case of beer under the bed. Counting the hours until sundown, lying in her bake-oven bed. Everything shut tight. Airless. Mon oncle John, Rosa's British

267

husband, is in the back shed. He roams between the kitchen and the shed. Bluebottles buzzing in and out of the knotted wood slats. Waiting. Puttering, whittling pieces of wood. Waiting for the news to break. Keeping an eye on his hiding place in the swamp. Killing time. Wondering when the heat of the day will end. Listening to the radio. Wondering what the Prime Minister has to say. "Peace in our time." Not much.

Aunt Rosa opens another warm beer. The cap flips. Ttt. Don't come near me, John. Don't come near. Two children was enough.

"Why are you so quiet, Bella?"

She brings the binoculars into tighter focus. "I'm looking. I'm looking." The blur turns to instant clarity. "I see ma tante Manna's house, my mother's third sister, the one with the prickly beard and the man's haircut. Cousin Anna's mother. Anna owns the Hotel at the end of the road there, remember Michael?"

Back to her binoculars and Manna's house. It too was a shack, tucked in beside and behind Grandmère Tombeau's shack as an afterthought. Funny, she had never thought of the little houses as shacks when she was growing up.

Mon oncle Armand is on the wine-coloured leather chaise longue in the front room. Bella smiled, remembering her aunt's love of the wild flowers that grew in the swamp. In consequence Manna brought the outdoors into the décor of her indoors. There were flowers everywhere. On the beige flowered wallpaper and the gleaming flowered linoleum.

Ma tante Manna is pickling cucumbers on the dining room table. As fast as mon oncle Armand discards the unread newspapers, she picks them up. It appears to be a game they're playing. He reads,

THE POINTE

shakes them out as if he's trying to open a paper bag, and finally scrunches them up in exasperation, with no hope of ever being able to make sense of the daily news.

Ma tante runs up the flowered walls and around the flowered floors trying to keep up with him. It borders on the insane.

Bella sees the scaffolded walkway, still there, leading to ma tante's outhouse, perched high up on the edge of the back swamp, with the honest smell of wood and shit. Mosquitoes had bitten her legs while she read about Betty Grable's legs. "They're insured for a million bucks! Wow!" She noticed how Gene Tierney's buck teeth really suited her. She wished she had buck teeth too. Makes for a wall-to-wall smile. Must've sucked her thumb a lot to get those!

Bella rests the weight of the binoculars on the balustrade for a moment and wonders if her mother had sat there studying the movie stars as she did. No. It was decidedly unthinkable. Rudolph Valentino in *The Sheik* and Ramón Novarro in *Scaramouche* were stars that had passed her by. Maman had never been interested in pictures that moved. Or men that leered openly.

Peering through the glasses she wonders why there aren't pictures of the back swamp pasted up there too. Her territory. It's scenic and just at the back door. Someone might have taken photographs after all and pasted them up. The most sacred place that she knows of, ignored. It was not recorded for posterity. She had floated on a raft past frogs, toads, lizards, and water snakes. Spent afternoons on her back studying cloud formations. Drifted unafraid. The stream would take her wherever. It didn't matter to her. It was all home. That's where she was happiest.

She readjusts the binoculars to the doorless outhouse. New images pasted on top of old images every which way. A tall, glistening tower and a huge ball beside it. She reads the caption, The World's Fair.

Pasted on the wall beside it, Jewish refugees walking out of Germany with paper bags and sacks. Sad faces that open up the heart. A heartrending sight. Devastatingly senseless. The world didn't make sense. But then, of course, it never had.

"What drivel in the newspapers. Only good for wrapping fish and chips," commented mon oncle Armand in perfectly cultured English. "Or using as wallpaper or wiping your ass with," he said as an afterthought. Bella smiles at the memories. The profusion of the world's confusion that was spread out over its walls merited his remarks.

Mon oncle Armand trashed another newspaper. *"Elle est dure à cuire, celle-là."*

Whaaat? Hard to cook? Meaning what? Hard to cook in French means stubborn. The facts are indigestible. It's the news that's hard to cook.

"Are they going to call us up?" mon oncle Armand asked her in his English-with-a-cultured-French accent. As if, because she's married to an English-speaking husband, that gives her clearer access to the world's international information. Well how should I know? But Bella nods in the affirmative.

"There, you see? You see what I mean?" This time he shreds the newspaper, glaring at his wife as if she's to blame.

Armand ran a tug, pulling booms. *La Pitoune*. The Loose Woman. His three sons, Norman, Ti-Loup (Little Wolf), and Henri all worked on the floating logs with their long wooden punt sticks. They manipulated these slippery, rolling logs, maintaining their balance as they did so. High up on the shoreline, her cousins had always looked to Bella as though they were dancing. They positioned the logs by stabbing at them with iron picks at the end of their punt sticks and then chained them together into huge islands. The tugs then pulled the chained body of logs downriver to the paper mill in Gatineau Mills. In winter they waited on tables at the hotel.

Mon oncle Armand glared into the swamp through the back window. "*Ben c'est pas notre guerre!*" It's not our war!

Bella puts down the binoculars for a moment. "Are we going to war, Michael?"

"Not if we can help it," he replies, and adds, gazing across the river, "I still don't understand these people."

She shrugs at his response while still struggling to understand Armand's craziness and ma tante Manna's nervous tidying up after him. Sensing that Michael is eager to take the ferry, she hands the binoculars back to him. "Why is it so important to you to know about family history?" She's being conversational. Instead, she unwittingly elicits the teacher in Michael.

"Because I don't want our children to question their lineage the way I do. I want to get it as straight as I can for their sakes. Knowledge of lineage is a key factor in the development of individuation. I don't want them growing up angry and frustrated, not knowing who they are. If we can't straighten it from my side of the family, at least we'll straighten it from yours."

An electric current runs from one end of her body to the other. For no discernible reason her legs turn to jelly. She sits beside Alma on the bench. She doesn't understand a word of it. It isn't so much the words as it is the intensity with which he speaks them. His passion gets in the way of her understanding. Some part of her shakes with its intention. Her only reassurance in the midst of her fear is that she, at least, knows who her father is. But how far was he going to take this thing? Truth causes fear to swirl in the belly.

Ambulance sirens resound across the water on the Pointe side. Echoing emptily across the water.

THE WORLD'S FAIR

Michael looks at Emer, who looks away as suddenly and leaps into mounds of crisp leaves. Children are uncanny in their ability to read thoughts. It's their clarity. Then again, it's not just children, it's Emer. He feels how closely she can follow his thoughts. It's almost too close.

Emer takes her brother's hand. Michael takes the other. She hums the latest number on the hit parade.

The dry, floating oak leaves glide with the lyrics through the rays of oncoming dusk. They crunch underfoot. The children laugh at the sounds. Michael sniffs the early, spicy smells of autumn in the air. Pumpkins. Halloween. Costumes. Disguises.

He holds his children's hands but doesn't feel connected to himself or to them. Fragmented like the crushed leaves underfoot. He feels loaded down with unanswered questions, his children bearing the overflow. He knows that resentment for his mother's silence fills him with anger, but simply knowing it isn't enough to control the surges.

"We'll see everything up close when we get there," Michael assures them. "Can't see anything from here." He settles his family into Monsieur Séguin's small yacht.

※

There are no suitcases. Emer has her chessboard and pieces under her arm. Bella has Grandmère Tombeau in her core, and Granny Longpré has nothing except her long black poplin dress, black beads, small round, black glasses, and money carefully tucked inside her corset. Her fuzzy white hair stands an inch off her head, giving the effect of a halo. Michael holds Zack in one arm, his violin case in the other. As they cross the Gatineau River they see the Ontario and Quebec shores at once.

THE POINTE

The sacred Chaudière is within view. Its presence affirms Bella's need for valuing the sacred. "Pipe Bowl Falls." she murmurs. Then suddenly she shouts, *"C'est éblouissant!"* There are no words to express its beauty in English.

Michael says, "Diamondly diaphanous?"

Bella smiles. "You can try, but you can't translate it."

The combination of spray and the hum of the motorboat bring Michael back to the days of their courtship. He feels good again. He notices Gran clinging to the sides of the boat, enjoying the spume of the churning waters. Only Zack's bottom can be seen as he paddles his hands through the foam. Bella cranes her neck, waiting for Memère Tombeau's house to come into view. Monsieur Séguin cuts the motor. The boat whispers into the sandy beach. A long, soft landing. They disembark along the beach and up the embankment to the dirt road, all holding each others' hands. Bella leads the chain with confident steps.

Home. For her, home.

Gran shakes the wrinkles out of her black cotton dress. "How do I look?" She turns her haloed head, inviting them to inspect her.

"Great!" everyone shouts.

"Now then, it's a white house with green shutters and a piece of etched glass in the front door. Do you see it? That's what the lawyer said."

Grandmère Tombeau waves at them from her front porch as though she's always been there waving, smiling smiles of welcome. *"Bienvenue,"* she calls.

Bella waves back. *"Je vais venir te voir tantôt."* See you later. Smiling her wall-to-wall happy smile.

Michael sees the house first. The frosted glass door. He counts. "It's three houses to the west of the Queen's Hotel," he says, "and four houses east of Memère Tombeau's, and faces *la rivière éblouissante*." He turns to Bella with a knowing wink. He loves to speak French but is self-conscious about his pronunciation.

Emer holds Alma's hand as they walk down the other side of the embankment onto the front lawn of the cottage. Michael stands for a moment looking back across the Gatineau River at the Lookout pavilion. Their gazebo, as Bella called it, sitting at the top of the cliff with its green tile roof. He sticks his head under the water pump. Magic remembered. Again and again and again. Had it only been his hormones? No matter, he smiles. Hormones are true of everyone. So what? He frisks his hair dry with light, swift strokes. "Don't look back," he chides; "might turn into a pillar of salt."

Bella observes him. He knows the look. She hopes this trip will bring them closer together, and he's no closer to knowing that it will.

Cooling off under the pump looks like a good idea, but she doesn't want to get her hair wet.

"Water's good tasting!" he says. "This is a good spot."

Once inside, they open all the windows and doors, letting the river breeze blow out the must. Alma lies on the wine velvet chaise longue in the sitting room, sneezing. The dining room is lined with hard-cover classics from ceiling to floor. He feasts his eyes. Emer puts her chessboard down on the table and joins him.

Books by Flaubert, Zola, de Maupassant.

Even some Alain Fournier, as well as Dickens, Jane Austen, Pope, mixed in with books by Rumer Godden.

"What's *The Black Narcissus* about, Dad?" she asks.

"Godden, hmm. I believe it takes place in the mountains of India and is about some women in a religious community." Michael turns to Alma. "Where'd he get so many books?"

"Horace was a teacher. Taught literature in both languages. At Ottawa University,"

Michael apologizes, "I didn't know." All he knew was what family voices had told him: "'Horace is your grandmother's old-crone-drinking-buddy."

"You never ast." She says it that way when she's being sarcastic.

"I was told he was just an old drinking buddy."

The old lady snorts. "You don't have to tell me who told you that one."

Michael feels his anger rising. So much for family voices. He turns to Emer. "If you're reading you can stay up as long as you wish."

Bella says, "We can go to the beach every day. *La plage est à la porte.*" The beach is at the door.

He detects reverence in her tone. There's a pervasive air of freshness in the little house that night. They all find their rooms upstairs and settle in very quickly and comfortably, considering Horace hasn't been in it for over a year.

Michael finds the axe in the shed, and pretty soon they have a roaring fire in the stove to dry out the house. Before going to bed that night, Emer peeks through the crack in Gran's door to make sure she's all right. She finds Alma in bed, praying and counting her money. She's sitting up in the dark, feeling each bill meticulously and stacking them all in different piles. Emer hears her thanking Horace and the gods "for the umpteenth time for all your kindness," as she takes a swig from her silver hip flask.

CHAPTER SIXTEEN

Downriver

IN THE DAYS THAT FOLLOW, Michael still does not approach Alma. His silence intensifies whenever they all sit down to eat. Bella needs a break away from the tension, and hides behind the activities of housekeeping. Her lower back pain reaches epic proportions. She has trouble walking. Maybe her mother could help out. But then she doesn't think so. It's not the kind of thing Maman can handle, and Michael is too preoccupied.

On Saturday morning she can't move.

"Stay in bed," he says. "I'll make some pancakes."

She lies there trying to distinguish where her boundary lines are, what belongs to Michael and what belongs to her. She bites her lower lip. Paternity isn't her issue, but at the same time it *is*, because they're married and share everything together. Where do I draw the line? What's mine and what's his? She tries to let her body relax further into the feather mattress. The base of her spine feels like a clenched fist. She cannot evade her discomfort. As she observes the tightness, she sees that it's centred around Pierre. This astonishes her. She sighs a deep, unfocused breath around the pain. If Michael ever found out, there would then be two divorces before she was thirty. She shivers. The thought is untenable. He would surely dramatize it into a tragedy of Greek proportions. He's fixed on getting to the bottom of everything. He can get to the bottom of things for himself if he wishes, but not to the bottom of my stuff

DOWNRIVER

as well. "*Point finale.*" To Bella, his obsessions with lineage are an affliction. As well, the reality of being back in her village with its memories enervates her. But then finally she needs to exercise her legs. There's only one road, and it leads to her mother's house.

The next day she takes Emer to visit Maman in Monsieur Séguin's boat, Upriver.

"Today we'll go *par-en-haut*." Upriver. "We'll meet with Memère Duval and walk back down here to visit Grandmère Tombeau. *Par-en-bas.*"

Maman lived opposite the grey stone church in the village. Little white houses clustered at the foot of the cruciferous steeple. Pierre bought the house for Maman. What with his savings from the café in Gatineau Mills and the offer of the Tecumseh job, he was able to pay for it fully, in cash.

The rich people lived Upriver, the poor Downriver, the reason being that most of them Upriver, in the village proper, were on the immediate bus route to Gatineau's paper mill, where the men in the Pointe worked. They had permanent jobs. Some had big important jobs with good money. They had steady jobs and the people down below didn't. The work of organizing the logs into booms on the Gatineau River, though it paid well, was seasonal.

As the boat docks at the pier, Bella sees Monsieur le Curé watching them from the circular front porch of L'Église St. Thérèse. The porch where she and her first husband parted after the ceremony.

She had miscarried shortly afterwards. Through hooded eyes Bella watches the priest watching her and shudders. The black-coated cassock had followed her home from the confessional many times. Bella clutches Emer's hand tightly to steady her gait as they walk past him.

Within three months she had been married in the Church, divorced by the State, and pregnant with no visible means of support. He had jumped her in the confessional when she had revealed her teenage truth. The unburdening of her soul had a price tag on it, she discovered. Thank God she hadn't ever mentioned Pierre to the priest too. She imagined that she would have had a parade of cassocks following her back to the house. And perhaps Maman would have begun to wonder. This episode gave birth to her famous chant, "I'll die with my secrets." Her divorce appeared on the front page of the *Ottawa Citizen*. How she reconciled notoriety with "dying with her secrets" was anybody's guess. Her logic was that she would rather die with her secrets than be humiliated by the clergy into thinking that she was a bad woman.

As a result, the word religion turned into a snarl whenever she spoke it. She had enough beautiful teeth in her head to express it that way.

In her view, once the cassocks determined they couldn't have her, their message became, "You may not have a divorce and you may not marry Michael Maguire in the Church." She did not like being limited by a set of rules that were not her own. She understood it to be an ecclesiastical vendetta. The Church canon did not interest her. Their man-made laws were lacking in compassion. Period. "You and Michael must live together as brother and sister," the clergy had intoned. Indelible imprint. Some imprints turn into snarls.

At first Maman doesn't hear them walking in through the side door. Bella and Emer discover her on her knees, beads rattling, praying to the steeple. For forgiveness? Relief from grief? Usually Bella can read it, but in this instance she can't. She's too absorbed with her own frustration over Michael.

Maman's rosary rattles as she hastily sneaks it back into the washing machine, where everything of any value is stashed. The crystal beads clink against the bottle of Johnny Walker whiskey. Not that she's a drinker. It's simply to keep her little snorts hidden from Pierre. He always makes a big case out of it, which sometimes goes on for days. "*C'est ennuyant.*" It gets tiresome.

"*Bienvenue, bienvenue,*" she shouts from the innards of the washtub.

They all sit down at the prepared table with radishes, spring onions, and olives. "*Du jardin,*" she says, proudly indicating the raw vegetables.

A greasy vegetable soup with dumplings, fresh parsley, and garlic is also served. Maman loves greasy soup, though why she does is anybody's guess. Probably to do with a residual belief that you need fat on your bones to contend with the below-zero weather in winter. So you eat the grease in summer too, just to keep in tandem with the intake of bodybuilding insulation. We're just lucky that it's summer and not the cold season, Bella thinks. In winter, the fare is great big chunks of boiled pork fat with minute strips of pink meat marbled through it. In any case, Maman's apple pies are better, though her doughnuts are as greasy as her soup. White flour batter, deep-fried in Crisco lard, sprinkled with lots of icing sugar.

Emer looks happy enough with the prospect of dessert, but the heavy feeling of lead couldn't be a better description for Bella. Pierre is a better cook than Maman, but he always makes a fast exit when she's in the kitchen. They argue over the greasy dishes she turns out. He doesn't care for arguments. So he isn't here today.

He's at the Tecumseh, cooking dinner for the executives at the mill. The golfers.

Bella is more at ease because of his absence. She doesn't have to scramble behind the furniture to keep up appearances. Maman ignores their "play" as infantile child's play, in any case. She protects herself by keeping her thoughts at that level. If she thinks anything more of it than that, she'll have a nervous breakdown. When confronted with the truth, she usually says, "*Tant qu'à ça c'est vrai.*" A passing acknowledgement meaning "so what?" Or, in demotic speech, "Ain't it the truth, though?" And leaves the room nervously humming, *Sur le plancher des vaches.*

On est heureux comme des poissons dans l'eau,
Sur le plancher des vaches.

A French song learned from Bella's father. Pure cover-up.
We are as happy as fish in water,
On the bottom of the sea (literally, on the cow's floor).

Or sometimes when she wants to let you know that you should mind your own business, it's a popular Bolduc song called *Le P'tit Bonhomme avec le Nez Pointu.* The little man with the pointed nose. Intended to remind one about being too nosy.

Conversation, in any case, makes Maman nervous. She never knows what to say in response. So, she runs. She runs because she really doesn't know what anyone is alluding to. They might as well be talking some foreign language. To some degree Bella learned how to use the same language fillers, such as "*Que voulez-vous?*" and "*C'est la vie,*" to let everyone know that she heard them. What can you do? That's life. That was the degree of Maman's socialization.

Whenever someone knocks at the door, the reclusive native in her tiptoes from window to window to see who it might be. As she peers silently at the intruder, fear grips her. When Bella sees her frozen in that way, it grips her too. Both are lost in their historically-conditioned passivity.

Maman cooks, she waits on tables. She washes. Hates ironing. *Ennuyant!* Such a bore! She chops wood. Loads the stove. Cleans the shed. Washes floors. Washed them in the Parliament buildings after the children died and George Senior left. Placed the two remaining, Bella and young George, with her mother *par-en-bas*. Got to meet some of the people in the House. *"Ca c'est du monde!"* Now there are some real people! Meaning the people she met in Parliament were interesting to talk to. Who she referred to was never really clear. What she might have said in response was never clear either. Bella presumed that they were some important political figures, because she knew her mother wouldn't talk that way about just anybody. Bella knows her mother well. Especially her pain.

Maman's pain, when it occurs to her to feel it, is "the white man's malice." It chokes her off at the throat. Their shared grief over family history bonds them.

Her Belgian father's brutality was beyond description. The reason she can't speak even now. The reason she looks the other way when she's addressed.

But for now, anyway, Bella is relatively at ease with Maman. Pierre isn't home. She doesn't have to pretend. All is well. It's comfortable being with Maman alone. Neither one of them ever discusses their past.

"What's past is past," they keep telling each other. Unaddressed pain. No discussion. *"Que voulez-vous? C'est la vie!"* They have an unspoken understanding that it's the most expedient way to go. When Bella was a young teenager, that approach worked. But presently, in the immediate moment with a crippling backache that won't let up, Bella wonders if she should put words to what is paining her. She knows that her situation is completely outside Maman's ballpark, but it's also somewhat outside Bella's as well. Her only support might not, after all, be able to be supportive.

At the table Emer faces a tapestry in the stairwell. Her eyes widen. "What's that, Mom?" she whispers.

Bella is distracted. She watches her mother hooking her gold ciborium-shaped earrings into her earlobes. "Do you have to wear those?" It seems in such poor taste to be wearing a miniature replica of a vessel intended to hold the consecrated bread of the Eucharist. From an aesthetic point of view it simply doesn't work for her.

"They're pure gold. What's the matter with you?" Maman says as she waggles her head in front of the buffet mirror. Madame Duval likes the darting gold tassels that dangle from the ends of the earrings. What's more, Pierre gave them to her in his courting days when Bella was in the convent.

"They're replicas of the Egyptian lotus flower," she says grandly.

Bella is about to say, "A piece of antiquity!" but decides to be quiet. She'd have to live with it, walking down the river road. Her mother might as well have her lower lip stretched and place a saucer in it to match the incongruity of those earrings. They unnerved her with their constant movement, even when her mother's head was perfectly still. Thank God it's summer and she's not wearing her famous itchy muskrat too! Sometimes Bella is ashamed of her mother's taste. The thought of it makes her swallow her soup too quickly, and she chokes. The coughing continues for a few seconds.

Emer pounds her back. "You okay, Mom?"

"I'll be all right in a minute," she says, her chest still heaving.

Maman runs for the tap. "*Tiens, prends de l'eau!*" Here, drink some water.

When it subsides, Emer nudges her under the table and nods at the wall hanging again. It isn't new, but it's new to Emer. It depicts several people scrambling to pull away from the food on the table when a bear appears in the casement, ready to gobble up everything in sight.

Bella has always hated it. It isn't art. Nor is it craft. Not that she knows that much about it. It just isn't anything. Seeing it through Emer's eyes. The most that can be said for it is that it inspires fear.

She notices Emer surreptitiously taking a glance at the side door as she dips into her soup. "*Est-ce qu'il y a des ours dans la région, Memère?*" Are there any bears in the area, Memère?

"*Non, mon enfant, il n'y en a pas. Fais-toi s'en pas pour ça. Mange! Mange!*" No, my child, there aren't. Don't worry about it. Eat! Eat!

"Eat! Eat! How can I eat? Eat when my stomach is in a clutch at the sight of a big, bad bear ready to grab my food?" she grumbles. "Maybe even grab *me* for dessert!"

Bella looks and sees a depiction of the proverbial wolf at the door. The story of life and mother. The story of having either no money to live or no man to live with.

Emer nevertheless tucks into the soup. "Good. No bears in the area. I can eat."

Not an appetizing thing to have in front of you at the dinner table, Bella reflects, but then meals with Maman had hardly ever been without some kind of fear-making tension. To her, the tapestry manifests the Duval family dynamic. She knows Maman doesn't think about it in exactly those terms. All she knows is that tension is activated in the kitchen at mealtimes. Where it comes from and how it happens Bella doesn't know, but that's her reality. Now that Maman is alone with Pierre, the tapestry still hangs there as a remnant, reminding Bella of the way things had been. She and her mother are the same person, she reckons. Her backache intensifies at the thought.

※

Afterwards the three generations set out to meet the fourth generation Down-Below. They hadn't told Memère Tombeau they were coming. Which was always the way it was in any case. Short of sending up smoke signals.

Maman sighs, *"Ah, qui fait donc beau!"* What a beautiful day! She chews hard on her spruce gum, which never softens and has a bitter taste. It's from the spruce tree and good for the teeth and the liver. *"N'est-ce pas?"*

What a beautiful day! She drinks in the water, the trees, the grass, the songs of wild canaries from the swamp in the back of the little houses. Smells of light frying butter on the river road mingle with the freshwater fish smells of the Gatineau River. The boom workers are occupied with their activities of strapping logs together to form islands. They bounce from one slippery log to the next in a bobbing dance. The sound of cicadas all around them herald the heat wave like pipe organs with all the stops out. Their droning sound assaults the dog days of summer.

She knows Bella doesn't care for her earrings but she wears them anyway. She likes the feel of the long icicle tassels splashing against her neck. She saw Bella wince when she put them on. They may be a trifle garish but they are in good taste, and what does Bella know about taste? Well, actually, her daughter does have good taste, but it isn't her taste. Is her daughter jealous? Hard to say. Maybe, though she can't imagine why.

They stop to watch the holidayers swim out to the booms, where they rest before splashing back to shore. Neighbours rush down to their little picket fences to say *"Bonjour"*—with the usual whispers that come with it: *"C'est qui ça?"* Who's that? *"Endimanché aussi et c'est Samedi."* All decked out in Sunday dress, too, and it's Saturday.

"C'est la belle Bella. La fille d'Anna." They wink knowingly at each other. The beautiful Bella. The *ménage à trois*, don't you know?"

Bella looks utterly beautiful with her upswept blonde curls against the backdrop of blue sky and rippling navy blue river. If you listen carefully, you can almost hear the current flowing swiftly past the mouth of the Ottawa River.

Her smile, disarming. Incandescently clear, and beautiful. Today there's something of Irene Dunne about her. She carries herself with an air of royalty as she walks the gauntlet of probing eyes.

Everyone knows Maman's story. Just as she knows theirs. It goes without saying.

She hums her tuneless tunes, just in case their questions get too probing. You never know. She reviews her text anxiously. *"Tant qu'a ça c'est vrai!"* *"Que voulez-vous?"* *"C'est la vie!"*

Simultaneously. Together. Or all mixed up.

They glance curiously at Emer, checking her out.

"Elle resemble à son père." Resembles her father. Nods of agreement. Mouths wreathed in smiles of approval. Paternity issue settled. Memère breathes a little easier. Enough to say, *"Ils sont dans la maison d'Horace pour le mois d'août."*

They all nod sadly, already knowing about his passing. Knowing that Alma Longpré has inherited Horace's house and that the Maguires are there on her invitation. Glad nods. Happy to have Bella back among them. Where they can keep an eye on Michael's unpredictable temper. They'd heard of that too. And his

TB: *"guérison."* His healing. They cluck sympathetically, knowing everything.

"*Et le p'tit?*" they ask pointedly. "*Où est le p'tit?*" The baby? Where's the baby?

"*Il est avec son père dans la maison d'Horace.*"

She starts to hum *The Little Man with the Pointed Nose* as she smiles her goodbyes and quickens her step.

Maman doesn't look at Bella, for fear of what she might see. Bella doesn't look at Maman. For fear of what she might see.

The parade continues all the way *par-en-bas*, with a smiling claque of well-wishers lining the river road. Mother, daughter, and granddaughter return their smiles.

There are a few sailboats gliding across the surface of the water, but mainly tugs, chugging along with their boom-load haul of logs to the paper mill.

The villagers are close-knit, much like the boom-logs. Lashed together. Silent. Knowing everything there is to know. On both sides of the river. Maman is in her element. She knows too.

If the word "collusion" had been mentioned, no one would have known what it meant.

They arrive at Grandmère Tombeau's house. Though they had been walking downhill all the way, Bella is tired. The steeple disappears as they gather at the front of the house in the shade of the enormous maple tree, which is surrounded by beige beach sand.

They fan themselves with their white gloves and Memère Duval's straw hat.

Emer recognizes the old wooden bench under the tree. She'd had her first formal lesson in French on that bench.

Grandmère points at the sky. "*Le ciel.*"

She remembers the river that day. Its exquisitely reflected diamonds. Glistening. Blinding in the sunlight. "*La rivière.*"

Today the grass grows, in long, dewy, green strands, up the sides of the unpainted wooden house. The thin panes of the two front windows are puttied into four equal squares. The hand-painted white enamel knob glows with its colourful flowers.

"*Non assieds-toi pas!*" Don't sit down! Memère reads her thoughts.

She sees a child standing nearby, watching. "*Va y dire qu'on est ici!*" Tell her we're here.

The two women stand formally at attention, waiting for the visit to begin. "*La vieille va être contente de nous voir.*" The old lady will be happy to see us. There's an air of respect in the tone.

In the branches above them, bumblebees are buzzing in anticipation. Grandmère Tombeau appears out of the side door. Slowly. Grey felt slippers whisper over the soft sand and tufts of grass.

Emer sees her walking on the outside, but running toward them on the inside. Silence. Imperceptibly the three women nod at each other.

She sits on the bench. They sit on either side. Emer stands in front of her. They haven't seen each other in three years.

"*T'es mieux?*" You are better now?

Emer nods.

Memère Tombeau takes her hand, leaving the other two to sit under the maple tree.

"*Entre!*"

Bella sits on the unpainted bench. She rubs the wood with her fingertips; it powders in her hand. Sometimes she feels that old too. Maman fans her with her hat. "*Elle a bonne mine, tu trouves pas?*" She looks good, don't you think?

Bella digs her fingers into the ridged wood. "Yes, when we consider her age and the hard life."

"*Ben c'était pas si pire que ça.*" Well, it wasn't as bad as all that.

Bella sighs. "Why must you continually minimize life's events?"

"I am not stupid, you know. I'm well aware that her life was a disaster, but there were always other things in life that were not. Those are the things I want to focus on." She starts to weep silently.

Are we one and the same person? Bella wonders and shudders. The very idea is too disturbing to think on.

"My life is certainly not what I expected it to be."

"I know." says Bella sympathetically, searching vacantly for something more supportive to say.

"Contrary to what you might think of me, I am not stupid," she repeats. "I think I will go crazy if I allow myself to see any more pain. *J'en ai assez!* I've had enough. My mother's life was a disaster. It's true what you say. What's it all about anyway? I did a little better with my own life, but Pierre can be such a fool sometimes." She tamps her cheeks with a small handkerchief. "In any case, he's a good provider, and that counts for something in my books."

Bella agrees limply. "Yes, I know."

"All I'm doing is trying to live with the cards I got."

Unexpected laughter.

Zack's laughter travels upriver toward them. Both women look up.

He's four doors over, out on the lawn playing ball with Michael. Alma is sitting in a rocker on the porch with the chessboard in front of her. Bella can see her studiously counting the squares. "Pawn to King two," she shouts finally. Michael goes running back to his game.

Bella is amazed. "Wait 'til Emer hears this. She'll want to play Granny a game."

Zack's gurgling laughter resounds in her ears. He's such a good-natured child. She isn't eager to return to brooding Michael.

"What's the matter?" Maman asks.

What if I told her? What if I suddenly confronted her with the truth and said, "Look Maman, your life was as good as it was because I slept with Pierre, because I knew if I didn't he would have left you. What if?"

Part of her scorns her mother for playing stupid, as if she doesn't already know. She must. Her lips curl in disdain. She doesn't allow herself to know.

Instead Bella's response is, "Nothing." And to herself, "*Je vais mourir avec mes secrets.*" I shall die with my secrets.

Zero.

Gravity pulls down the corners of Bella's mouth.

"Well, there's no reason for you to be down in the dumps. You're very lucky to have that man. Count your lucky stars."

"*Je suppose.*" Bella rubs her hands into the bench uncertainly. She glances at the wood fragments in her hands and then over at Michael. She squeezes the powder through her thumb and fingers as she watches him. Her fingers shake a little. She bends over the bench and examines the textured ridges of the wood with her nails. The bench was coming to its end. It had been a hard life, but a life nevertheless, desiccating its way to death as they spoke. Bella wipes the powder from her hands. She's angry because she can't confide the truth to Maman. She needs someone to talk to, but because Maman never lets anything in, it isn't possible. It has never been possible. Why is it, she wonders, that the most important things between them never get said? She changes the subject back to

Grandmère Tombeau, hoping that by talking she might communicate with her at some level.

"Elle a vécu une vie affreuse." She's had a horrible life. "Why can't you let the truth in for just a second?"

Memère Tombeau's life had been wretched. Bella understood that awfulness. She felt that hers too could have been considerably different if her mother had been more open to receiving her truth. Her grandmother's life would always haunt Bella. She'd been too young to remember it, but her mother knew all the details. She'd told it to her often enough as a child.

Family folklore they had shared together. Shared the shivering fear. Perhaps the biggest well-kept secret between them was that basically they were the same person. Their fears were the same. At that level their personalities were in many ways interchangeable, though neither one of them would ever have admitted to that.

Maman said that she had been sitting in the kitchen with her mother and young George, having a drink, when her father walked in the door. Unexpectedly.

"C'est défendu de boire l'alcool!" It's forbidden to drink alcohol here. He had made that clear.

Bella was a baby, somewhere upstairs in the house.

"Natives can't carry their liquor," he bellows.

He heats the poker over the stove as he walks up and down ranting and raving. Threatening. Turning it over. His horse and buggy are at the door. They thought he was going to shoe his horse. They all watch the poker getting redder by the minute, never thinking that he'd actually use it. Fear of his bad temper paralyses them.

He beat her with the poker. They all froze in horror. Memère Tombeau screamed and fainted. She never came back to them again. She came, but never the same. They lost her. She moved to another plane. The old lady never acknowledged Maman's father again. He didn't exist, and he was right there in front of her. He scarred her back. She has difficulty moving, even now. He went into the 1914-18 war in France after that. He never came back. Lost in action, they said.

She never touched a drop after that night. Never. Finished. None of them ever got over that beating. Ever.

Burnt flesh. The smell filled the room. They all threw up. So did Bella, upstairs in her crib. The house became a tomb. Memère Tombeau's downstairs bedroom became her coffin for a long time. She did not move from there.

Maman slept upstairs with Bella and George. This was just after the girls had died. Her sisters, Manna, Rosa, and Nina took turns waiting on her. They took turns treating Memère Tombeau's burns with "*l'Onguent.*" Ointment. They smeared it on every two hours for months. To this day, Maman plunges into turmoil whenever she smells it.

Memère Tombeau never stopped moaning. Day and night. For days and weeks at a time. No position was comfortable. Nothing they did for her could ease the pain. Stop her grief.

Maman grew to hate her lamentations. She blocked her ears at night. Bella watched her and did the same thing. It was too terrible for words that a human being could go on suffering in such a way. It was bestial. She couldn't stand a draft from an open window or door. The breeze pained her. And there was no breeze. The days were long and hot.

They mourned all over the house as if she was dead. Day and night they walked on tiptoes, wringing their hands, clutching their breasts and each other for support. Even the sound of their footsteps or breathing pained her. They never sat on the bed, or touched it.

They tried as much as possible to hold their breath whenever they came near her, to avoid giving her more pain. No one who tended her was ever the same after that. In the midst of their numbness, they had tried to save her as best they could.

A doctor came. He stood at the foot of the bed and shook his head in horror; he was in absolute disbelief that she had survived.

"*Histoire de sauvagerie.*" "This is about Native savagery," he said, and stomped out.

The savage was her father. He was drunk. Her own French father, Oscar Tombeau. Bella's grandfather. They both weep about it even now.

CHAPTER SEVENTEEN

Two Greats

BELLA TURNS the flowered enamel knob and slips in through the front of the house. After removing her white sandals and brushing the sand from her feet, she sits on a straight-backed chair in the shadow of the alcove where Memère's bed used to be. There's a small window overhead. It faces the wall of the neighbour's house. The flowered linoleum covers the centre of the floor, and there are four chairs on its perimeter. An icon candle burns on a wooden ledge, but there's no icon. Incense burns in the old smudge pot in its usual place next to the candle. It has a familiar exotic scent. She feels comfortable sitting in the coolness of the alcove listening to the murmur of voices. The door to the kitchen is slightly ajar. She moves to open it fully and watches from the shadows. It reminds her of her days on the raft in the back swamp, silently floating past people's open windows, hearing what went on behind closed doors.

She doesn't want to disturb them, because it's Emer's first visit with her great-grandmother since the San. But it's equally true that the native in her loves to sit behind the bushes and watch human behaviour from afar. It makes no demands on her and she can enjoy it freely.

Memère Tombeau holds Emer's hand. No words are spoken. Sunlight hums through the small kitchen window, resting on the red-and-white checkered oilcloth with four glass cruets centred on the table.

"I am ancient. From ancient people. I wouldn't walk down the stairs for anyone else. But for you, yes. From a small child you let me see into your soul. Your tears, your laughter, your excitement at being alive. Your great, great grandfather was a leader of men. I learned a lot of things in my father's tent."

"*Votre père était un Chef?*" Your father was a Chief? Emer asks in astonishment.

Memère butters thick chunks of warm bread and spreads them with molasses. "*Oui. C'est ça,*" she says, pouring the molasses out of the quart bottle as if she were pouring prayer. She listens to the child's voice, an overflowing stream babbling in response. Such words, and so many for one so young.

She draws the chair to the table, sits, listens, and folds her hands. They rustle like silk against silk. In the long silences she and Emer sip hot black tea.

There's a smell of hand soap in the air. Cashmere Bouquet.

Plates are stacked in the plate-warmer over the woodstove. No food in sight other than bread and molasses. Maybe some food on the back window ledge. The butter sits in a basin of cold water.

Emer can't sit still.

Neither can Bella in her dark corner.

Memère is solid. Present, like the maple out front, its vast leaves offering shelter. She cradles her tea, enjoying momentary sips. Her skin is wizened, weathered like tree bark with its dark brown furrows and crevices.

Emer suddenly feels cold and small.

Grandmère is large. Take it or leave it! Life is what life is. It's hard to swallow sometimes, but that's what it is. It is what it is.

Emer fights with this. "Where is the freedom in that?"

"Ah," says Grandmère, looking away. "Let go. Go with it."

She points to the river through the window and makes a rolling gesture. "Let it take you. Life will show you."

"But I want to do what I want to do."

"Do it then, and let that show you. Nothing is wasted. Nothing. Our answers are all present. For all of us. Everywhere. All the time."

"But you see how I can't sit still with you."

"Are you excited?"

Emer nods.

"Then use it."

"Can I?"

"Yes. Excitement is a feeling. That's all. Feelings are pure energy and can be changed. If you have the intention to change it. *L'intention est clef.*" Intention is key.

"How?"

"By simply willing it so. *Le vrai dialogue est avec soi.*" "The real dialogue is with oneself," she says softly in English.

In her head, Emer understands her great-grandmother. The real dialogue is with oneself. It's simple enough for her to understand. How and when to implement it would be another question. Another time. Another place.

"*J't'embrasse, Memère! J't'embrasse!*" In gratitude she kisses her.

The old lady's hands go up.

Palms flat out.

No emotion.

And she goes some place else.

She said, "*Quand c'est fini, c'est fini.*" When it's finished, it's finished.

The bare wood floorboards creak with her weight as she slowly climbs back up the stairs. Emer looks around the empty room. A cold water tap, a bucket under the drain, and an outhouse on the edge of the swamp.

The audience is over.

Sunlight streams through the small window. She notices that it rests on the chair where Memère Tombeau sat.

Bella slips out the front door into the brilliant sunlight. She squints at Maman sitting on the bench and beams her approval, though she hasn't understood all of it.

Emer appears from the side door. Both women embrace her. "*C'était bien?*" It was good?

"Yes," she breathes. "*C'était bien.*"

⁂

When she returns to the cottage, Emer looks in on Granny Longpré in the front bedroom.

She's snoring. Or she's pretending to snore? Hard to say. She's pretty good at pretending, Emer decided. For instance, pretending to see when she couldn't.

"That you, Emer?" she calls. See what I mean? She could see with her eyes shut.

"Yes, Gran."

"Hang on, jus' a minute here." She swings her feet over the edge of the bed and reaches down her dress into her corset.

"Here's some money. I want you to get me a forty of Melcher's now. Go to the Hotel ... an' here's some extra for a bottle of Pepshi. We'll split it and have a talk later. Put the money in your shoe."

Emer walks to the head of the landing, eyes squeezed shut, imitating Alma, deftly avoiding Michael as she squeezes past him.

"Where are you off to?"

"To buy a Pepsi." It was only a half lie. It didn't count.

He calls down the stairs as she rushes out slamming the screen door. "Your mother's over there making some phone calls." The teacher in him bridles. "And next time stand still and listen when I'm addressing you!"

"Ah, leave her alone. There'll be time enough to stand still when she hits my age," Alma sighs.

"Did you give her money to buy a bottle?"

Alma takes off her glasses and rubs the bridge of her nose as if it was a bump that needed a vigorous massage. God, would no one ever leave her alone? She couldn't turn around without some member of the family breathing down her neck. "She's getting me a bottle of Pepshi."

Michael decides to accept what she says at face value. He could take her to task, but not today. It's her sixty-ninth birthday. They're organizing a surprise party for her.

Spur of the moment thing. Bella's calling friends in Ottawa to come. It's not a good day for a quarrel over her drinking habits. Bella, in any case, is ordering a barrel of beer from the Hotel. A glass of beer won't do the old lady any damage. So he thinks. They'd water hers down with ginger ale. She'd never know the difference. He claps his hands and rubs them together.

Michael could be naive that way.

Celebration's in the air! August twentieth and countdown till classes start in September. Anticipation. The smell of autumn and new beginnings! Lots of ground to cover between now and then. He looks at his grandmother and braces himself for the right moment.

Alma feels Michael's energy hovering over the bed.

She braces herself too. "You happy you?"

Now is not the moment.

"Great! Just great!" he says, disappearing down the hallway.

THE WORLD'S FAIR

Emer sneaks under the saloon doors so as not to disturb the customers. She doesn't want to be noticed, particularly by her mother. Buying a bottle of liquor for Gran is not what she would have wanted.

Emer whispers her order to the bartender, no doubt one of her mother's distant cousins. She doesn't know this one. While he fiddles his time looking on the shelves for the gin, she leans backwards to catch sight of her. There is Irene Dunne in Anna's kitchen on the telephone, which is high up on the wall, shouting into the mouthpiece. Because after all it's long distance, don't you know!

Wilfrid, her husband, is cooking dinner for the six children while Anna controls them with a floppy pink flyswatter in one hand and a lacrosse stick in the other. Lots of shouting for *patates frites*. Which apparently are being fried up anyways. So what are they all shouting about? As she sneaks back under the doors someone plays Tino Rossi on the jukebox.

"Ama-polaaa...."

Silently she wishes her mother well. Above the din of the squabbling children, she imagines the plaintive love-song travelling across the Gatineau and well into the Ottawa River.

"Here you are, Gran," she says, placing the bottles on the washstand.

"Where's my change?"

Emer offers it boldly. "I forgot."

"Forgot, eh?" Alma fingers her change shrewdly. "What's this? That's not a dime. It's a red cent. You'd dare rob your old–"

Emer is paralyzed with fear. "Oh no, Granny! It's here ... I forgot...."

Alma presses Emer's head to her chest. "You know, I love you. You can rob people who can see, child—they can defend themselves and call you on it." She held her tightly for a moment. "But never a blind person. Will you remember that?"

Emer blanches, looks at her, and nods.

"I said will you remember that?"

"Yes, Gran.... Sorry, Gran."

"Good. Now you can have half of this Pepshi.... Drink it now. Only half."

Emer gulps the sweet, sticky liquid. It makes her mouth pucker.

"Is it half yet?"

"Yes." She wipes her mouth with the back of her hand.

"Then give it here. Tell me when, now. I don't want to pour it to spilling...."

"It's ... when."

Alma puts the Pepsi by her bed and the gin under her mattress, then opens the window a crack. At that moment a draft slams the door shut. "Emer, are you gone?"

She shakes her head but keeps her distance and her silence.

"The little divil: wait till I get aholt of her next time. Slammin' the door indeed! Ahhh, nobody cares. I'll pull her nose as long as my arm. Nobody really cares." Alma starts to snore.

Emer tiptoes closer.

"Ahhh, you're a long time dead ... an' ... an' ... paddle your own canoe." The last syllable gives her a start. "Ah Lord. Talkin' in m'cups again."

She leans over her to catch all the words.

"Old Horace's a blessed jewel. Kinder to me than me own flesh and blood. Hope Silvy doesn't find out where I am. Ahh, let her. I don't care anymore. But there's still a heap o' fight in me yet. They'll see they can't shift me around like baggage."

Emer steps back quickly as Alma sits up in the bed. She gently lets her feet touch the floor. Leaning over the washstand she takes a handkerchief and silver snuff box out of the drawer.

She takes a pinch, and waits for the sneeze. After it comes she lies back. "Ah, tha's what I needed."

Emer is mystified.

"Can think better now. I'm ready for anything. Bring on the gaddammed cat!"

The chugging of Monsieur Séguin's little yacht going to pick up passengers on the Ottawa side fills the room. Emer gently turns the door handle and lets herself out. Let the birthday party begin!

CHAPTER EIGHTEEN

The Arrivals

MONSIEUR SÉGUIN SITS on the balustrade of his spacious porch. His eagle's nest. He scans the clouds. Thick black clouds. Not a good day for ferrying people across the water. Summer lightning threatens. It doesn't look good.

His wife hands him a shot glass of rum.

The five-o'clock crossing would be just before his supper hour. Not a boat on the Gatineau. He knocks the amber liquid back with a loud, guttural "Ahhhh!" When he focuses the binoculars on the Ottawa shore, he's surprised. *"Y en a du monde là bas!"* Lots of people over there! It was only Wednesday and there was a crowd. The weekends were always crowded with people coming over for a drink, but today? With an oncoming storm? Didn't they know any better? "Aghh, city people!"

He lifts his yachtsman cap and scratches his head. "Well, they're waiting for me. Might as well move."

On the Ottawa side, Bert and his wife Lil stand by the water's edge. She wears a large natural straw hat with a few daisies under the brim. Her long brown hair streams from under the hat. She wants to see Michael again, now that he's out of the San. Mo isn't with them. He's at another yo-yo contest, where he won a typewriter the previous day.

Lil looks up apprehensively. "I hope those clouds don't crack open when we're crossing. Feels like it's going to be an electric storm."

Bert skips stones along the water's edge. "It'll probably pass. I hear the boat starting up now."

Silent buddy-boy Rex fidgets alongside him. His commissioned officer's hat and blues become him, but he isn't the same old sparkling Rex. Bert notices Silvy sitting on a log, sharing a box lunch with a white-haired lady.

Silvy feels the silk rustle of the grey poplars. She shivers. "I hope we aren't on the water when the storm breaks." She silently chants to herself, "Ma will be happy to see me," in the hope that repetition would wash away the fact that she'd put her out of the house.

Maura looks up at the swiftly moving black clouds. "The wind is high enough for it to pass straight over," she replies as she opens the lunch, brushing the crumbs off her blue-flowered crepe dress. It was nice of Silvy to invite her along to Alma's birthday. Without Meg it's easy enough to "let bygones be."

The motorboat hums up to the makeshift wooden dock and cuts out.

"Women and children first!" shouts Rex from nowhere.

Surprised, Bert looks around at him. Geez, the guy's moody. But he shouts back, "Even on thin ice!"

All three women laugh uneasily as they gather up their ankle-length skirts. High waves splash over the dock.

Monsieur Séguin and the two men assist them into the rocking boat one by one.

Shouts of "Watch your step! Watch out!" The river churns into a seething foam of blue-grey whitecaps.

Silvy and Bert greet each other while there are introductions all around. She clutches her tourtière for the party with one hand and shakes hands with the other, teetering from side to side. Maura, Rex, and Lil crisscross hands through everyone else.

THE ARRIVALS

Monsieur Séguin pulls the rope on the engine, eyeing the guy in the Air-Force uniform quizzically. As he guns the motor, an unexpected spray of water showers the passengers sitting at the back. Amid shouts of laughter, someone calls, "Hey! Tell the driver to be more careful! I'm soaking wet!" Above the motor's din are shouts and whistles from midway up the hilly incline.

Flashes of a red coat, khaki pants, and black boots through the trees interspersed with a woman who is running as if on one leg.

"It's Nelson Eddy and Jeanette MacDonald," Bert says. He'd met Michael's next-door neighbours briefly.

At which Rex spontaneously breaks out into an aria:

Rose Marie, I love yooo,

Always thinking of yooo.

Everyone laughs as Les Drake and Jean jump from the edge of the dock into the bobbing boat. Shouts of "Hurrah! You made it!" bounce across the choppy river.

Jean holds the hem of her dress down to hide her bad leg. She clutches a brown paper shopping bag. "We didn't bring June with us," she says volubly, as if everyone knew they had a twelve-year-old daughter. "She's visiting at a friend's cottage."

Les is happy to be off-duty. His Mountie hat slung over his back bobs in the wind.

By the time the boat beaches, the sun's out and there's a rainbow that seems to touch down on either side of the river. Bella and Michael wave from the embankment. Michael sees his mother in the crowd. "What in hell is she doing here?"

Without missing the beat of a wave or a smile, Bella says, "I thought it might be a good idea."

"You didn't consult me first!"

THE WORLD'S FAIR

Bella continues to extend her welcoming smile at the oncoming guests. "It's her mother's birthday!"

Michael's thrown. "Nevertheless, I wish you'd told me."

Before they know it the arrivals are shaking hands and exchanging pleasantries. The small group walks down the narrow road toward the house.

"What's with the Air Force suit?"

Rex kicks the ground. "Thought I'd do it before they made me."

"It's going to get that bad, is it?"

Rex nods and looks out toward the river. Michael casts Bert a glance for confirmation, and finds that he's further away than ever. Maybe if they didn't think about war it wouldn't happen.

Certainly joining up was not an option with a TB background. Michael knew that much.

Rex says, "I understand that DND is looking for people in math and the sciences. You might check into it."

"Here in Ottawa?"

"Ultimately, Quebec. Valcartier, that is."

"National Defence is it?"

Rex suddenly breaks rank, feinting a sparring match. "You're looking good!"

Joining him, Michael laughs. "So are you."

Rex stops for a moment to light his pipe. After a puff, he looks up and down the road at the little village. "You'd never know that we're on the edge of a war here," he says. "Never been here before. Bit of a time warp, a step backwards in time."

"They're mainly Bella's relatives," says Michael stiffly.

"That so? A segment of the Algonquin tribe, you know. Canoed down the river in the late eighteen hundreds. Some walked. They had to cut down the forest to build." He nodded toward the fringe of houses sitting on the edge of the swamp. "They were Algonquin dissidents, from Maniwake," he continues, "and they came here a number of years before the inception of the Canadian Industrial Paper Mill in Gatineau Mills. They followed the Gatineau River down to where the jobs were. Entrepreneurial bunch!"

The old history professor. "A segment of the Anicinaabe group." Michael smiles, remembering his friends capacity for historical data.

Rex knocks the tobacco out on his heel. "Yes. It figures! They build bridges too. Great people. They're not afraid of heights or water. They love to work at jobs that involve their feet and a sense of balance. Like the Incas....that is to say, not afraid of danger."

Michael casts a glance at Bella to see if she'd heard. She hadn't. "They own that hotel there, at the end of the road," he says.

Rex smiles. "Selling liquor to the Ottawans, huh?"

"Everyone comes over here for a drink on weekends."

He laughs. "I wonder what the law thinks it's prohibiting."

"Seems it's all perfectly legal."

Rex pulls on his pipe. "On this side of the Gatineau."

When they reach the house, Silvy puts her tourtières down on a garden table. "Where's Ma?" She wants to get the meeting over with. The sooner the better.

Michael, on his way to the beer barrel, says, "In the house."

Bella watches the activity from a distance, but also keeps an eye on the clouds as they bounce over the face of the sun, which is drying the heat of the late afternoon. She welcomes the guests to the hors d'oeuvres under the parasol.

"Here," Jean Drake says, thrusting the paper bag in Bella's hands, "I made you some hats."

Bella is delighted. "Thank you."

"You can give one to your birthday lady on my behalf."

Jean pops an hors d'oeuvre in her mouth. "Did you make these?"

"Let's say I assembled them."

"Mmmm, what is it?" asks Lil as she munches.

"It's cheddar cheese whipped up with home-made mayonnaise and dill."

"But the cracker?"

Bella twinkles at the culinary talents that Pierre had taught her. "It's my own secret recipe."

The beer is passed around in tankards. Horace's antique tankards with hinged lids.

Rex rotates the mug in his hand. "Nice piece."

"Glad there's somebody here to appreciate it," Michael says.

Les Drake eyes his mug. "They're quaint, aren't they!"

"Wake up, you clown. They're from Yurrup!" Jean says.

"Belgium, to be precise," Michael says.

Lil pretends to be interested. "Where's that?"

Jean knocks back a long draught and lets the lid on the mug snap shut. "In the Alps, where else?"

Bert ambles over from the barrel. "You're thinking of Bavaria, maybe?"

She waves her mug at him. "So who the hell cares?"

Rex blows smoke rings at the mosquitoes. "You might, in time."

Les gulps his beer down. "Well we're going back to the States. I'm a non-interventionist! Handed in my resignation this morning."

Jean winks at Bella. "Yes, we're going to try our luck in Chicago this time."

THE ARRIVALS

Bert sidles over to Michael: "The Peter Pan syndrome."

Michael studies the American couple. Avoidance? Clinging to the irresponsibility of youth? Making it work in their favour when the chips are down? He can relate to it, but he isn't sure he approves. It lacks altruism.

Rex holds forth. "No, I don't think it's the Peter Pan syndrome. Isolationism, as we all know, has been in effect ever since the arrival of the pilgrims to Plymouth Rock. Question is, how appropriate will the non-involvement US policy be in the light of the oncoming threat from Germany? Roosevelt's at the helm now. Let's see what he does with it."

All conversation stops. Heads turn to listen to more. There's an imperceptible hush.

Suddenly all the attention is focused on Rex, who turns to Les. "So you're going to Chicago, Les, is that right?"

Michael admires Rex's sense of diplomacy.

"That's right," says Les.

Without pursuing the matter any further Rex hops up onto the veranda and sings,

> Chicago! Chicago!
> That wonderful town.
> Chicago, Chicago,
> I'll show you around.
> I knew a man once
> Danced with his wife.
> In Chicago, Chicago,
> My hometown!

He sings to the end of the song, executing a snappy dance step to accompany it.

They all applaud and sing with him.

THE WORLD'S FAIR

Silvy opens the door to see what the commotion is about. The action tips Rex over the porch onto the grass. He somersaults in mid-air and lands on his back, tankard in one direction, pipe in another. Everyone gasps. The mug hits Lil on the side of the head, knocking her hat off.

No one knows who to rush to first.

Bella bumps into Jean. Beer spills down the front of their light summery dresses. Les suddenly comes to rigid attention.

Maura picks up the hat with the flowers. She hands it back to Lil. "Your hat protected you."

Lil rubs her shining bald head in a daze. "Yes, I think so."

"You're lucky you weren't knocked out by the blow," says Jean, to cover her laughter.

They all gather round while Rex moans, "Ohhh, my operation!"

"What operation?" Michael asks.

"I just had my appendix out ten days ago and the stitches are still healing."

Michael helps him up. "Let's go in the house and put your feet up."

Silvy runs around them in circles, shouting, "You'll be fine, you'll be just fine!"

The party walks into the house.

Alma sits at the kitchen table pouring tea into a teacup. She's playing chess with Emer. Bella runs to the shed to chip a piece off the ice-block. Lil ties her hat under her chin, still looking very pale. "What a sweet old lady," she remarks to Bert, attempting to cover her embarrassment, "drinking tea while the rest of us are drinking beer."

Rex sits in a chair groaning. "Oooh, my incision!"

Alma sips from her teacup. "What incision?"

He holds his side, his face contorted. "Here, do you want to see it?"

"Show it to me."

Rex pulls his shirttail out of his trousers. "There, look. Is it okay?"

The old lady whips her glasses off and makes a pretense of looking. Her nose is as close to it as she can get. "Looks healthy enough to me."

"Are you sure?"

She stands up. "Sure I'm sure. Here, do you want to see what I've got?" She starts to unbutton the top of her dress.

The room is silent. Emer, head down, moves her knight forward. "It's your move, Gran."

Rex stands up, to come in for a closer look.

Emer covers her eyes. "It's your move, Gran!" she shouts forcefully.

Undeterred, Alma takes a swipe in mid-air at what she presumes is his head. "You dirty pup! You dirty young pup for even thinking I'd show you."

Silvy breaks through the guests, shouting, "Ma, Ma, that's enough now!"

Outside, Bert mutters, "Well, Rex certainly asked for that one."

Everyone breaks out into nervous laughter.

Bella slips Lil a piece of ice, which she slides under her hat.

Bert's complexion is as grey as Lil's. "That's right," he whispers nervously, "keep some ice on it."

She drapes the tea-towel around her neck as a scarf and mops up the melt-down around her neck with an air of grace.

Attempting to hide his distress, Michael motions Bert to the edge of the porch. "What the hell's going on?"

Bert takes a step back as if he's astonished by the question. "What do you mean?"

"You know damn well what I mean."

Bert looks pained. "No, I don't."

Drained, Michael sits on the grass. "Jesus, Bert, can't you see it?"

"You mean from the blow?"

"No, no, not that. She's not well. Can't you see it?" he says in shock.

"She lost her hair because of the treatment. We're hoping that she's getting better now."

"But why have you never mentioned it?"

Rex comes tumbling out of the house with Lil by the hand and Silvy fast behind them. "That's quite a grandmother you have there, Michael. She's drinking straight cognac out of the teapot!"

Michael hides his displeasure with a grin. "It's her birthday, why not?"

Rex swings Lil's hand at them. "Some surprise party! I hope I live long enough to pull that kind of a number. Drinking cognac at sixty-nine."

Bert winces. "I hope we all do."

Rex straightens his jacket and looks at Lil. "Well I say let's all go have a shot of that on me at the Hotel."

Silvy bites her lips. "Michael, if you're going to do that, you better lock Ma in the house. Just to keep her safe. She's had too much to drink. She could walk right out of there into the road."

Sometimes she made sense. "Yes, I'll do that."

Bella clears the food off the table. "Zack's upstairs asleep. We won't be long, will we? Let's take Emer with us."

"No," she interjects, "I would like to stay here with Aunt Maura and Gran."

As Rex propels Lil toward the Queen's he shouts from the road, "Bring your umbrella, professor, it could rain!"

Maura sits in a deck chair and watches the black clouds moving overhead. "I'll sit here with Emer. Bella, you go on ahead." Silvy agrees that she'd do the same.

Emer comes out of the house. Michael locks the door behind her, calling, "We'll just be gone for a few minutes, Gran! Be right back!" He was eager to question Rex on his travels. Had he gone to South America? Had he seen the wholistic urban construction of Emperor Pachacuti? The Alexander the Great of 15th century Peru. The city dedicated to survive the torrential embrace of the elements. In a word the sacred.

The two women are left to sit under a tree. Emer sits on the grass by Aunt Maura's feet.

Silvy claps her hands in the manner of a delighted child. "Now tell me where in the whole world do you want to visit?"

Emer thinks for a moment and then says, "Peru." That's where her father had promised he'd take them, because of the dry climate in the mountains.

Silvy's face is flushed with excitement. "Is there any place else?"

Maura holds Emer's hand while she thinks. Not that she particularly needs to have her hand held, but it has a nice feel to it. A bastion of warmth. It feels good to have their attention focused on her.

Silvy persists. "Well?"

Emer remembers. She draws a ball and a tower in the earth with a stick. "I want to see that."

Silvy shouts, "That's it! That's it! We're going to New York to see exactly that!" She grabs Emer by the hands and swings her round and round in the air.

She puts her down and hugs her. "That's where we're going, my darling!"

The prospect of going to New York overshadows any sense of cloyingness Emer otherwise felt.

"I'll even make you a dress. A sailor dress." She had it all laid out and planned.

"When? When are we going, Gran?"

"The soonest I can make it is the first weekend after you've started school. Friday the seventh. How does that suit you?"

Emer hugs her. "Wonderful, Gran!"

An unexpected bolt of lightning illuminates them in its purple light. A deafening clap of thunder comes with it. The storm breaks over them in heavy drops as they run for cover under a tree. Thunder and lightning crash once more. The storm is directly overhead. "This is not a safe place to be," Maura says.

Silvy wrings the edges of her dress. "Let's run for the house."

"It's locked," Emer shouts above the storm.

Maura takes Emer's hand. "Under the parasol, by the veranda. Let's run for it!"

Closer in to the house they can hear banging on the other side of the door and Alma's voice. "Open up, you sonsabitches. Open up and let me out of here. How dare you lock me in, in my own house?"

They hear the rattle of the front glass as she pounds her fists.

Silvy runs up the stairs. "Hold on, Ma. Be patient. We'll unlock it. It was for your own safety."

Maura holds Emer tightly in her arms.

Emer can see her father's black umbrella undulating up and down through the shimmering sheets. "They're coming back!" she shouts.

"Your father's got the key and he's on the road now! The party's returning," Silvy says in a reassuring tone, though inside she wonders what her mother might do next. There's silence on the other side of the door. Silvy presses her ear to it, to hear what's happening. Apparently nothing. All quiet.

Maura calls to her. "Come away. Come away from there."

Pellets of hail the size of large peas start to clatter on the veranda and against the glass door. It makes loud pinging sounds like musical notes. Mixed in with the musical notes are the shattering notes of broken glass scattering in a deluge of diamond fragments onto the front veranda.

Lightning flashes across the front of the house. They all duck their heads. When they look up, they see Alma, black gown and beads, step through the aperture with her hand in a large vase. The sky thunders directly overhead.

She thumps her chest with her fist and shouts, "Go on, strike me dead! I dare you!" She waves her fist at the lightning. "Go on, I dare you!"

The birthday partiers stand dripping in the rain, gaping at her.

Rex emits a low whistle and whispers, "Nothing like smashing etched glass."

Alma's hearing is acute. "So what? I broke a pattern. So what?"

Michael runs up the porch steps. "That's enough now, Gran, I'm home."

"Don't touch me!" she screams over the thunder. "Don't you dare lay a hand on me."

"Okay! Okay! But let's go inside."

She fixes her unseeing eyes in his direction. "Going off and locking me in, indeed! Are you crazy?"

Michael casts a glance at his mother.

Silvy trembles under the parasol. "She's in her cups," she whispers.

"Everything's all right now," he says. "We're going inside."

"Don't you use that patronizing tone with me, mister!" She throws her vased arm up at the sky and waves her other fist in a threatening gesture. The guests stand riveted. Emer can't help noticing. It appears that Gran's menacing them. Maura holds Emer to her. Silvy silently cries into her wet handkerchief. The crunch of broken glass and hail underfoot makes it slippery.

Michael catches Alma just as she's about to go down. He gathers her up and brings her into the house. The storm begins to subside. However, the tempest within the hearts of the immediate family is barely contained.

They stand around drenched, staring at each other vacantly. Finally, it's Rex who gives everyone the high sign to go back. Silvy and Maura see them off at the pier with Emer.

On the way back, in the drizzle, Silvy squeezes Emer's hand. "Don't forget, you and me, we're going to see the World's Fair."

Emer has a hard lump in her throat. She feels badly that the party ended on such a sour note. "Yes, I know, Gran. I won't." But her eyes fill up as she waves back to the departing guests from the embankment above the churning waters.

By the time they get back to the house there's a light spray in the air, shot through with earth smells of freshness. The shattered glass lies in mounds like mica chips on the veranda. Silvy and Maura exchange doleful expressions. Silvy walks toward the back shed. "I'll get the broom and clean up this mess."

Maura sits under the parasol and waits. For what or for whom? No matter. She waits. Ever present. Emer pulls away to sit on the porch steps. She smells the comforting aroma of coffee. Sounds of quiet sobbing from the upstairs bedroom. It's her mother. It makes Emer feel sad to hear her crying. Zack has apparently slept through the whole scene. Her father and Gran are in the kitchen. Their silence is total.

Her father stands on the threshold. "I'll clear this mess up later so that you can get in," he says.

She watches as he walks down the long dark hallway into the lighted kitchen. His back fills the doorway. He gives Gran a cup of coffee. As he leans over her, he asks, "Who is my father?"

She replies, "Toussaint."

Silence.

The name crashes around in his head. It can't be. The truth hits him like a riptide sweeping him off his feet.

"My uncle?"

Alma nods.

"My mother's brother?"

Silence.

Emer sees her father crumple into a chair. Sobbing, he holds his head in his hands. Silvy stands in the back doorway, her hand over her mouth in horror. The memory she has tried so hard to keep at bay slowly floods into her brain, blotting her sensibilities. Her body wavers as she slumps on the threshold with bowed head.

Alma continues, "I couldn't stop them. I could not put a stop to it. I tried everything. She thought I didn't know. Still thinks so."

Emer hears her father say, "I'm so ashamed."

"Why? You didn't do it. Silvy no more asked for it than he did. It happened. And it happened whenever my back was turned. They were children. First she had Andrea and then you. You, she fobbed off on John Maguire, which was a joke in its own way. Not that I see it as funny now. But hell, being a woman without a means of supporting oneself is a challenge that no man can understand. She had to do something. So she married John as a cover. The marriage didn't work. Obviously, how could it? That's all. I helped her as best I could without letting her know that I knew it all. We all have our pride. I let her have hers as best I could, which perhaps wasn't always my best shot. But I tried." She waves a long, bony finger at Michael. "An' if I'd to do it over again, I would."

Michael looks at his mother. He doesn't know whether he wants to shout obscenities at her or console her sobs. He feels his stomach churning. His heart pounds in his head. He looks through the smashed-out front door. The river is still there. Still flowing. How strange. Life goes on? How come? How could it, when the world, his world, has stopped? Where to go from here? "How shall I begin to spit out all the butt ends of my days and ways? And how shall I presume?" Eliot? Am I thinking T.S. Eliot at a time like this? What else? What else is there to think about? I feel numb.

He hears Tom's voice whispering by his ear. "Pranayama, Michael, Pranayama." Breathe? Why? Conscious breathing is for people who have something to live for. What's there to breathe for? It's a mess. My life is a mess. Where to go from here? This cannot be fixed! It's what I have to live with. Waves of shame run through him like an electric current. His mother's sobs fill the room, and with it, surges of violent rage from his belly. His roaring spent, he stares out the doorless doorway in the silence that exhaustion brings. He knows that the wall is down between them, but the clarity of the view is overpowering. He doesn't know if he can handle it. He clenches and unclenches his fists in an attempt to control his temper.

The seed of his rage is born.

Michael looks at Emer sitting out on the front steps with mounds of sharp glass between them. It's in the blood line. How appalling. The sins of the father are visited unto the seventh generation, Father Bruneau intones. How far back had it gone? How far ahead would it move? Not any distance if he could help it.

"Where's Bella?" he says thickly.

"She's upstairs, Dad."

Emer watches him move like an old man to the foot of the stairs.

Silvy rises as if coming out of a deep sleep.

"Bella, I want you to come down here, please."

Bella holds the edge of the banister in pain, barely able to walk.

"Did you hear that?"

Bella nods that she did.

Michael seats her opposite him at the kitchen table with Alma and Silvy. His voice is hoarse. "What we know now will not move on into our children's lives." He looks at Emer darkly.

Emer is expressionless. The inside of her head is white-hot lead. Heavy and light at the same time, it floats above her shoulders. She hears the words, but they are only words. Sounds, but no reality. The gravity of her father's tone tells her that something is wrong. Questions. She has a lot of unformulated questions. She understands that whatever Gran has said impacts her father in such a way that she wants to run inside and throw her arms around him. Fear stands in her way. Fragmented glass between her and her father. The good thing is that finally his bad dreams are over, she thinks. That's a relief. But does that mean his good ones are over too? The solving of Fermat's last theorem? The prize money? Peru? A jumble of questions fight within her to be heard.

Bella sees Emer's thoughts flickering across her face.

Silvy's sobs travel through the doorway to the river.

Michael rises and walks toward the aperture. When he sees Maura still present, he feels that he wants to die. He looks at her woefully.

Maura knows his thoughts. "It was an accident," she says. "The whole thing was an accident from beginning to end."

"This?" he asks, nodding his head toward the kitchen.

"Yes. They were children when it happened. Things could have been worse."

"Are we saying they didn't know any better?"

"It was unconscious."

Michael thinks for a moment. "You've known it all along."

"Yes."

"How?"

"Toussaint."

Michael looks at her in bewilderment. "Really?"

"That's right."

Michael hangs onto the door jamb.

"You could have been our son."

With glazed eyes Michael looks at her. "I killed him."

Maura stands up with resolution. "I saw you. That was pure accident."

Michael is horrified. "You saw me?"

Maura nods.

"But I hated him."

"You may have, but it was not your intention to kill him. You were being the mischievous boy that you were."

"I thought I was being funny."

"You were being the prankster that you've always been and still are. That was Toussaint in you!"

"If you knew all this, why didn't you tell me?"

"You had to first get it from its source. And you did. Alma," she says quietly.

"I need time to absorb this."

Maura smiles. "Join the human race, Michael," she whispers softly. "We've all got a lifetime to absorb our experience of life."

The blur that had been the river comes into Michael's view. "All of this may take a couple of lifetimes."

⁓

In the upstairs bedroom Bella kneels by the front window. She rests her eyes on the flowing Gatineau River. So near she can almost touch it.

She inhales deeply, supported by the fresh breezes after the storm. The Chaudière Falls are a ten-minute row-boat distance away. She doesn't have to think it. She knows it.

The Falls affirm her love of validating the sacred.

The Creator's Pipe, *les Chutes de la Chaudière*, is still there. Nothing has changed.

Her heart swells with pride and joy.

Grandmère Tombeau takes her. *"Viens on va y'aller."*

They go when she's old enough, after she has lost her three sisters and then again after her arm has been broken.

Together they row on the Ottawa, or the "Outaouais," as Grandmère names it. Nature's boundary line between Quebec and Ontario. They row through the swift currents to the mist-engulfed

Horseshoe Falls. The power of the roaring rush of waters combined with the fog knocks the breath out of her. They dock the boat. She accompanies Grandmère closely as she climbs to a high promontory to throw her blessed tobacco leaves, an offering to the swirling waters. An offering for the healing of all creatures.

As they return home together Grandmère explains. "Great amounts of water flow through an underwater cavern there, and that's the pipe-bowl part of it. It re-energizes the downstream. The narrowness of the river represents the narrowness of the pipe stem where it meets the bowl." After a pause she says, "It's a powerful healing place."

Bella nods in awe.

Revisiting the joining of the pipe and the stem from the window, she allows herself to feel the power of its strength.

Silently, she whispers Grandmère's words, "For the healing of everyone, everywhere."

The energy downstairs had not gone unnoticed.

CHAPTER NINETEEN

Epilogue

THEY RETURN TO PROSPECT STREET on Friday, August 31st, the weekend before school starts. The street is teeming with energy as usual, but Emer isn't excited about being back. Her father is in a state of dismal apathy.

The vegetable peddler is conducting good enough business on the street, though. The end of the season has brought in a bumper crop, judging from the overladen wagon. There are crowds around his cart shouting prices down to a penny a bunch or a pound. They walk away with boxes and bags crammed full of vegetables and fruits that would be stored for autumn and winter.

Jocelyn-Gosselin-with-the-ringlets hauls away a basket of huge tomatoes in one hand and bunches of carrots in the other. Her sausage curls bob up and down on her shoulders as she scrambles out of the crowd. She reminds Emer of Madame Pompadour in *The Three Musketeers*, but somehow the romance of both the novel and Jocelyn has evaporated. Where, Emer can't tell.

June Drake lounges on her front porch eating pink candy floss with one hand, playing jacks with the other, and watching the crowd through thick glasses.

As they pull up to the curb, Emer notices that the oak leaves in front of their house are beginning to turn a crisp orange and brown. Poupoune is standing tall in the tree as if she'd always been there, waiting for her to come back. The unexpected vision is a heartening sight. But when she gets out of the taxi, Poupoune vanishes. Percy and Arnie are on their front porch counting out their pencils, scribblers, and books. Ho hum. Humdrum.

Michael walks around the house in a somnambulistic state. The truth is harder to digest than all the questions he's ever lived with. He tries to prepare his lessons, but his heart isn't in it. Fermat's last theorem is dusted off and silently tucked into the bottom drawer of his desk. "For future reference," he says in a miasma of vagueness. "So much for the Master's degree." "For now," he adds as an afterthought.

Emer is disappointed in her father. She wonders about the negative feelings that hover in every corner of the house. How would Grandmère Tombeau respond to them?

Emer feels as if Grandmere Tombeau is in the room with her. "Feelings are pure energy and can be changed. Intention is key." If she could somehow get this idea across to her father. His grief is infectious. Even Zack looks sad.

To kill time Michael takes to sculpting pieces of wood. A completed piece stands proudly on the windowsill.

"What do you think?" he asks Emer.

She had a few art lessons while in hospital. She looks at it. It's a globe of the world resting on a footstool.

"It's not in proportion," she says. "The world is larger than the stool can carry."

Michael shrugs. "Perhaps so … perhaps so."

The violin resonates throughout the house. They're all gut-wrenching pieces. Emer can't bear to listen to them.

Finally, with some money that Alma gave him, he buys a telescope and occupies himself with the study of astrology. His grandmother's response had either derailed him totally or set his

EPILOGUE

wheels back on track. He wasn't sure which. Certainly the telescope took him off planet earth, if only for a while. It was a good way of getting a rest from emotional chaos within.

Silvy packs up the cottage for the winter months. Alma is back into her middle-of-the- road mode again. The drinking has subsided, and consequently Silvy has taken her mother back with her to the Beechwood house, with Maura's approval. Meg would no doubt go into a furor, but that was her problem. Alma wanted to leave the cottage on the Gatineau open for the autumn for the family's use, but Silvy said Michael would be teaching, and she was taking Emer to the World's Fair for two weeks in the fall.

Whenever Emer walks past his bedroom, Michael is bent over the tripod, exclaiming about the wonders of the universe … the dark patches on the face of the moon, the nearness of Mars.

It's either that or the violin, or sculpting. His engagement in these activities continues until he starts back to teaching. The distraction of teaching then substitutes for the other distractions. His way of coping with his pain. That aspect hasn't changed, with the one exception: he engages himself knowingly.

His magic tricks become more and more polished, and he gives dazzlingly professional performances, especially on birthdays. He dabbles in hypnotism, and works on Bella for a while, but she's an unwilling subject. He even tries ventriloquism with hand puppets. He's good at it but it doesn't grab him enough to pursue it. Edgar Bergen was doing a good enough job with his puppet on Sunday night radio.

Every night Zack and Emer sit up and watch "the Show" before bed. Michael has turned an old butter box into a puppet theatre. He turns all the lights out except two small table lamps on either side of the "Puppet Theatre" on the dining room table. Christmas tree lights serve as footlights and a spotlight defines stage centre. The script varies from night to night. One memorable night he plays a fight between Sneezy and Dopey over the love of Snow White. He teaches Zack and Emer how to make their puppet heads out of papier mâché with newspapers and flour. Bella sews the costumes.

With great panache, he pulls out his violin and begins the production with a short overture, then ducks behind the stage to be the puppeteer.

SNEEZY (whistling and sneezing): Now where is that old Dopey? I hope he isn't out having fun with my Snow White. He better not be or I'll bop him one. (looking behind bushes for DOPEY) Let me catch him, just once! (sneeze)

DOPEY (yawning and stretching, not seeing SNEEZY): I'll bet that Sneezy has been wondering where we were. OHO-HO! (whispering to audience) I took Snow White by boat across the river so that he will never see her again. But don't *you* tell him. I'll just hide and wait for him in the bushes here. (so saying he backs into SNEEZY)

SNEEZY: AHA! So there you are! Where is my girl?

DOPEY: She isn't yours, she's mine!

SNEEZY (runs for a stick in bushes): The heck you say!

DOPEY (picks up a stick and shouts): On guard! (they fight, lots of pratfalls, gasping, and struggling to the death)

SNOW WHITE (her face appears over the bushes): Now boys, do stop it, for heaven's sake! (they continue to fight) If you don't stop I will go far away and never come back!

The puppets get into intense dialogue while Snow White,

EPILOGUE

played by Michael with a blonde pigtailed wig, comes between them and tries to part them in their conflict.

After these shows they always go to bed willingly, with hearty guffaws. His improvisations are cathartic. Good therapy for everyone.

Even Bella stands watching the show in the kitchen doorway, tea towel in hand.

The radio in the Truro Apartments continues to blare as it had before they left. This time it isn't music so much as the news of the day. The announcer's tone is ominous. Dark. "This is the BBC from London." The British Broadcasting Corporation. Pure, round, authoritative vowel sounds. Striking terror in the heart. People walk slowly past the Truro on their way home from work. Heads down. Listening.

Monsieur Larocque sits on his front porch as ever, picking his teeth with a matchstick. Grinning.

The rabbi attacks the Torah with renewed vigour as he stands in front of his bookstand, chanting a lament by the open window. Sometimes the wailing rabbi and the radio announcer coincide. When that happens, people scurry past the commotion as quickly as they can. Windows are gently lowered. This world of confusion is of a different variety than the personal one that they're accustomed to, and so goes largely unrecognized. Everyone stands around helplessly, allowing the world's chaos to live its life. They don't know what else to do.

Monsieur and Madame Larocque go indoors after sunset. The only thing that can be seen of them is slow motion movement on the other side of the thick lace curtains. Emer has to strain her eyes through the mesh to see them. They grope around the furniture in the dark.

Monsieur Chapelle grins through it all, as is his usual habit. He parrots the popular refrain, "*C'est pas notre guerre.*" It's not our war. Not because he believes it, but because he has not yet formulated an opinion of his own.

Through it all, Madame Gosselin shakes her carpets with vehemence and batters them with a broom for good measure. Getting ready for the long, hard winter ahead.

The Drakes are packing already. One foot out the door, preparing to leave for Chicago. June whines, "But I don't want to leave here." In the ensuing days their confusion can be heard across the laneway with loud swearing and broken dishes.

The biggest change was with the Sarrazins. Poupoune's family. Emer goes to check them out through the broken slats at the back. All is quiet.

A new family has moved into their back shed. She sees through the half-open shed door that they had wallpapered the walls with newspapers. Protection, she guesses, against the cold in autumn and winter. Not that it would do much good as insulation, but it fills in the cracks between the barn boards. Emer sees a baby and two young children. One is still crawling. The interior of the shed is strung with a clothesline that dips dangerously close to the earth floor with the weight of wet diapers.

A man appears in the doorway. "*Qu'est-ce que tu regardes?*" What are you staring at?

Emer is embarrassed. "*Rien.*" Nothing.

"*Ben on n'est pas à vendre!*" We're not for sale! "Scram!"

Bella happens to see the scene. "C'mon in and have a bite to eat before bed." And with the best support she can, she gives it. "Forget the rudeness. He doesn't really mean it. He's having a hard time. Come to bed. Tomorrow's another day."

EPILOGUE

When Emer climbs into bed and her mother is tucking her in, she hears strange music in the distance. "What's that?"

Bella leans out the window. "It's coming from the bazaar at the corner of King Edward and the next street over. In that empty lot. It's the time of year for bazaars."

"What's a bazaar?"

"It's a cross between a small fair and a small circus."

Emer sits up on her elbows. "What kind of music is that?"

Bella smiles, remembering. "It's calliope music."

"Cal-ee-oh-pee!" She liked the sound of it. "What's that?"

"It's a set of steam whistles activated by a keyboard that forces the sound out. It's the same kind of music they played when I drove around the corral on the Shetland ponies in Sault Ste. Marie. They played it for me when I was small to calm the real horse I was sitting on … and me too, I guess!"

"It's lovely!"

"Yes. They're probably setting it up for the merry-go-round tomorrow."

"But the horses aren't real, right?"

"They've got real hair. But no, they're made of plaster. Painted plaster of Paris."

"I loooove the music,"

Out of nowhere there's the sound of a loudspeaker and a man's voice coming over the system.

Bella sounds resigned. "That's the barker selling his wares on the megaphone. I guess we're going to be hearing that for a while now!" She pulls the quilt up under Emer's chin. "Try to sleep, love."

Emer nods, not minding the noise. It's exciting.

As Bella gently closes the door and goes downstairs, Emer hears her say, "There's no peace at either the front or the back of the house!"

Michael is playing chess in the dining room.

She sits opposite him. "I'd really rather be living in the country."

Studying the "men" on both sides of the board, he says, "Don't know that there'll be any country left by the time we get through the mess we're in right now."

"I mean the 'country' country."

"I know, I know," he says irritably.

World chaos reflects his own inner demise. He knows it. He doesn't yet know how to address it.

The next morning God is barking at Emer on a megaphone. His voice reverberates from one end of Ottawa to the other.

Parliament is not in session yet, but the empty seats in the lower house are quivering even so. Apparently God is hustling the members into a big tent. He wants them to see his wares. He's a man in the sky with a long white beard and He appears very wise. Once inside the tent He picks up a long broom handle and unhooks every picture from the walls in one fell swoop! They lie in several heaps at the Members' feet. They stare vacantly at a collage of their own fragmented images on the floor.

Emer wakes up sweating, but she doesn't tell her father, because she knows it's just fear. No need to worry him on that account.

"It's only a feeling," Grandmère Tombeau had said.

Like passing clouds, Emer thinks.

A voice fills her bedroom. "Collapse. Collapse it! Collapse that platform. You brought the wrong one. Won't work."

The angry voice fills the whole of Ottawa. Maybe even the whole country. It's that loud.

EPILOGUE

"Tighten those guy ropes over there, or those things will come down on our heads, Lee!"

"Testing, testing. One, two, three. Rhubarb, rhubarb. Over and out!" And then, "It's not working, Joe. The right amp's busted."

"Busted?"

"Blown ... whatever."

Emer looks out the window. There are colourful pennants and flags beckoning her to the fair-grounds.

Her father's voice calls up to her. "Emer, it's Saturday. I'm making pancakes. Want some?"

She can hardly wait to get dressed. "Pancakes and maple syrup! Yippee! Thank youoooo!"

Bella moans from her bedroom. "Don't shout, you'll wake Zack. And I'm trying to sleep in."

At the breakfast table Michael says, "Why don't you go watch them setting up?"

"Is that what they call it? Setting up?"

He flips the pancakes in the hot butter. "Yup!"

"How do you know?"

"Because when I was just a few years older than you are now, I got a job with a travelling circus."

"What doing?"

"I sold three balls for a nickel to knock the fat lady over."

"Did you make much money at it?"

"Let's say I broke even."

"How did you get the job?"

The spectre of his misery reappears for an instant. "Your grandmother. Granny Silvy."

She pours syrup over the hot pancakes. "She's pretty good, you know. She's taking me to see The World's Fair."

His Adam's apple bobs a few times. "I know. Tell you what. You go on ahead to see them setting up. I'll stay here and do the dishes."

Emer steps forward, daring it. "Did you know, Dad, that feelings are like clouds passing over the face of your sun?"

Michael smiles at her broadly. "Really? Thanks, lady!"

"I'm out of here," Emer calls. "See you later, Dad."

"Your milk!" he calls.

She gulps it down quickly and ventures out even further. "We're creative, you know, both on Mom's side of the family and yours. Pretty exotic, huh? My intention is to go to Europe and study theatre. What's your intention, Dad?"

Emer is out the door, milk-white moustache and all. Although it's only eight-thirty in the morning, she sees Poupoune already ahead of her. She runs to catch up at the corner.

Her Saturday's brace of chickens hangs over the edge of her covered basket.

"Are you going to sell those at the Fair?"

Poupoune shakes her head. "Noh. I go to Bywar Mark-et."

"When you come back?" Emer thinks that if she speaks in broken English, her friend has a better chance to understand her.

"Dunno. *Jusqu'à ce que je vends tous les poulets.*"

"When you've sold all the chickens?"

Poupoune nods. "*A tantôt.*" See you later.

Tantôt. It sounds like the Lone Ranger's Indian Buddy, Tonto, but she says, "Okay, see you later!"

Poupoune speeds down the long tree-lined boulevard, leaving Emer to explore the fairgrounds on her own. She races across the street right after the breadman's buggy, careful not to step into the horse droppings.

EPILOGUE

The grounds are wide open on all sides. Emer walks around the outer rim. One of the rides reads "CATERPILLAR." The men are testing the speed of the cars and the operational closing of the umbrella over the ride.

A man shouts through a rolled piece of cardboard. "Not dark enough, Joe!"

An exasperated voice mimics him: "Not dark enough, Joe!" Presumably it was Joe. The disembodied voice continues, "Come here, Joe. Go there, Joe. Not good enough, Joe!" Joe is obviously a one-man show.

A man with a megaphone begins. "Step right up, kids. Today is Saturday and all the rides are five cents." He signals to her. "Here, kid! Here's a candy floss for you!"

At the same moment a woman throws three rings at her. "Three throws," she hollers in a Cockney accent. "'Ave a go, luv."

Emer throws all three rings.

"Dead ringers!" the woman shouts. "And 'eres a tawffy apple for you, luv!"

The merry-go-round is still in the set-up stage, but the calliope is pumping its tunes anyway.

There are freak shows in tents at the far end of the lot, but the garish pictures upset her stomach.

Home has started to look good to her. As she makes it over to the middle of the King Edward, she sees Poupoune running toward her with an empty basket. "That was fast. What happened?"

"I sell everything to Bywar' Mark-et!" She claps her hands. "Like that!"

"Like that! Wow!" Emer waves the apple and floss at her. "Here: which one do you choose?"

Poupoune takes the pink floss. "This one."

"Do you want to come back to the fair with me and have a look?"

She taps the pocket of her dress. "No. I go to Routhier's to buy coco-a and *mélasse*."

"Molasses and cocoa powder? For the family?"

She nods, her face nose-deep in the floss. "*Oui*."

Madame Sarrazin welcomes Emer into the house; this time she's wreathed in smiles.

"*Pis?*" she says to Poupoune. "And how did it go?"

Poupoune puts the quart bottle of molasses down on one end of the table, the money on the other, and grandly places the cocoa powder in the middle.

Her mother eyes her. "*C'est quoi ça?*" What's that?

She tilts her chin. "*Du Coco-a.*"

"*Pourquoi? Qui t'a demandé d'acheter ça?*" Why? Who asked you to buy that?

Emer, sensing trouble, ventures forward. "Me. I told her to buy it."

She ignores Emer. "*Ma p'tite chienne! Où on mange de la mélasse ou du Coco-a, mais pas les deux a la fois!*" You little bitch. It's either cocoa or molasses, but we can't afford both at once.

While Madame shouts at Poupoune to decide which one to bring back to the store, Emer tries to hold her balance on the rickety sloping floor. There are squalling babies everywhere, including the new arrivals in the back shed. The stench of urine fills the air, from the steaming diapers in an open cauldron on the wood stove.

The kitchen cabinet, with its open roller doors and drawers, teeters precariously in the middle of the kitchen. Empty. The sticky spiral of flypaper, black with flies, hangs from the light bulb. Madame Sarrazin slaps a mosquito on her upper arm. The blood dribbles

EPILOGUE

down to her elbow. "*Va*," she says, grabbing the cocoa. "Échange-moi ca pour du pain!" Go. Exchange this for bread.

Poupoune ducks behind her candy floss. "You come? I change for bread."

Together they run to Routhier's, and back with the loaf.

There's a lull in the house when they get back.

She whispers, "I show you my room." As they walk up the uneven stairs, she says, "My mother, she rents my room to a woman with baby." She throws open a door. "This is my room."

Emer holds her breath. Afraid to breathe. The room smells of bleach, disinfectant, and Barsalou soap. Poupoune's smell. They are in the bathroom. There are rags on the floor where she sleeps. No pillow.

"It is very good here," she says, letting the floss melt in her mouth. "Very quiet." She stands on the toilet seat and points to the window. "And has beautiful view."

Emer hops on with her, holding on to her tawffy apple.

"Testing, testing. One, two, three. Charlie, Abel, Baker, one. It works! Hey Joe, it works!"

Emer figures that at last Joe must be happy.

A barker's voice immediately begins:

> A loaf of bread
> A pound of meat
> And all the mustard
> You can eat
> For ten cents!

℘

With that the brass fanfare starts up and a rag-taggle group of musicians marches behind a moving truck with cables and a sound

THE WORLD'S FAIR

system. They march up and down King Edward Boulevard with the drummer pulling up the rear. Bong! Thwack! Bong! Thwack!

Emer feels the vibrations of sound in the pit of her stomach.

The Ferris wheel starts to turn, the merry-go-round's coloured horses bobbing up, down, and around to the sounds of the calliope.

"Crank up the sound, Joe! Crank it up!"

Delighted squeals can be heard from under the closed parasol of the Caterpillar ride. Emer feels butterflies in her stomach. The experience is as good as being there. Still on the toilet seat, Poupoune and Emer hold each other by the waist. Emer holds onto the chain for balance as the toilet flushes its heart out. They laugh to hear the churning waters below their feet. As the band moves past them, the sign at the front of the parade reads, WELCOME TO THE BIGGEST LITTLE FAIR IN THE WORLD!

※

On the following Monday, September 4th, 1939, Labour Day, the BBC announces from the Truro Apartments that Britain has declared war against Germany. The streets hush. The fairground closes.

On Tuesday, Emer goes to her new school. At three-thirty her mother is in the schoolyard to greet her. Emer is surprised to see her.

"You didn't have to meet me, Mom. I know my way home."

"Just wanted to be sure," says Bella, and holds her hand tightly.

They laugh and talk as if nothing in their lives has changed. When they arrive home her father is talking animatedly on the phone.

Emer has not seen him like this for months. She looks at her mother questioningly: her face radiates certitude.

Michael hangs up, claps his hands. "That's it! We're out of here."

EPILOGUE

"Peru!" Emer shouts.

"Noooo .... not exactly!"

"Who was that, Michael?'"

"It was D.N.D. They offered me a job in Quebec."

"Doing what?"

"Heading the math department for National Defence." He looks at Emer. It's an intermediate step to Peru ... in a lot of ways it's a mixed blessing.

Everything is beginning to happen at once. Emer is unsure.

"Working for the war effort has its drawbacks, I know ... but with any luck it'll be short. We'll win and get ourselves over the financial bump at the same time. Then, Peru, we're on our way."

Bella, rooted in nature, silently purses her lips into the roaring power of Pipe Bowl Falls, honouring its strength. Her stock is established in the promotion of endurance and peace.

The phone rings. It's his mother. "Phone's been busy for so long."

"Yes, I know," he says.

"What's going on?"

He tells her.

"A mixed blessing," she observes.

"Yes, I know. As soon as we pack up we're out of here."

"That fast?"

"Yes."

"Let me speak to Emer, please." He hands his daughter the phone.

"Emer, you heard the news?"

"Yes, Gran."

"If we go to war, I'm not so sure it's a good idea to go off travelling."

THE WORLD'S FAIR

"Why, Gran?"

"Well, we don't know exactly what can happen."

Emer is silent. Silvy clears her throat. "I'm so sorry, my love."

"Oh well, that's all right, Gran. I've already seen the World's Fair. I saw it from my girl friend's bedroom window. It was very beautiful! Thanks anyhow."

"Let me speak to your father now," Sylvie says.

She hands the phone back. "Gran wants to speak with you. She says you can go over to pick up your books."

Michael smiles in approval. There's only one way and that is forward. "You can keep them, Mother."

Emer always knew that her father could turn things around. She could bank on it.

The proceeds from sales are being donated to the education of the men and women who wish to work in an improved Canadian Mental Health System.

AUSTRALIAN REGIONAL FOOD GUIDE